A Year with Edgar Cayce

Daily Wisdom from His Readings
and
Events That Shaped His Life

BY

Lenore Vinyard Bechtel

Copyright 2020 Lenore Vinyard Bechtel

First Printing Library of Congress # 2020918407

ISBN 9781735703923

Cover: James J. Carey

Write-On Creations
15235 Scenic Woodland Drive
Conroe, TX 77384

Acknowledgments

This book could never have been written without many wonderful books and articles which preceded it. At the top of the list of people to be thanked is Sidney D. Kirkpatrick, author of *An American Prophet*. Without his wonderfully researched book, complete with dates of important events in Edgar's life and footnotes for every single fact, I would never have dreamed of attempting a day by day account.

I also relied heavily on the following books:
There Is a River by Thomas Sugrue
My Years with Edgar Cayce: The Personal Story of Gladys Davis Turner by Mary Ellen Carter,
The Sleeping Prophet by Jess Stearn,
My Life with Edgar Cayce by David E. Kahn as told to Will Oursler,
Many Mansions by Gina Cerminara.

I am grateful for *Venture Inward,* the magazine published by the Association for Research and Enlightenment, and the many fine stories that guided me to the exact reading numbers I needed for particular topics. In particular I would like to thank Elaine Hruska, Kevin J. Todeschi, and John Van Auken.

Of course, my biggest gratitude is for Edgar's 14,306 psychic readings for their continued inspiration as a true and ongoing blessing to humankind.

PREFACE

As an Edgar Cayce ambassador, I am amazed at the many people who have an unfavorable impression of this outstanding psychic who wanted only to help humanity.

A longtime friend, who acknowledges that our souls must have been together in previous lives, worries that I teach classes about this man, who surely had the devil in him. My minister, who acknowledges that Edgar was an outstanding Christian, will not allow me to present an introduction to him to church members. His reason is that he disagrees with Edgar's claims, though Edgar made none. Any claims came to him in a hypnotic trance—enlightenment given by the Creative Forces, the Universal Consciousness, the Infinite Intelligence, the Akashic Records—the presence most of us call God.

If people with such preconceived notions truly looked into this special man, they would change their minds. Most would not consider reading one of Edgar Cayce's fine biographies. But perhaps they will read his wisdom one day at a time and learn about his life's sacrifices to bring this knowledge to the world. Perhaps one day at a time they will recognize that his tips for improving both their health and their spiritual journeys can be life-changing.

Definitely, if they spend *A Year with Edgar Cayce,* they will recognize his greatness and wish they had discovered him much earlier. I am humbled by this opportunity to write this book and help his insights continue to serve humanity.

Lenore Vinyard Bechtel

January 1

All power, all love, all faith, all hope, all honor, all grace, all mercy, is within Him - and He hath promised to meet thee within thine own SELF.   1362-1

Edgar Cayce, age 67, heard joyful horns celebrating the beginning of 1945 as he lay on his bed in his Arctic Crescent home in Virginia Beach.

Sitting at his bedside, Gladys Davis, who had documented most of the 14,306 psychic readings he had done in his lifetime, told him "Happy New Year! We're going places and doing things in 1945!"

"Maybe. Maybe, if the Lord is willing," he answered. "Miss Gladys, don't forget me."

Gladys, who had been Edgar's stenographer since she was eighteen, lived with Edgar and Gertrude and was like the daughter they'd never had. She was still at his side when he awoke during his sleep and said, "This world's in an awful mess, and we've got to control it. I just hope I am worthy."

His lifelong goal had been to use his unusual abilities to help others, always cognizant of trying to please the Source from which they came. "Your will, not mine" was an affirmation that guided his life.

***

On this day in 1906 Edgar—found unconscious in his photographic studio—died after being given injections of several strong medicines. Two doctors declared him dead, but Dr. John Blackburn kept talking to him anyway. See Dec. 29 for details about how he came back to life

January 2

Passing from the material consciousness to a spiritual or cosmic, or outer consciousness, oft does an entity or being not become conscious of that about it; much in the same manner as an entity born into the material plane only becomes conscious gradually of that designated as time and space for the material or third dimensional plane   5790-31

On this day in 1945 Edgar talked so movingly to his wife Gertrude about his love for her that she burst into tears. Gladys was the one sitting with him as he slept that night. He awoke and said, "Who is that man?" Then he told her someone who looked like a musical conductor was playing beautiful music.

"What is he playing?" Gladys asked, and he confessed he didn't know.

"I don't know much about music," he said, but Gladys corrected him on that statement.

"You know about the harmonies of the universe," she said. Gladys knew that his last reading had told him, "Ye have much work to do." After his death she dedicated herself to continuing that work by organizing all his readings, making their wisdom available to the masses.

***

On this day in 1906 a lovely floral arrangement was delivered with a card expressing deep sympathy. Edgar's obituary was in the morning newspaper. News of his impending death has reached the paper's staff, but they had not been told of his remarkable recovery.

January 3

For, as given to self often, Know Thyself and what thou believest; and to WHOM thou wouldest turn for aid, counsel and guidance. For, a few years in this mundane sphere is little compared to eternity.   257-123

On this afternoon in 1945 Edgar's pulse quickened, he perspired profusely and pushed away an offered oxygen mask. As Gladys and his sister Annie watched over him, they could hear Gertrude's incessant sobbing from the dining room downstairs.

Holding back tears of her own, Gladys warmed his feet with a heating pad. Annie succeeded in getting him to sip a few drops of oyster stew.

At 7:15 p.m. he transitioned to the realm of the voices who had spoken to him throughout his lifetime. A few hours before his death, he had awakened and said, "How much the world needs God today!"

* * *

On this day in 1924 Edgar began readings to write a screenplay about a man remarkably like himself. The plot revolved around Abe, a New York young handyman. While delivering firewood for his wealthy employer, he is persuaded to let a dinner guest hypnotize him.

In a trance he becomes an accomplished musician, plays heavenly music, and gives provocative answers to questions about how humanity's destiny is determined both by fate and free will.

These five readings expounding intelligently on the meaning of life became the screenplay called *Why*.

January 4

No limit may be set as to the abilities of an entity who puts self - in purpose, in desire, in hope - on the side of the creative forces of the ONE God.   2795-1

    For nine days in January 1924 Edgar did readings on writing the screenplay *Why* at the urging of his friend Tim Brown. Brown frequently had ideas for Edgar, who was plagued with financial woes, to use his psychic skills to make money.

    A reading convinced Edgar that Brown's proposal would not be a violation of the use of his God-given gift.

    Brown had actually met in Los Angeles with the producer of Famous Players Lasky (later Paramount Pictures) to propose using Edgar's psychic abilities to plot movies.

    This attempt at screenplay writing was not Edgar's first. In 1917 a screenplay Edgar dictated from his sleeping state was accepted by film producer Thomas Ince, though it had not been produced or earned Edgar anything but publicity.

    Edgar now gave Hollywood another try. These five readings with Abe expounding on life's meaning were never made into a movie, but producer Jessie Lasky consulted Edgar for a physical reading and was given a diagnosis of heart disease, later confirmed by a doctor as "perfect." Edgar and Brown had received no feedback about *Why* when Brown asked him to write another suitable for superstar Gloria Swanson.

January 5

For we are joint heirs with that universal force we call God—if we seek to do His biddings. If our purpose is not in keeping with the Creative Force, or God then we may be a hindrance. And as has been indicated of old, it has not appeared nor even entered into the HEART of man to know the glories the Father has prepared for those that love him. 5755-20

This day in 1945 was the perfect day for Edgar's funeral: it was the day he had told Jane Williams, an Association for Research and Enlightenment member, that he would be rejuvenated.

Jane was there with many others crowded into the Cayce home to memorialize the man they had so admired.

At the request of the family, the Reverend Joseph B. Clower Jr. conducted a beautiful service, saying he was tempted to eulogize, but at the family's wishes he chose to "confine myself to passages from the Book which Edgar Cayce knew so well."

When he was age 10, Edgar vowed to read the Bible every year of his life, and he did. He taught Bible study classes in every church he belonged to all his life. His knowledge of scripture was astounding, if not unparalleled.

Clower later wrote to Hugh Lynn, Edgar's first son, "Nothing...has meant more to me than your request to have me officiate at the funeral service for Mr. Cayce."

January 6

FATHER, GOD, KEEP THOU ME IN THE WAY THAT I SHOULD GO, THAT I MAY FULFILL THAT PURPOSE THAT THOU WOULD HAVE ME FILL AT THIS TIME. 281-23

From a very young age Edgar knew he was different, and he realized his purpose in life was to help others. By the time he was a teenager, he realized that his difference was the vessel with which he would deliver that help.

He probably hadn't figured that out when fairies and little people came to play with him, or even when he injured himself in an accident and prescribed his own cure during his sleep.

Maybe not even when he won at card games because he could read the minds of other players. Or not even when his anger set a sofa afire when he was sleeping on it. Or not even when he enjoyed conversations with his deceased grandfather whom no one else could even see.

When he learned that under hypnosis he spouted information way above his educational level, he might have begun to key in on his purpose in life. But when his trance readings gave information that healed people, he was certainly sure because he never wavered from what he called "the work" after that.

His mission was to share the enlightenment of his readings for the benefit of humanity, encouraging all to be better Christians, Jews, Buddhists, Muslims, Hindus, or any other religion.

January 7

(Q) What is the state of the physical forces of this body while giving this work? (A) They, the physical, are under subjugation of the subconscious or soul forces. As we see in the body we have the trinity for an entity. We have as this: the physical forces and mental mind; we have the spirit or soul force with the superconscious or soul mind; then we have the spirit that is the mind of the soul force, just as the soul occupies the body in its same form and manner. Just as the body of an individual that has passed beyond may be seen by others in the physical plane only when their physical or mental, material or mental are subjugated like this body here we are speaking of, Edgar Cayce, the physical is subjugated or laid aside, we find the soul forces give the information, and the body is under the subjugation of the soul and spirit forces. 3744-3

While using psychic skills to find cures for ailments, Edgar didn't realize until October 11, 1923, that the infinite intelligence that came through him would also answer philosophical questions. The above quote explains how his subconscious mind retrieved information from the universal consciousness and the soul force of the person getting the reading.

In later years he referred to the etheric body which lay suspended above his physical body during the readings. He also reported being drawn to the Akashic Records, a vibrating energy record of everything that ever happened. Data sometimes came directly from angels amid wind and clattering window panes.

January 8

> (Q) Where does the soul come from, and how does it enter the physical body? (A) It is already there. "and He breathed into him the breath of life, and he became a living soul," as the breath, the ether from the forces as come into the body of the human when born breathes the breath of life, as it becomes a living soul, provided it has reached that developing in the creation where the soul may enter and find the lodging place. All souls were created in the beginning, and are finding their way back to whence they came. (Q) Where does the soul go when fully developed? (A) To its Maker.   3744-5

Humans have an innate need to connect with their source. Our purpose for being created was to be a companion for the Creator, and to do so we need to show ourselves worthy of that companionship.

Edgar, like most devout Christians of his era, thought that at one's physical death, one's spirit—if one had lived a righteous earthly life—went back to the Creator. One ascended to God in heaven with glories too magnificent to be comprehended in this three-dimensional world.

Then readings revealed a different story. Mortals who have not qualified to dwell in eternal bliss get another chance by being reincarnated for another try. Souls know when they come back what lessons they need to learn, and if they don't master those lessons, they have to come back to earth again. Because souls travel in groups, they meet each other over and over again until their group has achieved its earthly purpose.

January 9

Keep the will in that of the spiritual development, if the physical would manifest to the better advantage in the present plane, keeping this ever before, that all work in present plane will be judged to that individual and the classes, masses, as to the individual's manifestation of spiritual forces in and through the individual action in and before men.   294-8

On this day in 1888 Edgar fell on a stick which pierced through his pants and went through one of his testicles. He developed an infection that made his recovery long enough to read the entire Bible three times —quite an accomplishment for a 10-year-old.

The Cayces lived in Beverly, a small village outside Hopkinsville, Kentucky.

Both of Beverly's two doctors were unable to cure him, but the daughter of Edgar's grandfather's former slave concocted a folk remedy spiked with spiderwebs, and he drank it and recovered.

He would remember this injury as the most painful of his life, and it would be responsible for other ailments that afflicted him as an adult.

One of the doctors that tried to help him had a daughter that Edgar was attracted to as a teenager. The doctor objected to his daughter seeing Edgar, not just because he was different mentally, with his clairvoyance and mental telepathy, but because he might not be able to father children.

Finding that out was as bad as being called "freak."

January 10

Moderation in all things, excess in none. In excess, when through good or bad is conceived, the wrong impressions are given the souls of the earth plane. Develop the soul forces by contacting those of the vibrations necessary to give the best to the Maker's realm, and present itself wholly and acceptable unto all men, that none may question either the acts of the physical, the soul or spiritual purposes within this individual.
797-1

Edgar made his first medical diagnosis on himself after an incident that happened at school.

He tried hard to fit in with his classmates, participating as best he could in recess games. One day while playing Old Sow, the ball hit the end of his spine.

Back in the classroom he acted queerly—laughing, making faces, throwing spitballs. On the way home he rolled on the ground, jumped in ditches, and stood on the road stopping buggies.

During supper he threw things at his sisters and made faces at his father. His father Leslie made him go to bed.

In his sleep Edgar gave instructions for a poultice of corn meal, onions, and herbs to be put on the back of his head, near the base of his brain, explaining he was suffering from shock.

His mother made and applied the poultice, and the next morning he was well. At school he already had a reputation as a weirdo and the children started calling him freak. School was not a happy place for him.

January 11

Keep level, don't talk too much, do talk sufficiently to know where you are at all times.   5259-1

On this day in 1912 Edgar opened a photography studio in downtown Selma, Alabama, for H.P. Tressler Company. The studio was above a drugstore and under an apartment for his family who would come when Gertrude was fully recovered from tuberculosis. (See June 10)

He left his Hopkinsville business because he couldn't succeed without Dr. Wesley Ketchum, who had used Edgar's psychic diagnoses to cure patients. Edgar refused to continue working with Ketchum after discovering he'd used readings to get tips on horse racing. (See Oct. 9-13)

Edgar had still given readings, but most were charity cases instead of doctor referrals which paid $25. His father Leslie later sued Ketchum and the other partner Noe for breach of contract and back rents of $28,000 which he and Edgar were stuck with.

Back from Alabama for the court ruling, Edgar was enraged when the judge dismissed the case, ruling that the original contract was illegal. Edgar was so angry, he said something he later highly regretted. He told the judge, "For the lie you have this day enacted, the worms of your body will eat you up while you are yet alive!" Indeed, the judge did later die of intestinal worm infestation. Did that happen because Edgar willed it, or did he have precognition that it would happen? Or was it coincidence? Edgar wished he hadn't said it.

January 12

For this entity should comprehend and KNOW, and NEVER forget, that life and its experiences are only what one puts into same! And unless the activities, the thoughts are CONTINUOUSLY constructive, and the experience well-balanced, the entity CANNOT, WILL not fulfill the purpose for which it came into the present experience....an individual is EACH DAY meeting his own self - either in the mental, the material or the spiritual.... 1537-1

On this day in 1912 Edgar joined the First Christian Church in Selma, Alabama, and quickly became a deacon and a teacher for both a Bible study class and Christian Endeavor.

His Christian Endeavor program received a national award for having the most active participants in a single chapter in the movement's history. Many members became missionaries in Mexico, Japan, and India.

Edgar's studio became the hangout place for his church friends, and he invented a game for them to play, *DrinX*. From one trump card and the fifty-nine cards representing different non-alcoholic drinks, participants tried to collect all of a particular fruit juice, ginger ale, or soda.

He had learned a lesson by losing rights to *The Pit*, the first game he'd invented for which Parker Brothers paid him no royalties. (See April 6)

This time Edgar had *DrinX* copyrighted, but as popular as it became in Selma, its momentary fame did not spread.

January 13

At times we find these conditions get on the nerves of the body, as it were, and the body ceases to care to put up the resistance, feeling as if there is no use. This should be dismissed, for the body should acquire and gain, and set before self, that all building and replenishing for a physical body is from within, and must be constructed by the mind of the entity; for MIND is the BUILDER; for each cell in the atomic force of the body is as a world of its own, and each one - each cell - being in perfect unison, may build to that necessary to reconstruct the forces of the body in all its needs, and in this body, as given, there is then necessary to add that vibration to that being administered, that would give this incentive, necessary in rest, necessary in blood building, necessary in the cellular forces of the body, for these to coordinate the more properly, would we bring the better forces to the body.   93-1

Edgar's physical readings are packed full of medical terms and unique remedies, but they also point out the patient's responsibility in the healing process.

The above idea that thoughts in the mind affect the body's cell was revolutionary then. Edgar certainly earned his title as the Father of holistic medicine.

In his words, "If your mind holds to it, and you've got a stumped toe, it will stay stumped! If you've got a bad condition in your gizzard, or liver, you'll keep it - if you think so? But the body - the physical, the mental and spiritual - will remove same, if ye will LET it and not hold to the disturbance!" (257-249)

January 14

> KNOW in whom, in what THOU believest. If the desire of the heart, the soul of self is constructive in thine own consciousness, then that thou receivest in thine OWN consciousness may not come save from that sphere, that soul, that may - too - be constructive in its progress through that journey that is before each soul in its activity in eternity in which each soul finds itself in a physical, a mental consciousness.   5752-3

On this day in 1887 Edgar received his very first Bible. He first heard about the Bible from the woodcutter Crazy Bill, who told him the story of Samson. Edgar liked to read and became fascinated with his Aunt Ella's illustrated Bible.

His father Leslie told Elijah Hopper, bookstore owner, how much his 10-year-old son Edgar yearned for his own Bible. Hopper generously gave Leslie a Bible to take home to Edgar as a gift.

He began to spend many hours reading the Bible, carrying it with him wherever he went. He read it once a year for every year of his life, making up for the nine years before he had one. He also taught Sunday school in each church he joined.

When the concept of reincarnation was first mentioned while he was doing a physical reading, he rejected the idea until he found scriptures in the Bible to support it. Holding out as long as he did was remarkable because he knew the voice he called the Forces was never wrong.

January 15

As ye would then that men would do to you, do ye even so to them. As ye would that thy God would be patient, be thou patient with thy neighbor, yea with thine enemy - for in so doing ye heap coals of fire upon thine enemy and make thine own self happy in doing GOOD unto others. For as ye do to others, ye do it to thy Maker.   1362-1

One day in school in 1890 Edgar, age 13, was unable to spell "cabin." The teacher made him stay after school and write it on the board five hundred times.

His furious father Leslie took it upon himself to tutor Edgar that evening, but Edgar was not doing well. Leslie — perhaps a bit inebriated for he was known to drink excessively—backhand slapped his son and knocked him out of his chair.

Edgar begged for time to rest and laid his head down on the McGuffy's Reader that was giving him so much trouble. When he lifted his head after a short rest, he could spell every word in the book.

He had no trouble in school after that. He told his teacher that after sleeping on a book he could see pictures of the pages.

This newfound ability did not endear him to his classmates who taunted him, saying, "Old Man, how about sleeping on our lessons for us?"

Old Man is what Edgar was called by his family and friends at a very early age. He took things as seriously as a child as he would later take "the work."

January 16

Be angry and sin not. Be patient. Seven times forgive; yea, seventy times seven. And, being dead, being crucified to the things that pertain to the earth, looking for tha acceptable day of the Lord..   262-59

On many occasions throughout his lifetime, Edgar forgave his father Leslie, who was called the Squire—a title he was entitled to use for an office he once held.

When Edgar was a child, the Squire was not always a loving father. If not for his mother Carrie's protective affection, he probably would have slapped Edgar around even more than he did.

He certainly was not a good provider, going from one money-making scheme to the next. Certainly his problem drinking contributed to his inability to make a steady income. When Edgar dropped out of school and started working on his uncle's farm as a teenager, he became the Cayce family's major breadwinner.

When Edgar and Leslie were selling insurance, Leslie would not allow Edgar to sell to a black person. He was a devout racist—totally unlike Edgar himself. (See Jan. 21) Yes, Edgar had much to forgive, and he did, watching out for his father until his death.

A reading he gave when Leslie was 70 said he died in the hold of a trade ship "at the hands of those in the rule of Hannibal."

His death in this incarnation was also not a good one as it was brought on by burns from a house fire. He would still have his racist karma to overcome.

January 17

Man from the purely material sense only becomes conscious through the sensuousness or through the ability of attunement of the sensuousnesses of the physical body, or through the five senses. Yet ever is that sixth, seventh or eighth sense of the entity alert to the various responses as received by the inner self through the various experiences of life. Hence we find in many various phases of same these - taken as an oneness - become as it were branches or lines of study sought out by individuals and classified as the keynote; yet no ONE is superior to the other in its influence....
900-359

In early 1899 Edgar accompanied his father to Madisonville, Kentucky, on business. Leslie was now an insurance agent hoping to sell policies to the Odd Fellows fraternal organization.

When a smallpox outbreak quarantined everyone in the hotel for three days, a fellow guest, a hypnotist, put on a show to help relieve the group of boredom.

He hypnotized Edgar easily and told him to play the piano. To everyone's amazement—especially Leslie who knew Edgar had never touched a piano—Edgar played beautifully, in spite of never having had a piano lesson.

Edgar later realized that his latent musical talent existed in his soul memory, but this was before the Forces had mentioned anything about previous lives.

He later learned that in this third dimension, "man hasn't the ability EVEN TO IMAGINE anything that isn't a part of the living physical organism's activity!" (470-22)

January 18

Be not impatient with those even that would hinder thee, from gaining something of this world's pleasures; but know, he seeks to do the biddings of the Creative Forces in a manner that is constructive, gratifies that which is the soul development.   257-123

On this day in 1914 Edgar's first son Hugh Lynn had an accident that could have left him blind.

He came down from the family's third floor apartment to Edgar's studio to see a box of squirrels Edgar had photographed.

Edgar had inadvertently left out a box of flash powder, used to shorten exposure time for the squirrelly squirrels, on his camera stand. A cleaning lady had knocked it off to the floor.

Hugh Lynn, a mischievous six-year-old, sprinkled the stairs with some of the powder to play a trick on the cleaning lady. But as he struck the match, its head broke and ignited the whole box, exploding directly in his face.

When doctors said he would never see from his right eye and wanted to remove it, Hugh Lynn told them, "My daddy, when he's asleep, is the best doctor in the world. He'll tell you what to do."

Edgar's reading said to add tannic acid to the solution the doctors were already using. When the doctors objected, saying it was too strong, Edgar and Gertrude pointed out if he were to be blind anyway, why worry? After two weeks of frequent treatments in a darkened room, Hugh Lynn could see.

January 19

In earth, then, as has been seen, we are GIVEN - Men, Women - are given an OPPORTUNITY - see what you do with it all! 331-21

On this day in 1934 a reading hinted, but never said, that Edgar was supposed to let the world know the need for the brotherhood of man. The reading's topic, world affairs, was requested by a group of New Yorkers and recorded on an Edison phonographic cylinder.

The reading described where geographical earth changes would occur and warned that "the rottenness of those that have ministered in places will be brought to light, and turmoils and strifes shall enter. . . Armageddon is at hand." As always, though, it contended that free will could prevent such a disaster.

Through the Archangel Halaliel's voice, the reading said a spiritual awakening would begin when the Prophet John returned to earth to become a channel to usher in the "Day of the Lord." Surely the New Yorkers must have grasped the possibility that Edgar, who at that moment was channeling an Archangel, might be the one bringing the divine message to the world.

"That has been delivered unto me to give unto you. . . know that He will make thy paths straight if ye will but live that ye know this day...Love the Lord thy God with all thine heart...Love thy neighbor as thyself."

Halaliel predicted, "The young king will soon reign!" The reading identified the young king as Hitler and the problem country as Germany.

January 20

But first KNOW ye the Lord, for the cattle and the gold and the silver are His, and all ye have is lent ye of the Lord! Only that ye give away, of self, of money, of time, of patience, of love, do ye possess!   1362-1

On this date in 1927 Edgar, Gertrude, Gladys, and Edgar Evans went to the Caribbean Island of Bimini, all expenses paid by Thomas Peters and A.C. Preston.

A reading Edgar gave the partners on August 14, 1926, revealed that huge quantities of gold, bullion, and silver that had been aboard a mutinied ship could be found on the 12,000 acres they owned on that island. Edgar had identified landmarks to pinpoint the treasure's location but before a search began, a destructive storm devastated the island, rearranging its geography, wiping out the landmarks sited in the reading.

Four readings during this trip didn't locate the treasure, but went into great detail telling why. "The trouble lies within," Edgar repeated from the Forces.

Basically, Peters' and Preston's motives were not pure, and the Force behind the information that came to Edgar chose what and what not to tell him.

The fourth reading on February 7 told Edgar to go home, stressing the priority of "inner riches."

Edgar considered this trip a profitable one for the moral lesson that had been reinforced.

The Bimini readings also pinpointed the exact location of Atlantis—evidence that the continent was real, not mythical.

January 21

For know, the Lord is in His holy temple. If thou hast, as His child, desecrated thy temple - in word, in act, in deed - know that ye alone may make those corrections, and that thy body is the temple of the living God. Act as though it were, and not as if it were a pigpen or a place of garbage for the activities of others. 294-208

In 1900 Edgar became his father's field representative selling insurance for Woodman of the World. He had left J.P. Morgan on good terms and was now selling items from their catalog. His combined income was some $50 a month.

He found the insurance business distasteful because Leslie, a devout racist, would not allow policies to be sold to Negroes. Edgar could not understand racism. He loved his black nanny who had healed his childhood testicle infection when doctors couldn't and respected the black man who had saved him from drowning.

During January through March, Edgar suffered severe migraines. Unaware of any physical reason for the headaches, he thought perhaps he was being punished for not fulfilling expectations of the angel who had visited him in his childhood. (See June 15) He knew he was not using his God-given talents the way they should be used. He also looked upon his headaches as divine punishment for working for a company which openly discriminated against black people and openly advocated the purity of the white race. This job didn't last long.

January 22

But take time to work, to think, to make contacts for a social life and for recreation. This old adage might well apply: After breakfast, work a while, after lunch rest a while, after dinner walk a mile. This as a recreation may be a helpful, balanced experience for this life. As these purposes are set in motion, let it not be "Well, I'll do this sometime" but set all of these in motion for at least a week.   3624-1

In 1898 at the Holland Opera House Edgar was invited on stage at a hypnosis show starring Stanley Hart, who had been coming to Hopkinsville regularly, billing himself as Hart the Laugh King.

Hart's show revolved around leading the audience in a relaxation induction during which he could spot people who looked like good hypnotic subjects. Then he would invite them on stage, hypnotize them, and order them to do silly things to keep the audience laughing.

Hart got no laughs out of Edgar because he was unable to hypnotize him. No one would have expected that years later, Edgar would easily be able to slip into a hypnotic trance.

Who would have dreamed that the boy who couldn't be hypnotized would one day devote his life to going into trances, and—instead of entertaining people with his ability—spending his life receiving information about healing, overcoming karma, exploring ancient mysteries, and uncovering metaphysical truths?

No one would be more surprised than Edgar.

January 23

There is no greater factory in the universe than that in a human body in its natural, normal reacting state. For there are those machines or glands within the body capable of producing, from the very air or water and the food values taken into the body, to take from or to reproduce ANY element AT ALL that is KNOWN in the material world! 1800-21

Edgar gave four major tips for maintaining a healthy body. Dr. Harold Reilly summarized them with the acronym C.A.R.E.—circulation, assimilation, rest, and elimination.

Circulation includes exercise, massage, and adjustments. Assimilation concerns eating the proper foods in balanced combinations and with the proper amounts of water.

Rest includes relaxation and recreations, with a recommended eight hours of sleep every night.

Eliminations include not only a dietary program to keep the bowels working regularly, but also colonics, certain natural laxatives, steam baths, and other forms of hydrotherapy.

The readings abound with potion-making directions, and Edgar did not hesitate to share these with companies to make them to sell. Members of the Health Home Remedies Company brought two new formulas for a reading which told them how to improve them and why. The company profited, but so did the product's buyers. Edgar's help to humanity spanned many directions.

January 24

> . . .referring to those...elements within the system, the BODY, the PHYSICAL body, of the GLANDS of the body - for, as has been given, the KINGDOM is within YOU! This, then - that the SPIRIT, the soul, the ELEMENTS of the ACTIVE forces, use those portions OF the physical body as their temple DURING an earth's experience. 311-4

The highest requirement for maintaining a healthy body is good circulation, and that is impossible without good digestion.

"Most of all," a reading said, "train self never to bolt the food. Take TIME to assimilate, masticate, so that ASSIMILATION is well...with an EVEN balance between those that produce acid and those that make for the alkalin...."

Edgar's source stresses the benefit of drinking plenty of water both before and after meals because "when any food value ENTERS the stomach IMMEDIATELY the stomach becomes a storehouse, or a medicine chest that may create all the elements necessary for proper digestion within the system. If this FIRST is acted upon by aqua pura, the reactions are more near normal."

He recommends each morning upon first arising to drink a half to three-quarters of a glass of warm water to clarify the system of poisons. Occasionally, add a pinch of salt to the water.

Both keeping the digestive system working correctly and keeping physically fit with proper exercise are vital for keeping blood flowing properly through the veins.

January 25

Take more outdoor exercise, that - that brings into play the muscular forces of the body. It isn't that the mental should be numbed, or should be cut off from their operations or their activities - but make for a more evenly, more perfectly balanced body-physical AND mental.
341-32

Edgar's source stressed exercise as the key to good circulation, the first requirement for a healthy body.

"Be a well-ROUNDED body. Take specific, DEFINITE exercises morning and evening. Make the body PHYSICALLY, as well as mentally, tired."

If we do so, we will eliminate sleep problems, laziness, poisons in the system from non-eliminations, but best of all—the body responds to dieting.

"Each cell of the blood stream, each corpuscle, is a whole UNIVERSE in itself. Do not eat like a canary and expect to do MANUAL labor. Do not eat like a rail splitter and expect to do the work of a mind reader or a university professor, but be CONSISTENT with those things that make for - even as the UNIVERSE is builded."

One patient complained of being too tired in the evening to put any pep into exercising. Edgar's Forces responded, "The best way to acquire the correct amount of pep is to take the exercise!"

Attitude toward physical fitness matters. "Through diet and exercise the greater portion of all disturbances may be equalized and overcome, if the right mental attitude is kept." (288-38)

January 26

> But never think more highly of self than ye should. Know thy ideal, in whom as well as in what ye believe. Know who is the author of thy ideals, spiritually, mentally, materially. Budget thy time more; first in the care for the physical being, recreation, improvement mentally, spiritually, also socially. Take time to be holy.
> 3393-2

Rest and recreation are crucial for maintaining a healthy body. A good night's sleep should come easily to anyone following Edgar's instructions for circulation and assimilation.

Edgar diagnosed one patient's sleeplessness as a nerve condition causing restlessness or insomnia. "The nerve force in attempting to gain its equilibrium, gives over-taxation rather than the correct distributing or equalizing itself for rest, and it apparently makes the brain more active, because there is more blood flow."

He blamed a lesion in the 9th and 10th dorsal region and prescribed a simple exercise to eliminate the problem: a circular bending motion of the body each night and morning, and rubbing the body well after each exercise with very cold water down the spine, rubbing the spine briskly.

"The circular motion would be with hands on hips, forward, backward, right and left, circle. Stooping, bending from the hips, and give the exercise to that portion of the body."

Another patient asked why he couldn't sleep, and the answer was "Worry!" A solution wasn't suggested.

January 27

There should be a warning to ALL bodies as to such conditions; for [if] would the assimilations and the eliminations would be kept nearer NORMAL in the human family, the days might be extended to whatever period as was so desired; for the system is builded by the assimilations of that it takes within, and is able to bring resuscitations so long as the eliminations do not hinder.
311-4

The above reading promises longevity if what goes in and what goes out of our bodies are kept normal. Bowels should cause no problem if one is eating and exercising properly.

Edgar's first recommendation for constipation is hydrotherapy which takes toxins out of the body—something that readings recommended for many ailments.

After hydrotherapy a reading advised: "Take varied things, not just taking one alone! As figs, Syrup of Senna, prunes and such natures; even Inner Clean or such would be well to be taken at times when such disturbances have bothered the body."

One can conclude that had current brands of laxatives been on the market then, he would have approved of several, but definitely the ones with the most natural ingredients.

He warns that laxatives are "not something to be kept up daily, daily, daily, or even weekly, but when the exercises and the activities have been indiscreet so as to cause an upset in these directions." (257-249)

January 28

> *Know, all that may be added to the body is only to enable each organ to reproduce itself in a consistent way and manner, and it will get rid of drosses with its reproduc-tion.... For, have ye not heard how that constantly there is the change, and that the body has in a seven-year cycle reproduced itself entirely? No need for anyone, then, to have ANY disturbance over that length of period, if - by common sense - there would be the care taken.* 257-249

Edgar's Forces contended that our bodies would take care of themselves if our minds would cooperate.

When treatment is needed, "The MIND will be much better! Let the body ITSELF KNOW the source from which these treatments are instructive, and what is to be accomplished by each!" (394-1)

Edgar said, "No one can hate his neighbor and not have stomach or liver trouble. No one can be jealous and allow the anger of same and not have upset digestion or heart disorder."

He said one could catch a cold just by getting mad. Anger can make the body do "that which is contrary to the better influences of same."

All healing comes about by changing vibrations. "This alone is healing. Whether it is accomplished by the use of drugs, the knife or what not."

Each cell reproduces itself every seven years, so one should never have ailments because "the body - the physical, the mental and spiritual - will remove same, if ye will LET it and not hold to the disturbance!"

January 29

Know that there is within self all healing that may be accomplished for the body. For, all healing must come from the Divine. For who healeth thy diseases? The source of the Universal supply. As the attitude, then, of self, how well do ye wish to be? How well are ye willing to cooperate, coordinate with the Divine influences which may work in and through thee, by stimulating the centers which have been latent with nature's acti-vi-ties.   4021-1

Edgar's overnight cure for the common cold is complicated and time-consuming, but many testimonials attest to its success.

He said to first take "an eliminant of about 1800 drops of the Castoria but not at once. Take it in very small or broken doses (a half teaspoonful every half hour.)"

"After the first container or bottle has been taken in these proportions...THEN take the Turkish bath... first the sweats, the salt rum rubs, and then the alcohol rub after the oil rubs....keep more of an alkaline diet. No white bread. Principally use fruit juices, and citrus fruit juices at that! A little coffee without cream may be taken as a stimulant, or a little whiskey and soda later in the evening... The body should feel physically fit by morning." The Forces expected a lot.

Castoria contains Senna, sold as an herbal supplement. Edgar specified that the rubs should be concentrated on the lower dorsal and lumbar area, though the cold manifested itself in the nose and throat.

January 30

Remember, healing - all healing comes from within. Yet there is the healing of the physical, there is the healing of the mental, there is the correct direction from the spirit. Coordinate these and you'll be whole! But to attempt to do a physical healing through the mental conditions is the misdirection of the spirit that prompts same - the same that brings about accidents, the same that brings about the eventual separation. For it is LAW. But when the law is coordinated, in spirit, in mind, in body, the entity is capable of fulfilling the purpose for which it enters a...physical experience. 2528-2

Emotions can have a direct effect on health because "there is an activity within the system produced by anger, fear, mirth, joy, or any of those active forces, that produces through the glandular secretion those activities that flow into the whole of the system. Such an activity then is of this endocrine system...." (281-38)

"Endo" itself means internal, and "It may be easily seen, then, how very closely the glands are associated with reproduction, degeneration, regeneration; and this throughout - not only the physical forces of the body but the mental body and the soul body." (281-38)

Edgar called the endocrine system the gift of the Creator to man—to be nurtured by positive emotions and hopefully not hindered by negative ones. To keep our endocrine systems functioning correctly is just one more reason to remember that mind is the builder and physical is the result.

January 31

Only that each soul turns not to self alone and cry for strength, but that each soul LIVES in such a manner that there may be the awakening to the needs, the purposes, the causes for the nation coming into existence! That such is, and to be, a part of the experience of America is because of unbelief! 3976-24

The above quote was an answer to a question concerning what could be done about the turmoil and unrest in the United States in June 1939. The answer is as correct today as it was following the Great Depression.

The questioner then stated, "Money is the root cause of the general economic unbalance of our country. Will you give specifically the reasons for this statement and the approach that can be made toward correction of the money order as operated today?"

Edgar answered, "Fear on the part of those who control or direct the investing of capital into channels that give the greater outlet of their characters of outlet."

As usual, his Source had the solution. "As to how this may be corrected - it is only through patience, persistence, and a RETURN to the trust in God, and NOT in the power or the might of self.... Unless there is, then, a more universal oneness of purpose on the part of all, this will one day bring - here - in America - revolution!"

Asked how to protect our democracy, he answered, "Raise not democracy nor any other name above the brotherhood of man, the Fatherhood of God! We are through. through." Source got tired of dumb questions.

February 1

Study well, then, the influence ye have upon those ye meet day by day. For, again, with what measure ye mete, with what judgment ye act, so comes it back to thee. For, to have love one must manifest and show love in one's life and one's dealings with others. To have friends one must show self friendly. 2560-1

On this day in 1928 Marion L. Stansell came to Edgar for a reading. When he was a 35-year-old engine mechanic dying of mustang gas poisoning and flu, he met Jesus. Jesus agreed to his pleas to live, telling him that he would be given a formula for a device to save the planet from destruction. He had been pronounced dead, but twenty minutes later came alive again.

The reading this day confirmed his miraculous healing and said Stansell would need Edgar to channel the motor's design from the deceased De Witt Clinton, who had been instrumental in the Erie Canal design.

A March 7, 1929, reading told them their invention could generate a payout of $10,000,000. The first of 21 readings happened the next day.

With design details nearing completion, Edgar's source refused to give the last needed information, saying, "There must be determined for what purpose these are to be used before ye may be given."

Even without the complete design, his associate Tim Brown built many prototypes from these readings, and in spite of failures, he, Stansell, and financier Morton Blumenthal had the invention patented.

February 2

And above all, KEEP that ability to see the humor in any experience, whether it is the most sacred, the most cherished experience, or that which comes as a trial or as a temptation from outside influence. 2560-1

In 1901 most Hopkinsville residents knew about Edgar's inexplicable inability to speak above a whisper. (See April 18-19) Many encouraged him to get help from Stanley Hart, the Laugh King, who was in Hopkinsville for a show at the Holland Opera House.

Hart had been informed of Edgar's problem and probably relished the idea of creating a stage sensation by bringing Edgar's voice back. He apparently wasn't worried that his hypnosis hadn't worked for Edgar before.

This time when he invited Edgar on stage, he slumped into a trance very quickly. Audience members were ecstatic when, under hypnosis, he spoke with a strong, clear voice.

They, like Edgar, were dismayed when he could only whisper upon awakening.

Backstage after the show Hart put the blame on Edgar's inability to go deep enough into hypnosis to accept and follow suggestions. Edgar thought he was probably right.

He offered for $200 to keep working with Edgar on posthypnotic suggestions until he was cured. *Kentucky New Era*, the largest local newspaper, offered to pay.

Unfortunately, Hart's suggestions still failed to help, and the paper didn't get the story it had wanted.

February 3

Keep then the faith in those things that pertain to creating in the mind and in the body a helpful experience; see in those ye dislike the most that ye would worship in thy Creator. For, each soul's manifestation in the earth is in the image of its Maker.... as thou art in his image.   3246-1

The readings have health tips on a variety of subjects. The most famous is to eat three almonds a day to prevent cancer. This practice may work because almonds have laetrile, which is still promoted, but not verified, as a cancer cure.

Castor oil packs absorbed through the skin relieve abdominal congestions due to sluggishness of the lymphatic circulation and strengthen some deep organs of the abdomen—or any body part they're applied to.

Soak three thicknesses of soft flannel in hot castor oil. Apply to the spot needed, and cover with heating pad or heat lamp to retain the heat. Apply for three consecutive days each week for one-and-a-half to three hours per day. Take olive oil for the next three days.

For psoriasis drink yellow saffron tea and increase all yellow foods—carrots and anything made with corn meal. Yellow peaches should be the only sweets. After bathing, apply Cuticura ointment followed by Resinol. After three weeks hold ultraviolet ray rod applicator in each hand about three minutes each. One hefty patient reported success in a week, plus the loss of seven pounds. Flareups can happen if one is careless with one's attitude or diet. Patience and right thinking work.

February 4

He that leads, or WOULD direct, is continually beset by the forces that WOULD undermine. He that endureth to the end shall wear the Crown. He that aideth in upbuilding shall be entitled to that that he BUILDS in his experience. He that faltereth, or would hinder, shall be received in the manner as he hinders.   294-208

Dr. William Girao, who saw Edgar on stage at the Holland Opera House, became interested in his case. Edgar out of desperation allowed Girao to experiment with him, often having Edgar hypnotized in a funeral home window—receiving much media coverage.

Giaro gave multiple press interviews and sent many newspaper clippings to a noted New York hypnotherapist, John D. Quackenboss, who requested more specifics about Edgar's case. Expecting he could help, he traveled by train to Hopkinsville to give Edgar's case a try. He came, he tried, and he failed.

Experiments with Edgar continued through February and early March. Girao enlisted Al Layne, a Hopkinsville man studying osteopathy by mail order, to help.

Since his voice problems started, Edgar's weight had dropped from 165 to only 85 pounds, and he admitted to being a nervous wreck.

Girao was now out of the picture, but Layne wanted to keep trying, and the family agreed.

FAST FORWARD: See March 31 for the cure that happened in 1901.

February 5

> Man alone, of all His kingdom, abuses the gifts that have been made his through the love that the Father would show, in that he (man) might be a companion, one with Him; not the whole, yet equal to the whole, able in that realm to magnify, glorify, even as the *dragon fly, that love the Father bestowed upon His sons.*
> 254-68

Sometime in February 1921 Edgar gave a demonstration for Dr. William McDougal, Harvard psychology chair, with master-magician Harry Houdini one of many in attendance.

Edgar did so many correct medical diagnoses that McDougal was highly impressed. He recognized that some kind of higher intelligence had to be manifesting itself through Edgar, whose formal education had ended after eighth grade.

With the many others who were present, Edgar went after the demonstration to Houdini's lavish Harlem town house.

At this stage of his career, Houdini was getting lots of publicity by exposing fraudulent mediums, spiritualists, and pretenders who rang bells from afar, levitated tables, and performed other such tricks.

Because Houdini never made a reported statement about the unusual 44-year-old Kentucky psychic, it seems probable that he truly believed Edgar was genuinely communicating with a higher, spiritual power.

If anyone could spot a phony, Houdini could.

February 6

Just as in the present, in keeping in that way of one ideal, one purpose, to do, to be that thy Maker would have thee be, the entity may bring peace and harmony into the experiences of many. For as ye do it unto the least ye do it unto thy Maker. And unless ye find peace and harmony within thyself, as ye did in that experience, ye cannot make it ye cannot bring it into the experience of others. For as ye sow, so ye reap. As ye measure to others, so is it measured to thee. 3250-1

The Universal Mind that spoke through Edgar harped repeatedly that everyone should have an ideal pleasing to the Creator. That ideal should become one's life's purpose.

"Who may tell the rose how to be beautiful?" the above reading continues. "Who may tell the violet where to grow? Who may know the works or the place of the wind? Only in Him is there found purpose.

"Keep thy faith, thy purpose, thy hope in Him - if ye would know the way to keep in peace and harmony in the Christ-consciousness. That alone counts."

Edgar's Forces spoke to him in the stilted language style of the King James Version of the Bible—appropriate because Edgar himself was a devout Christian and Bible scholar. Had Edgar been Buddhist or Muslim or Jew, the communication would no doubt have been given in those sects' vernacular.

The truth expressed would have been the same. All should live in love to earn the right to return to God.

February 7

Then, the mental attitude: Keep ever that as of the constructive; that is, knowing there is much for thee to do as a witness for the Creative Forces, for God, for Christ. These ye manifest by thy relationships with thy fellow man. Be happy - be in that attitude of ever being helpful to others. These will bring that peace within that is the promise from him. 1968-7

Edgar's Source asserted that nurturing a sense of humor helps both in healing and in developing favorable relationships.

"Not as one to be long-faced," the Forces affirmed. "For, the earth is the Lord's and the fullness thereof - in JOY! Do not see the dark side too oft. Turn it over - there's another side to every question."

He advised cultivating a sense of humor, pointing out that all enjoy wit in others, and "others enjoy it in thee. But too oft it becomes to thee foolishness. KNOW that thy Lord, thy God, LAUGHED - even at the Cross. For He wept with those who wept, and rejoiced with those who rejoiced." (2995-1)

But how does one become witty? "Do read comic papers. Do study those things...pertaining to the humor of all the wits, and learn to repeat them and say them; not merely as something as an entertainment but in which there is a story; and they may be a helpful force, not only in the life of self but as an entertainment, and as an attraction to others...." (3197-1)

Edgar gave both life and life-of-the-party advice!

February 8

Then let thy desires be in the ways that...demonstrate to others where thy heart and thy purpose lies. For, though ye gain the whole world in EVERY way of fortune, fame or what not, and lose hold of that love that cometh from just being kind and patient, ye have lost that harmony, that peace which comes from being at one with Him. The way grows brighter, if ye will come with Him into the light of thy own under-standing!   262-121

On this night in 1917 Edgar participated in an experiment to plot the screenplay for Universal Pictures. The occasion was arranged by his friend Edwin Williamson, whose ambition was to write for Hollywood.

As preplanned, promising actress Violet Mesereau was at Churchill's, a New York nightclub on this night, with many reporters invited to hear a speech by a doctor who was reputed to be an authority on hypnotism and mental telepathy.

The entertainment started as Violet wrote the type story she desired for her next film and placed it face down on a table.

Back in Alabama Edgar said some 450 words, which were wired to Churchill's.

This first five-reel scenario transmitted by a psychic received lots of publicity, but the film never got made.

Because of the good press, Williamson and his family were paid to move to Hollywood, where he sold two screenplays and his two children pursued show business careers.

February 9

> We have first the direction to the body wherein we have communication, or communion with the control we have gained to the ethereal [etheric?] world; that is, outside, the minds of all matter. It is the mental capacity of all matter… The development of each is to be gained by its control, which is gained by its material work shown to the material man…And action gained from the ethereal [etheric?], or mental, without its production through the material has no effect on the man. 254-1

On this date in 1918 Gertrude gave birth to the Cayces' third boy, Edgar Evans.

Not that day but soon afterwards Edgar lost his voice again. Gertrude conducted the reading to restore it, and for the very first time, Edgar remembered what happened while in a trance.

He saw boys who told him how they'd been killed and gave him messages for their families. Then he saw his dead son Milton Porter. He felt the dead were alive in another plane of existence, and a dead friend told him "death" should really be called "birth." When he awakened with his voice restored, he discovered he had not said one word during his trance.

***

On this date in 1924 Edgar, having dire financial problems, was persuaded to do a life reading for himself. He was described as "one given to make manifest in the present plane much of the forces of psychic and occult forces," but to face challenges of ordinary men. (294-8)

February 10

(Q) What will help me most in coming to right decisions as to my life? (A) Prayer and meditation, to be sure. For, as He has given, "Behold I stand at the door and knock. If ye will open I will enter in." 3250-1

(Q) Is it possible to meditate and obtain needed information? (A) On any subject! whether you are going digging for fishing worms or playing a concerto! 1861-12

Guidance can be ours on any subject if we are living our lives to please the Creative Forces. "For He faileth not to keep the peace He has promised in thee if ye walk in the light of His ways."

Prayers and meditation are keys to making good decisions. Edgar gives very specific directions. "First seek to know self as to what is the impelling desire in thine inner self... But ask in self, 'What IS my purpose? What IS my desire? Is it an experience that I may exalt my inner self? or that I may glorify my Maker, my Redeemer, my Lord, my Master?"

After answering this question mentally, "know that the Father liveth in thee, and will rightly guide thee in thy seeking and in thine steps day by day, if thou hast prepared His temple in thee for the place that He may abide…. if thou keepest the temple clean and decorated in the spirit of love, and in the light of truth, then it will shed its light abroad, even as He has given, 'I will not leave thee comfortless but will come and abide with thee, that ye may be my children and I will be your god.'" (440-4) If we're good, we'll receive guidance.

February 11

> First, analyze self and self's purposes. Know, study, analyze what is thy ideal - in body, in mind, in spirit. Not as to what ye would like for thy neighbor to be like; not what ye would desire thy friend or thy foe to think; not what ye would like for thy Creator to do - but rather "What sort of neighbor am I?" And "Do I live that I would have my neighbor be? Do I think, do I act in a way and manner that I would wish my friend, my foe, to do toward me? IS my ideal indeed in Him, who is the way, the truth, the light?"   2326-1

On this date in 1929 the Cayce Hospital officially opened. The facility had been dedicated on November 11, 1928, but was not until now opened for patients.

Over the many years of giving psychic diagnoses of physical problems, Edgar had found that if the recommendations of readings were followed, clients were cured. Finding a doctor willing to follow the advice was so often the problem.

Now doctors were on site to carry out the treatments as the readings directed. The goal Edgar had sought for so many years had been achieved. He was elated!

Charles Dillman, who was afflicted with a chronic sinus condition, became the first patient. He was cured and released on February 20.

The time would come when the waiting list for readings was more than a year long, and more staff had to be hired to handle the deluge of mail and phone calls.

February 12

> (Q) What is meant by "The soul must feed upon dead patience that it may grow into an abundant life"? (A) For, ...we become aware of our souls through patience. Then, patience that is crucified of self in service to another is as dead in the sense of the earth's activity... Be angry and sin not. Be patient. Seven times forgive; yea, seventy times seven. And, being dead, being crucified to the things that pertain to the earth, looking for that ACCEPTABLE day of the Lord.   262-59

Forgiving should be easy to all who understand the concept of the Law of One. We are all equal in the eyes of our Creator—the Creative Forces or God.

"Because there are contentions, because there is the lack of the giving and taking as to others' thought, does not change God's attitude one whit; neither does it make one above another; for, as has been given, there IS ONLY one - the others are as those acting in the capacity of the thought that was given to them through that same power...." (364-9)

We should forgive those who belittle us in any way. "Study, then, to show thyself approved, EACH DAY! DO WHAT thou KNOWEST to do, to be aright! Then LEAVE IT ALONE! God giveth the increase! Thy worry, thy anxiety, only will produce disorder in thine OWN mind!

"For the application in self, the TRY, the effort, the energy expended in the proper direction, is all that is required of THEE. God giveth the increase." (601-110)

For that promise, we forgive all, and thank God.

February 13

We have into the world all bodies subject to ethereal control....The development of each individual has this. in itself. The condition that we have [Edgar Cayce?] to help the individual bodies are through their individual self, assisted by material objects.   obtained into the mental mind of the material man. We have this body here, this mind, this matter, that we have here, of Edgar Cayce, Jr., through the ethereal world, as it gathers from the force given out either from the present, the past, and given back to the material man through the subconscious self...   294-1

A reading this day in 1911 explained how Edgar received information to help heal patients. Three months earlier he had started a partnership to psychically diagnose Dr. Wesley Ketchum's problem patients. It was the first reading on "the work."

With the new partnership Edgar for the first time charged a fee for his services. This reading made it clear that those receiving help should "give of their means for personal gain" to keep the business operating.

Edgar's Forces emphasized that when patients came for help "We answer both to his inner conscience and to the physical man, and to the outside world, whereby we gain credence...And the minute we gain credence and give credit to ourselves we lose it all."

The wordy admonishment seemed to be: Do good but don't take credit for it yourself. Edgar always obeyed.

February 14

Let thy light keep bright within thine own purpose. Analyze thy purposes oft; not as to become self-centered, not as to justify anything. For, He requireth not sacrifice… but that ye GLORIFY Him not others.
2560-1

On this date in 1927 Edgar gave another reading for A.C. Preston, whose previous reading for finding treasure in Bimini had failed because an impure motive kept Edgar's inner voice from sharing information.

This reading about a search for treasure along Lostman's River, in Monroe County, Florida, located some gold, silver, and jewels on an island near an old tree stump with a young tree growing out of it. The spot to find it was six miles above the river's mouth, where the river divided into two.

A second reading March 5 gave more explicit directions, warning that local inhabitants might be antagonistic toward treasure hunters.

The search party became lost in July, and the search stopped, but Preston continued to believe the treasure could be found if he could only find the right island, out of "the thousands" along the river.

Preston had great faith in Edgar and later became business manager for the Association for Research and Enlightenment, which was formed after the Cayce Hospital closed and the Association of National Investigators disbanded. (See March 29)

February 15

Then budget the time, that there may be a regular period for sustaining the physical being.... Do not court the flesh, but do give voice and heed to keeping the body as the temple of the living God, as indeed it is. Purify it. Keep it clean - in physical, as well as in mind, that it indeed may offer that channel through which thy Maker may speak to thee. For as He has promised, "I will meet thee in thy temple of thine own body." 3691-1

Edgar's formula for a good complexion comes with directions for treating ourselves as we would be treated in a professional spa.

The formula is 3/4 cup peanut oil, 1/4 cup olive oil, 1/4 cup rosewater, 1 tablespoon lanolin, dissolved.

Start with a tepid 15 to 20-minute bath, "giving the body a thorough rub with any good soap (Sweetheart, Castile, Ivory) to stimulate the body-forces."

Shake the solution well, pour some into an open saucer, and dip fingers in same. Massage the face, neck, shoulders, arms, and then the whole body, "especially in the limbs—in the areas that would come across the hips, across the body, across the diaphragm."

This treatment will "give the body a good base for the stimulating of the superficial circulation, but will aid in keeping the body beautiful; that is, as to any blemish of any nature." (1968-70)

Edgar recommended this self-massage at least once or twice each week. Two years previously his advice had completely cured this patient of dermatitis.

February 16

For, the warnings have been given again and again as to how to keep the body fit - as to the foods, the diets, the exercise, the recreation, the rest, the building of the mental body, the time to play and the time to work, the time to recuperate the mental body, the time to make holy and the time to pray.... All of these must be observed, if there would be a well-rounded, a well-centered life.   257-229

On this day in February 1944 Edgar gave the above advice to an adult male, an active A.R.E. member. This reading's admonition might very well have been meant for him to heed himself.

He had been working too hard, doing many more readings than he should. He couldn't find it in his heart to turn down parents who wanted news of their military sons overseas. He couldn't turn away an ailing person who hadn't been helped by a doctor.

Sick with a cold and cough, he needed a chance to recuperate away from Virginia Beach where he simply couldn't stop working. He went to Florida and spent ten days visiting Tom Sugrue in Clearwater, enjoying fishing and sunshine. He recovered from his cold and cough.

Returning to Virginia Beach, he resumed his usual hectic schedule, and before March he was bedridden with pneumonia.

The psychic diagnostician wouldn't or couldn't follow the advice he knew was always right. He couldn't say no to anyone who needed his help.

February 17

Do stay close to the Ark of the Covenant which is within thee; knowing the Father, the Son, the Holy Ghost must move within and through thee if ye would bring thyself closer to the fullness of thy purposes in the earth.

5177-1

Edgar gave readings to many people who had past-life ties to the Ark of the Covenant, the holy chest that held three sacred objects and was an energy source.

Barthuel, talented in both metal and wood works, helped build the Ark, and "in the present... certain things to be done at certain times, that become of themselves as a sacred duty to the entity...." (1747-3)

Emeliel was among "those who bore the ark as it passed through and over Jordan...." In the present he was advised "to show thyself approved unto God, a workman not ashamed, rightly dividing the words of truth and keeping self unspotted from the world." (5275-1)

Belda helped prepare for "the hangings of the Holy of Holies, for those wherein the ark was again to be reestablished...." In the present her "inner self an expression that is hard to give voice to, even in determining its effect upon the body or the mind of the entity." (1000-14)

The Ark readings made two things clear. Past-life experiences *do* influence present-day attitudes. We all have the Ark's boundless energy and power within us.

February 18

Happiness then is knowing, being in touch with, manifesting in the daily life, DIVINE love…. And Happiness is as much a law as is error or goodness or day and night; for without it man is a dreary being indeed.
262-109

Happiness comes from being a good person, by—as the above reading put it—keeping the law of the Lord.

"Keep thy purposes then, keep thy aims, thy desires, of a material, of a mental, of a spiritual nature…For these temporal things must pass away, but that spiritual house, that temple - that cleanliness so akin to godliness - is that which lives on and on….Then steer thy course to that… that brings peace, and the calm that brings Happiness in thy daily life."

The Forces that spoke through Edgar thought whiners couldn't find happiness because "what is the first law? Like begets like!" If we let direct love direct and guide us, we will not let trivialities bother us.

"What matter if there is no new dress, hat, shoes, or even the house rent paid? They are of the moment. If you are happy that you are alive, you still have the opportunity to say, 'Blessings be on thee,' and these are what live forever.

"Shadows pass. Only the light and truth lives on. Disturbances and distresses pass. For you say 'God is in His holy temple, let all the earth keep silent.' What do you mean? Is it just a saying because you have heard it oft, or do you really believe it?

"Then, as His children, ACT THAT WAY!"

February 19

FOR, THE EARTH IS ONLY AN ATOM IN THE UNIVERSE OF WORLDS!

And man's development began through the laws of the generations in the earth; thus the development, retardment, or the alterations in those positions in a material plane.

And with error entered that as called DEATH, which is only a transition - or through God's other door - into that realm where the entity has builded, in its manifestations as related to the knowledge and activity respecting the law of the universal influence.

Hence the development is through the planes of experience that an entity may become one WITH the first cause....   5749-3

    Earth is a school, and our souls keep reincarnating until we've learned all its lessons. Between sojourns on earth, our souls sojourn on other planets to learn the particular lessons offered there.

    The First Cause was that the created would be worthy to be the companion for the Creator, and it should be the first cause for every person on this planet. The same celestial spark exists in all of us. All is one. It is a universal law: the law of one.

    "The purpose of life," Edgar said in trance, "is not the gratifying of the appetite, nor of any selfish desire, but it is that the entity, the soul, may make the earth, where the entity finds its consciousness, a better place in which to live." (Creation: April 25-30, May 1-5, 7-17, 19-20)

February 20

Hence each soul finds itself ever in the hands of a LIVING Intelligence, a living God....While all depend one upon another, we find that the three phases of human exper-ience... body, mind, soul - the three phases ...for the freedom of same - knowledge, interpretation, application - all of these work together from those experiences....   1096-4

During the early l940s when many of Edgar's Bible study and Christian Endeavor students were overseas fighting World War II, Edgar discovered the voice that came from his mouth when he was in a trance could speak another language.

As Edgar gave readings for these students throughout Europe, his reputation grew abroad, and he began receiving reading requests from foreigners.

Every word he said in a reading for a wealthy woman in Palermo came out in Italian, which the stenographer was unable to record. The reading was stopped.

Hugh Lynn searched around Selma until he found a fruit vendor who sat in on a second reading and translated as best he could. He missed some words in the Sicilian dialect he didn't understand.

Afterwards, he complimented Edgar on his Italian fluency. From then on, Gertrude as conductor specified up front, when readings were for foreigners, that Edgar was to give the reading in English.

That command didn't prevent a foreign language word or two from slipping in now and then—and sometimes unknown languages no observers could identify. Edgar never doubted the Force's intelligence.

February 21

> *We have a body, one capable of attuning even to the masters of the holy place, or holy mount, such a one may gain for self an experience...beyond description in words, only feeling may express same.*   126-83

Edgar never seemed to be bothered by the strange things that—for no apparent reason—happened to him.

Once in a Hopkinsville barbershop, a playing child gazed at him strangely and then hopped into his lap and hugged him.

The child's father, who was being shaved, said such an action was highly unusual for the little girl. He was amazed that she seemed to be so familiar with Edgar.

At this point in his life, intelligence about reincarnation had not yet been revealed, so Edgar may have been as amazed as the father.

Once while giving a scheduled reading, the Forces gave him diagnoses of the physical problems of eight additional people. He didn't have to wonder very long about the reason because their requests soon arrived in the mail.

Once he passed a stranger on the street and had an urge to call him by name. The man asked, "How do you know my name?" Being the honest guy he was, Edgar explained that he had psychic skills, but the man scoffed at that idea.

"I am a bank president," he said. "Tell me the combination for our master safe, and I'll believe you."

Edgar did, and they quickly became friends.

February 22

Having given free will, then - though having the foreknowledge, though being omnipotent and omnipresent - it is only when the soul that is a portion of God CHOOSES that God knows the end thereof. 5749-14

Edgar was summoned on two top secret trips to Washington, D.C., during World War II. His memoirs said he gave information to "one high in authority."

He further surmised what the first reading said "must have been at least interesting as I was called a year or so later for the same purpose."

The irony of this occurrence is that Edgar surely came away from those meetings without knowing a single word of what he had said in a trance.

Certainly if he was being consulted about battle tactics, only authorities with high security clearance would have been present. If being investigated for his correspondence with Italy's consul general, the same is true.

During World War II Cayce *did* do readings for and carry on correspondence with Italians who discovered him through the many GIs he helped by remote readings.

The latter is the generally accepted theory for the trips' purposes because such an investigation was confirmed by the U.S. Department of Military. But would that investigation require a second trip a year after the first? And would an investigation into himself have been top secret and required a reading?

We'll never know, and neither did Edgar.

February 23

Mind is the Builder. Then, if ye would have less strife and more harmony, build same in thy daily relationships. For when ye complain of the faults of others, do ye not build such barriers that you cannot speak kindly or gently to those whom ye have felt or do feel have defrauded or would defraud thee?   412-9

We should let go of resentments and grudges against any whom we perceive to have hurt us.

"And when ye consider what disappointments ye have had in individual associations, think how thy God must have been disappointed in thee when thou hast spoken lightly of thy brother, when thou hast condemned him in thine own conscience...

"Hast thou prayed with them? Hast thou spoken kindly with them?...Why art thou impatient? For the carnal forces are soon given over to the lusts thereof, but the spirit is alive through eternity! Be not impatient, but love ye the Lord!" (262-63)

The Creative Forces agree with the Biblical command, "If thine enemy smite thee, turn the other cheek," and "only in the manifesting of same, and bringing into materiality such experiences, may ye indeed KNOW the joy even of living." (412-9)

If we keep busy with activities uplifting to the spiritual and mental associations with others, we will "lose sight of overconsciousness in disappointments, disillusionments in individuals." (3250-1)

In simpler words, we will forget what hurt us. Good!

February 24

Then the purposes, the aims, the spiritual life - this should be considered first and foremost. Know thine own ideal, spiritually, mentally, materially. Thou knowest in Whom thou hast believed. Then in thy mental life and in thy material life, make practical application of the tenets and the truths of same, in the choices of thy daily activities; knowing that He, the keeper of the way, is in accord with all that is. For, without Him there was not anything made that was made.
2925-1

Spiritual is the life, mind is the builder, physical is the result. This universal truth was heralded in the readings often enough to warrant being a universal law.

Edgar repeatedly makes the point that cooperation among the spiritual, mental, and physical can achieve great things: health, happiness, abundance, success, whatever. As long as our ideals are in accordance with spiritual laws and expectations, we will receive the help we need to reach our goals.

"Yet study to show thyself - in thy activities, in thy thoughts - approved unto that thou hast chosen, or may choose, as thy ideal." (900-331)

"And in the spiritual, know that the ideal must be that which is able to keep whatever may be committed unto it against ANY experience. In the mental, it must be ever constructive, creative in its influence, in its activity….These…should be studied, analyzed, thought through; and.. should be lived up to, in accordance with that ideal." (2021-10)

February 25

Set an ideal; as to citizenship, as to parenthood, as to neighbor, as to MANNER of church service, as to manner of neighborly activity; as to thy spiritual, thy mental self. ...then so live thine own life in those relationships that others would never question... what thy ideal is.
1745-1

Abandoning spiritual ideals can cause societal woes. In a reading during the Great Depression, Edgar was asked the cause of the economic depression and when conditions might become normal in the United States.

"As it, the United States...is the leading nation in attempting to give an understanding of the principles of 'Thou shalt love thy neighbor as thyself,' it stands above all others in its financial, in its social positions in the world; yet it has faltered, and...when troubles arise, when fearful conditions beset thee, the same answer as was of old, 'Know ye that SIN lieth at THY door!'

"When there are, then, the greater number that would SEE that the IDEAL is again MADE the STANDARD, then may CONDITIONS be EXPECTED to improve. This not as MEN count improvement, in dollars and cents, but in contentment and understanding - and ONE is the fruit of the other!" (3976-9)

We all have the responsibility to demonstrate our ideal for the benefit of our society and the world at large. "For TODAY, in the experience of EVERY soul manifested, is the OPPORTUNITY to make manifest that which IS ideal, in the experience of that individual entity." (816-10)

February 26

Do learn music. It is part of the beauty of the spirit. For remember, music alone may span that space between the finite and the infinite. In the harmony of sound, the harmony of color, even the harmony of motion itself, its beauty is all akin to that expression of the soul-self in the harmony of the mind, if used properly in relationship to body. 3659-1

Edgar's Forces compared music to all harmonies in the universe and advised playing, listening, or dancing to music as aids for imbuing spiritual, mental, and physical balance.

"So, begin with this. Get this thoroughly, and begin with the simplest, but of ever interpreting the emotions of the body, the mind, the soul. And we will come into symphonies then, to be sure. For these are those upon which the greater interpretation of the soul and mind may attune the body to the infinite." (3053-3)

"Music is as color, as tone, as a destructive or creative force, dependent upon that to which it appeals in the influence of individuals." (3509-1)

When asked if music, poetry, and art were just worldly and illusory, Edgar answered, "Know they are of the realms of creative energies which are of the Maker." (5265-1) "Music should be the life giving flow, the interpreting of the emotions... of the body." (3053-3)

Music and art are "the varied experiences that may be taken of that as necessary to make for an exceptional individual." (403-1)

February 27

(Q) Does the soul ever die? (A) May be banished from the Maker, not death.   3744-1

On this day in 1925 a reading revealed that 7-year-old Edgar Evans developed the mechanical skills he was already demonstrating in Poseidia during the Atlantean era. By this time the Cayces believed in reincarnation, so the revelation came as no surprise to them.

Had they received such information at their healthy baby boy's birth on February 9, 1918, they would have met it with genuine skepticism. No reading exists for Edgar Evans at his birth, perhaps because at that time Edgar was run down and again losing his voice.

The next reading given was for Edgar himself, and it turned out to be the first he remembered when awake.

He saw graveyards in India, but then he was in France, at graves awaiting three former Bible study students who gave him messages to deliver.

He again changed places and saw his own dead son, Milton Porter, on the third or fourth row up on a stack of babies. Milton smiled his recognition.

Then Edgar saw a family friend about to be buried at that very moment in a local cemetery. She told him where he would find $2.50 that should be given to her daughter. Next a fellow church member talked to him about his son, and he woke up. Gertrude said Edgar uttered not a word while asleep, and when he awoke his voice was fine.

He found the $2.50 exactly where the woman had told him, and he gave it to her daughter.

February 28

Do not hold resentment. Do not get so mad at times when things are a little wrong. Remember that others have as much right to their opinions as self, but that there IS a level from which all may work together for good.   1819-1

On this day in 1931 Morton Blumenthal asked the board of the Association of National Investigators to turn the hospital property over to him.

The Cayce Hospital, in operation for just a few days more than two years, was in dire financial trouble, but not for lack of patients. People whose doctors had been unable to help them found the Cayce Hospital, Edgar diagnosed their ailments, and on-site doctors stayed true to the reading's recommendations in treating them.

The problem was that Edgar could not turn anyone away, no matter whether or not that person could pay. Edgar gave 210 readings the first three months, and the appointment waiting list stretched for months.

Far too many patients had not paid, and Blumenthal wanted the property in exchange for his and his brother Edwin's paying the hospital's large outstanding bill.

The proposal was voted down, with Edgar abstaining. Then he said, however, that if Morton, who had financed the hospital, needed the hospital property, it should be returned to him, and a second vote did just that.

Within a few weeks papers were signed that closed the hospital and disbanded the ANI.

February 29

Know thyself first. Look within thine own heart. What is it ye would purpose to do? Satisfy thine own appetites? Satisfy thine own desire for power or glory, for fame or fortune? These, as ye have experienced and as ye know within thy deeper self, easily take wings and fly away. Only those things that are just, those things that are beautiful, those things that are harmonious, that arise from brotherly kindness, brotherly love, patience, hope and graciousness, LIVE.   1776-1

Selfishness may not only keep us from helping others, it may keep us from achieving our own goals.

When a young man asked if he would be successful in his field, Edgar answered, "These are channels, these are opportunities. For what purpose? For fame or fortune alone? Or that ye may be a helpful influence? If the motives are selfish, little success. If they are for the universal forces or sources, that God may be the greater glory in the lives of others through thine own feeble effort, then success. For know, ye alone with the Lord are a GREAT majority!" (1494-1)

Success we seek must be in keeping with our ideals, which must be in keeping with the higher good.

"Study to show thyself approved unto Him. For if the heart is singing with the beauties and joys that may come in the service to the fellow man, it bespeaks of those things that answer from within as to the life being made as a channel of blessing to the fellow man - and IN the path of glory for the companionship with Him." (683-10)

March 1

Truth the light! These are but words to many. Make them as frontlets upon thy brow, that those who meet thee even in the way - may be DIRECTED ARIGHT!   254-83

On this day in 1932 the kidnapping of Augustus Lindbergh Jr., son of a famous pilot, initiated a request from David Kahn—a friend of a friend of the pilot—to ask for Edgar's psychic help. The first reading saw a man lowering the baby to the ground. It traced their travel to the Cardova district near New Haven.

He saw the child was at 437 Scharter Street with three men (one named Megleo) and a woman named Madge Beliance. David and friend couldn't find the address. On March 10 another reading gave specific directions, describing the house with two goats in the yard. Megleo was now at the Taft Hotel having a coke.

Unable to find the house, Kahn and his friend wired Edgar, who called them "little minds" and said, "The directions have been given...It will be too late after a while!" Edgar had always doubted success with such searches unless requested by the ones deeply concerned.

He gave March 12 and 13 readings while Kahn and his friend kept looking. One said the Lindbergh child—now ill—had been moved to Jersey City in a car with a license plate 2M217, but directions to the house were fuzzy.

A March 26, 1932, reading said Kahn should give up the search for the Lindbergh baby, and he did.

March 2

> (Q) Please discuss, "How and What are the manifestations of the Father?" (A) The fruits of the spirit. Gentleness, kindness, the loving word, patience, hope, persistence, and - above all - consistency in thy acts and in thy speech. Be ye glorious in thine activity. Be ye joyous in thy words. For, HAPPY is the man that knoweth that his life bespeaks that the Son and the Spirit of Truth directs the words and the activities of his body! 262-58

Manifesting the fruits of the spirit is keeping the new commandment that Christ gave to humankind: to love one another.

"What, then, are the fruits of love? The fruits of the spirit; which are kindness, hope, fellowship, brotherly love, friendship, patience; these are the fruits of the spirit; these are the commands of Him that ye manifest them in whatsoever place ye find yourself, and your soul shall grow in grace, in knowledge, in understanding, and that joy that comes with a perfect knowledge in Him brings the joys of earth, the joys of the mental mind, or joys of the spheres, and the GLORY of the Father in thine experience." (436-2)

The fruits of the spirit have opposition. "The spirit of hate, the anti-Christ, is contention, strife, fault-finding, lovers of self, lovers of praise. Those are the anti-Christ, and take possession of groups, masses, and show themselves even in the lives of men." (281-208)

Avoid these, "For these take hold upon the gates of hell and are the torments to man's soul!" (1776-1)

March 3

Use that thou hast in hand today; for, as the opportunity, as the time comes for the giving out, be sure it is ever seasoned well with the words of truth that make for developments in the experiences of others towards constructive influences leading to God - for he that abides in Him shall want for nothing. 2136-1

Readings repeated three concepts for vocational guidance.

The first was to determine our ideal, our inner life goal, and seek to accomplish it.

The second was to strive to be of service to others. The third was to use that in hand—to start where we are.

An interest thoroughly developed in past lives points toward success in the field again. Whatever attracts us most, we should explore further.

An Irishman who was asked if he knew how to play the violin answered, "I don't know. I've never tried it." That reply was very wise because the subconscious contains reserves we don't know we have—like a bank account we opened as a child and forgot about.

Edgar's inner voice gave assurance that we all have the ability to tap into our souls' memory, either through hypnosis or meditation.

Child protégées don't need these techniques. They remember! Who knows what good karma awaits us, ready to bring us joy? Bad karma will always find us, but we might have to search for the good.

Edgar's very smart Source would say, "Do it!"

March 4

(Q) What should be our attitude toward the Negro, and how may we best work out the karma created in relations with him? (A) He is thy brother! They that produced, they that brought servitude without thought or purpose have created that which they must meet within their own principles, their own selves…. These should be taken in the attitude of their own individual fitness….. For He hath made of one blood the nations of the earth.
3976-24

Edgar didn't need his inner voice to tell him that the black, brown, red, yellow, and white races are equal to each other and to God. However, he lived in an era of extreme racism, and the above questions and answers emphatically made the infinite truth known.

His own father Leslie was not only an outspoken racist, he actually tried to perfect an organization to preserve the supremacy of the white race.

Edgar and his father had heated debates on the subject of black equality. In a letter to his son in November 1928, Leslie wrote: "I feel that God created only one man and one woman, and not races of men."

He quoted Bible passages saying they supported the fact that "This beast was made for man's servant to develop the earth. Man was given control of the beast, as he was of everything created."

Edgar, a supreme Bible scholar, certainly set his father straight, but to no avail. Leslie died with racist karma to face in his next life.

March 5

Ye have to do the do. God only gives an individual the ability to choose, but you do the choosing. He does not choose for you 257-249

On or about this day in 1917, Edgar's Forces said the only cure for Alfred Berry Butler was an organ transplant—35 years before the first transplant was performed.

This reading, considered preposterous at the time, has disappeared, but here's how Berry's son wrote about it: "The reading described the disease with which my father was affected exactly, which was in non-technical terms a cancer."

"Mr. Cayce made a statement that the bladder, stomach, kidneys were affected and that the only cure would have been an operation by the Mayo Bros. and a substitution of the diseased parts from some living animal. We were unable to convince my mother that this course was practical so the disease developed rapidly and was fatal within sixty days of the reading."

The transplant idea was too radical an idea for Mrs. Butler to consider even though she had good reason to believe in Edgar's predictions. Once before she was worried that Mary Butler had not come home at the expected time from a trip she had taken alone.

A reading told her Mary's letter, which had been delayed, would reach home tomorrow—and so would Mary. She was fine. Many relieved family members sought readings after that and poured kudos on Edgar for years to come.

March 6

As we see, all visions and dreams are given for the benefit of the individual, [if they would] would they but interpret them correctly, for we find that visions, or dreams, in whatever character they may come, are the reflection, either of the physical condition, with apparitions with same, or of the subconscious, with the conditions relating to the physical body.   294-15

    Edgar interpreted dreams for both of the Blumenthal brothers. Most ended up being stock-market tips.

    On this day in 1929 Morton reported a dream in which he saw a bull chasing his red-dressed wife. The reading's interpretation was that Morton should take the bull by the horns. The bull market was leaving. His wife's red dress warned of danger.

    On April 6, 1929, Edwin reported a dream in which an angry crowd was injecting him with poison. They were inflicting this punishment upon him for killing a young man, though he was not responsible for the murder.

    He felt the needle and expected to die.

    Edwin himself interpreted this dream to represent the battle then within the Federal Reserve Board that could affect the financial market negatively. His stockbroker clients would blame him when their stock values fell. A reading said his interpretation was right.

    Both brothers were stockbrokers by day and obviously took their work home with them, even while sleeping at night. Edgar's interpretations of their dreams made them rich.

March 7

Rather be in that manner as learned in the spiritual sense, with that UNDERSTANDING that to do good is to LIVE good, and NOT to APPEAR good. BE good - not just APPEAR good. To LIVE love is to be love. To be one with the Father is to be equal WITH the Father, and as the understanding of the entity is gained in the application of truths gained the consciousness OF truth is apparent - for, as has been given, to love is to LIVE love - not the answer of desire or of amorous affection, but is ALL in one - for love is law, law is love.   900-331

On this day in 1897 Edgar proposed to Gertrude, who said she loved him, but would have to think about his proposal of marriage.

When Edgar tried to pinpoint a date that might get him an answer, she told him March 12—five days away.

He would have her answer before his twentieth birthday on March 18 and he would probably ride his new bicycle to get it.

He bought the bicycle when his salary was raised from ten to fifteen dollars, and rain or snow didn't keep him from riding it.

At this point in their relationship, they had never even kissed, but they had been seeing each other very regularly. They never missed seeing Gertrude's brother play shortstop for the local baseball team, and they seldom passed up a performance at the Holland Opera House. When Edgar visited The Hill, they were usually around many others and busy with many other activities. Perhaps they'd had no suitable moment.

March 8

As the body-physical is purified, as the mental body is made wholly at-one with purification or purity, with the life and light within itself, healing comes, strength comes, power comes.

So may an individual effect a healing, through meditation, through attuning not just a side of the mind nor a portion of the body but the whole, to that at-oneness with the spiritual forces within, the gift of the life-force within each body. 281-24

On this day in 1914 Edgar had an emergency appendectomy in Selma, Alabama.

While out on an earlier photo shoot, he had felt cramped and nauseous. Dr. Gay diagnosed appendicitis and gave him drugs to correct it.

He took the drugs and felt better, but for some reason he decided to do a reading on himself. Had a voice in his head urged it? Was his precognition at work?

Whatever! His decision to go into a trance for himself may have saved his life.

The reading ordered an immediate operation that would be difficult. It also suggested the surgeon treat a clot caused by his childhood testicle wound.

That same night doctors reported difficulty with his appendix twisted around his intestines, and they could not remove the clot, which continued to bother him off and on all his life.

March 9

The ...sixth sense activity, is the activating power or force of the other self. What other self? That which has been builded by the entity or body, or soul, through its experiences as a whole in the material and cosmic world, see? ...Hence... does the subconscious make aware to this active force when the body is at rest, or this sixth sense, some action on the part of self or another that is in disagreement with that which has been builded by that other self, then THIS is the warring of conditions or emotions within an individual. 5754-2

Edgar called dreams the sixth sense, which allows our consciousness to mesh our present lives with the activities our souls have had throughout eternity.

If we go to sleep sad and awaken happy, our soul has traveled into the realm of past-life experiences, correlated a present experience with that, and judged our present experience to be good.

"Hence we find the more spiritual-minded individuals are the more easily pacified, at peace, harmony, in normal active state as well as in sleep. Why? They have set before themselves...awareness of the divine or creative forces within their experience."

The opposite is true. If we awaken in low spirits, "The experiences of the soul are meeting that which it has merited...If one has set self in array against that of love as manifested by the Creator, in its activity brought into material plane, then there MUST be a continual - continual - WARRING of those elements." (5754-2)

March 10

For remember, as ye sow so shall ye reap. And when that thou hast sown in thine mind (for thine mind is the builder)... brings that thou hast sown; some sixty, some forty, yea some an hundredfold.   1183-1

What Edgar sowed in 1919 came back to him multiplied in 1961 though he wasn't alive to realize it.

A pregnant woman in Selma was dying, and two doctors said her baby had no chance of surviving. It was mid-July, and the baby was not expected until August.

Her sister contacted the South's most famous surgeon for consultation, and he agreed with the two doctors. The woman was too close to death for the baby to have any chance.

By the time Edgar was consulted, it was definitely too late to save the mother, but the Forces said the baby could live. The reading prescribed "an unheard of concoction of simple ingredients with brew made from the bark of a slippery elm."

Upon drinking the unusual beverage, the pregnant woman immediately became more comfortable, and a few days later the baby came prematurely without complications as the woman died.

A Christian woman who had herself recently given birth sympathized with the family's tragedy and nursed the baby with her own child until the baby was put on formula at six weeks.

The baby grew up, married, had two daughters, and at age 41 joined Edgar's organization, the A.R.E. Payback!

March 11

We find there are no coincidents, or chance coincidents. Each and every individual follows out that line of development of the entity in the present earth plane as it has received from the preceding conditions, and each grain of thought or condition is a consequence of other conditions created by self.... 900-2

Skeptics of Edgar's unusual abilities felt obligated to put him to the test, and sometimes his skills were simply obvious.

A priest didn't know the contents of a package he'd just received in the mail. Edgar quickly told him the package contained altar candles. The priest opened the package, saw the candles, crossed himself, and fled.

Another test was to determine if Edgar could perceive the sex of a fetus, and Edgar did so correctly for nine expectant mothers and their doctors. One doubts they trusted him enough to purchase pink or blue baby clothes, but they surely would with the second child.

Edgar was always welcome to go fishing with a church buddy who kept a small boat at the Norfolk marina. His buddy loved telling how Edgar would quietly concentrate on the water around the boat, and the fish would come. Did he communicate telepathically with trouts and muskies?

He *did* communicate with plants that he talked lovingly to. His garden was a horticulturist's dream—the biggest, best of everything. Admirers lavished him with praise for his gardening skills.

March 12

By the creating of a normal balance within the body for its physical and mental and spiritual well-being, we not only create a normal physical balance but then give - in the expressions of what has been indicated for the physical and mental body - an OUTLET for the beauty of sex. Do not look upon sex as merely a PHYSICAL expression! There is a physical expression that is beauty within itself, if it is considered from that angle; but when the mental and the spiritual are guiding, then the outlet for beauty becomes a NORMAL expression of a NORMAL, healthy body.   1436-1

On this day in 1897 Gertrude accepted Edgar's proposal of marriage, and an awkward silence followed.

Instead of giving her the expected kiss, Edgar confessed he had never kissed anyone before.

Probably happy to know she was the first girl he'd ever kissed, Gertrude showed him how.

Within a few days after Gertrude and Edgar became engaged, Edgar had a small diamond ready to be cut and mounted. For some inexplicable reason, he sent the diamond to Romania to get this job done.

FAST FORWARD: The ring was back for Gertrude to wear by summer, but they couldn't set a wedding date because Edgar lost his bookstore job. The Hopper Brothers had a new partner, so they no longer needed Edgar, who was stunned by his dismissal because his employers loved his work. See June 27 about his job.

March 13

There are centers through which those of one solar system may pass to another, as we have indicated in information for individuals. There are also those experiences in which individual souls may seek a change. As He gave, as the tree falls so does it lie. This is not only material, it is also mental and spiritual. Is God's hand short, that there would not be all that each soul would require? 5755-2

Gertrude certainly knew that Edgar was different, but when she accepted his proposal of marriage, she could not have realized how drastically his unusual skills would affect their marriage.

The ability described in the above quote is one Edgar's Source asserted that we all have, but Edgar certainly had it from early childhood. Not only could he contact high souls, souls also seemed to search him out.

Once in 1932 Edgar was disappointed that so few regular students had arrived for his Bible study class. As he started talking about Joshua, his carefully prepared subject, the empty seats began filling up.

His father Leslie didn't see the new attendees, but he could tell from Edgar's expression that something astounding was happening. The seats were filling with ghosts—perhaps arriving to show a well-meaning teacher his effort had not gone unappreciated.

Ghost guests filled the pews at Virginia Beach's Presbyterian Church again in 1934 when Edgar was talking about the second coming of Christ. Gertrude quickly learned to accept such presences in their home.

March 14

Let love be without dissimulation. Abhor that which is evil. Cleave to that which is good. As ye walk in the light, so may ye guide others in their seeking, in their understandings of that they seek. Let the love in Christ constrain thee that ye may be more and more a channel of blessings to others. 281-23

On this day in 1944 the Archangel Michael shouted from Edgar's mouth accompanied by the usual window pane vibrations and wind gusts that always came with his presence.

"BOW THINE HEADS, YE CHILDREN OF MEN! FOR I, MICHAEL, LORD OF THE WAY, WOULD SPEAK WITH THEE! YE GENERATION OF VIPERS, YE ADULTEROUS GENERATION, BE WARNED! THERE IS TODAY BEFORE THEE GOOD AND EVIL! CHOOSE THOU WHOM YE WILL SERVE! WALK IN THE WAY OF THE LORD OR ELSE THERE WILL COME THAT SUDDEN RECKONING, AS YE HAVE SEEN! BOW THINE HEADS, YE WHO ARE UNGRACIOUS, UNREPENTANT, FOR THE GLORY OF THE LORD IS AT HAND! THE OPPORTUNITY IS BEFORE THEE! ACCEPT OR REJECT! BUT DON'T BE PIGS!"

Eight people witnessed this reading which was supposed to be about Edgar's health.

One of the witnesses was a troubled young man named Harmon Bro, who now worked for Edgar and whose story can be found on the March 15 page along with more details about this reading that ended with Archangel Michael's outrage.

March 15

They that seek GOD may find Him! Would ye have mercy shown...be merciful UNTO those YE contact. Would ye be forgiven, forgive them that know not what they say, what they do; for "As ye lift Me IN thine life, so shall YE be lifted IN the life here, now, and hereafter."
262-3

On this day in 1944 Edgar prayed for forgiveness with the group who heard Archangel Michael's scolding in yesterday's reading. Harmon Bro knew he was one who needed prayers. He was a University of Chicago graduate student prone to emotional outbursts and contemplation of suicide.

His mother, Margueritte Bro, whose story about Edgar in *Coronet* had brought him many clients, hoped he could help Harmon with his emotional problems. Edgar hired him as secretary.

The reading about Edgar's health first admonished him to take care of his physical body, then proceeded to his personality traits. Harmon recognized himself when the voice said, "Be patient with those who are weak. Be kind to those who are even ugly." He had once punched Edgar's solar plexus during an argument. Edgar's reaction was to work harder to help the troubled youth.

The reading continued, "Thy body is the temple of the living God. Act as though it were, and not as if it were a pigpen or a place of garbage for the activities of others."

Even a celestial voice couldn't persuade Edgar to stop helping so many others and start helping himself.

March 16

> Just so a SOUL enters an entity... taking on a form, coming in the dimension of that plane in which it finds - through its awakened forces, by the various spheres of relativity of forces - to make manifest ITSELF, or - as it were - it has flown out from its source to try ITS wings, to seek ITS own doing - or undoing; dependent upon that as has been builded, and the use it makes of that given it. 311-2

On this day in 1907 the Cayces' first son, Hugh Lynn, was born in the small apartment they'd moved to after Edgar's photography studio was destroyed by arson. Edgar was working long hours setting up another studio.

Gertrude's mother Lizzie helped take care of the baby, who cried incessantly until Edgar did a reading and found out why. He found that Hugh Lynn—named for both of Gertrude's brothers and called both names his entire life—was not getting enough nourishment from Gertrude's milk. A wet nurse solved the problem.

A reading many years later chided a man who too often had "neglected or forgotten what the first feeling was when thine own offspring caught hold of thy hand! This was not of sex - this was not of emotion only, but an answering of that which is the birthright of each soul to be made aware of the love of the heavenly Father to His creatures!" (1901-1)

The above quote was Edgar's Forces speaking. Today Edgar knew that truth without help.

March 17

Beware of wrath in self, and in grudges as may be builded through wrath's influences in the relationships of the fellow man; for discontent comes first within self by what is the seeming cutting off of the privileges, or of the freedom of self's movements in that thought as of self's interests. Weigh same well. Take counsel oft of self, as to whether those desires are in keeping with creative forces that are of a spiritual understanding, or have they become of the secular nature that build for CARNAL forces rather than spiritual.   1735-2

Hugh Lynn learned soon after he started school that he would never be able to keep a secret from his father.

Bullies at school taunted Hugh Lynn, calling him the son of a freak. For a while he followed Edgar's advice to ignore the boys or just to laugh with them, but as he grew bigger and stronger, he started fighting back—not only with words, but fists.

Many days he came home from school with torn or bloody clothes, his skin defiled with bruises and scratches. He hated school. He was only happy hanging out alone down by Selma's river.

One day he played hooky and took a swim in the river. Edgar knew the minute he walked into the house what he had done. He immediately recounted Hugh Lynn's entire hooky experience, right down to the place he'd put his clothes before jumping in the water.

Not only did the poor boy have classmates who taunted him, he had a father who could read his mind.

March 18

Each entity, each soul, enters the material experience for purposes. These are not individual or of a selfish nature, though they are very personal in their application and their practice.   1436-1

    Edgar was born on this day in 1877, described by his proud father Leslie as "an exceptionally fine baby, healthy...fat rosy cheeks, and a remarkably cheerful face." He was named Edgar Jr. to distinguish him from his uncle with the same name.

    He cried so much during his first month that one of his grandfather's former slaves pricked each of his nipples with a sterilized needle, allowing a liquid to seep out. During that era "milk breast" malady—a hormonal imbalance—was common after birth.

    Her treatment transformed Edgar from a squalling, angry baby to a cooing, happy one.

    Edgar was Carrie and Leslie's second child, but the first to live. Leila Beverly was born on December 24, 1875. Ten nights later Leslie got drunk and stormed out of the house. Leila was found dead in her crib the next morning, and no one ever knew if the two incidents were connected in any way.

    Edgar's mother Carrie inherited a 116-acre farm, which was lost to creditors because of Leslie's inability to farm it properly. She gave up an affluent lifestyle to marry him, and he surely did not live up to her expectations, but she was a wonderful wife and mother.

March 19

(Q) Please give a definition of the word astrology. (A) That position in space about our own earth that is under the control of the forces that are within the sphere of that control, and all other spheres without that control. That is astrology, the study of those conditions. 3744-4

On this day in 1919 Edgar gave a reading because several astrologers precicted it as the year's best day for a reading of "more interest to mankind."

Both Edgar and Gertrude felt the study of astrology conflicted with their strong Christian beliefs and had probably decided in advance what questions to pose.

As conductor, Gertrude asked if the planets have anything to do with ruling humanity's destiny. She probably was surprised when Edgar said, "They do." He went on to explain that the planets' ruling of all matter began when Earth was set in motion and the planets took their places.

The strongest power is the sun, then the planets closest to any individual at birth. The reading made it clear that no planet's action surpassed a person's willpower, thus ruling out complete predestination.

An analysis of Edgar's own astrological chart noted the moon on the opposite side of the earth resulting in many opposites for him: very good or very bad, very rich or very poor, very religious or very wicked. But it affirmed that "the psychical" had always been with him.

The Cayces kept this reading secret until they were willing to reexamine the subject four years later.

March 20

He that is without an ideal is a wanderer; and if the ideal is set in material things it will soon play out and fade. The ideal must be in spiritual things!   323-1

By mid-March of 1923 Edgar faced a crucial decision about his and his family's future. His successful Birmingham psychic diagnostician practice convinced him that giving readings should be his full-time vocation.

In January he had wanted Gertrude and the children to join him, but the readings indicated Birmingham was not the best location for a hospital. Virginia Beach would be the best location. He had been told the same in two previous readings.

He thought he was out of the oil business until Tex Rice entered his life. Edgar, who still controlled 25,000 acres of oil-rich land, ended up transferring his shares to Rice's Penn-Tenn Company. He did fundraising, but Rice's heavy drinking, marital problems, and hypertension hindered progress.

The venture ended when Rice was indicted for grand larceny for defrauding investors. Edgar and Penn-Tenn were not named in the indictment, but Edgar felt responsible because many had invested because of him.

Edgar left Birmingham and wired Gertrude to bring the children and join him in Selma. The oil business was behind him except for the many readings he gave to help others locate good drilling sites. Edgar, age 46, had made up his mind that "the work" needed to come first in his life.

March 21

Be it true that there IS the fact of reincarnation, and that souls that once occupied such an environ are entering the earth's sphere, inhabiting individuals in the present. 364-1

    Edgar's Penn-Tenn fundraising efforts led him to Dayton where he met Arthur Lammers, whose readings expanded their scope from only the physical to the philosophical. He no doubt remembered a 1910 reading in Anniston that said "the work" would begin in Dayton.

    Lammers asked Edgar's inner voice many questions about how it communicated through his body and if the information given was always correct. The answer indicated that the mind of the reading's conductor could influence the result. The intent of the inquiry could cause the source to withhold information.

    Asked if readings should be used for anything other than curing physical problems, the answer was that they must adhere to the "law of love." The information should not be used selfishly, but "given to the world."

    None of the above was news to Edgar, but what he found in Lammers' reading on October 11, 1923, certainly was. Lammers was not only told how planets at his birth had affected him, but that "this body was upon this plane, this is the third, and before that as the monk…."

    When Edgar awoke and was told what he'd said, he was distraught. He didn't believe in astrology or reincarnation, but the Forces were never wrong! He would certainly have to give the idea serious consideration.

March 22

> *When one understands self, and self's relation to its Maker, the duty to its neighbor, its own duty to self, it cannot, it will not be false to man, or to its Maker. Give then more thought, FOR THOUGHTS ARE DEEDS....What one thinks continually, they become.*   3744-5

Edgar had his astrological signs evaluated by Evangeline Adams, a famous New York astrologer of the 1920s. His curiosity was aroused because planets were mentioned more and more frequently in the readings.

She took the date, time, and place of Edgar's birth, and she pinpointed the latitude and longitude of his Christian County, Kentucky, birthplace on a globe. She consulted a large volume to find the stars' and celestial bodies' positions at 3 p.m. March 18, 1877.

From that information she told Edgar the influence planets had and were still having in shaping his life. When he recalled her findings in later years, he was impressed that much what she said proved to be true.

Hundreds of life readings told clients their natural inclinations caused by the planets at their birth, but they also always stressed that free will was the deciding factor in a person's destiny.

Astrologist Adams told Edgar to resign himself never to achieve complete success or to be materially happy, but he surely didn't dwell on that downer. The brilliant voice that came through him had said time and time again, "Mind is the builder, spirit is the life, physical is the result." He knew better than to think negative thoughts.

March 23

With a body surrounded with those elements that do not give the vibration that is in accord with the work attempting to be accomplished, there is not the best given off through the work itself.   3744-1

In March 1911 Edgar was invited by William Randolph Hearst himself to visit Chicago as his guest—the result of an article written by Roswell Field, whose story in the *Chicago Examiner* prompted the top man to want more.

Ketchum, Noe, and father Leslie accompanied Edgar on this trip, but—though it was clear from the moment they arrived at the LaSalle Hotel—the paper's intent was sensationalism, they didn't seem to mind.

Edgar was expected to perform before a crowd ensconced in the bridal suite, though Hearst himself was not among them. The readings he gave were filled with preposterous questions, and days passed before a doctor arrived—the same one who earlier punched a hypodermic needle into him.

Soon three doctors couldn't agree on what Edgar should do. Leslie objected when one wanted Edgar to solve several local mysteries, insisting upon a physical reading on one of the doctors' patients. At 2 a.m. he finally was permitted to do a reading, about which the doctors were noncommittal. One who insisted Edgar find information about a sick family member liked it.

Edgar was dismayed that partners Ketchum and Noe (See Oct. 12) showed no support for his ability and integrity.

March 24

Ridicule of such forces rather than being condemned, those are to be pitied, for they must eventually reach that condition where the soul awakens to the elements that are necessary for the developing, for without the psychic force in the world the physical would be in that condition of "hit or miss," or that as a ship without a rudder or pilot, for that element that is the building force in each and every condition is the spirit or soul of that condition which is the psychic or occult force. No healing is perfected without some psychic force exerted.   3744-2

The travesty of Edgar's interlude in March 1911 in Chicago culminated in a second section bold headline of the next day's *Chicago Examiner*: He Came, We Saw, But He Did Not Conquer.

The story quoted doctors—without naming them—as saying the physical reading that was finally arranged for Edgar to do at 2 a.m. in the morning had nothing of help in it. The stenographer, who had not written anything at all, called the words out of Edgar's mouth "gibberish" and a lot of "bunk."

A doctor who had been pleased with Edgar's diagnosis of his ill family member had refused to sign a statement for reporters, and the incident involving him never made it into print.

Testimonials praising Edgar's help were printed in the next afternoon's paper—probably never read. Edgar was no doubt unhappy, but he also pitied all involved.

March 25

(Q) Have I known any of the people in a former life with whom I have come in contact? (A) Most we meet. We meet few people by chance, but all are opportunities in one experience or another. We are due them or they are due us certain considerations.   3246-1

Sometime in late 1881 or early 1882 Edgar became friends with his first human playmate—Hallie Seay, who was called Little Anna. Up until this time he had played only with the "little folk" who came in great numbers to play games with him when he wasn't in the barn talking to his deceased grandfather.

Although his aunt warned, "He's got the Devil in him," his parents dismissed the little folk as figments of Edgar's imagination. How great it must have been for Edgar to have a real live friend who also enjoyed playing with the little folk!

Edgar and Little Anna had many adventures together, including a trip to Little River, where they met colorful fairies who were even smaller than the little people. They were best buddies until the Cayces moved in December 1882.

At age 14 he was distraught when Little Anna died of pneumonia in January 1892.

FAST FORWARD: In the 1940s while giving a long-distance reading, Edgar suspected he was reading a reincarnation of Little Anna. He later met her in person and they tearfully confirmed their childhood relationship.

March 26

Realize the influence that is shed even by the careless word that may be spoken; how that the smile makes a day entirely different for those who are burdened with the cares oft; how that the handshake may strengthen those who have in themselves lost hope, discouraged by the lack of the strengthening influence that may come from those who walk oft with their God - and their God not of themselves; needing not justification but glorification, in the manner in which ye measure to thy friends, thy foes, thy acquaintances, that blessedness of the love of God which passeth all understanding. 2560-1

In the spring of 1895, 15-year-old Edgar fell in love with 16-year-old Bessie Kenner and sent her a letter, which she answered.

Emboldened by her response, he singled her out at a church picnic, told her about his plans to be a minister, and suggested she'd be a good minister's wife.

Bessie laughed at him, making it clear her father had said that marriage to a person "not right in the head" was out of the question.

Edgar actually visited Dr. Kenner and found that Edgar's suspected mental problem wasn't his only objection. With Edgar having had his testicles injured in childhood, there was the possibility he wouldn't be able to have children.

Edgar was devastated. He quit going to school so he wouldn't have to see Bessie again. He had completed eighth grade, and his formal education ended at this point.

March 27

> *Know, however, that no urge, no influence is greater than the birthright of the entity - the will; that which is given to the soul to manifest in the beginning, as to be active within itself, independent of or in coordination with its source, or divinity itself. Yet the very gift of the Maker is divine. But this may be used or abused. It may be applied or laid aside...thoughts are deeds and bcome crimes or miracles in the application....* 900-331

In 1893 after Bessie Kenner had spurned him, Edgar decided he didn't want to be different. He wanted to be normal like the guys who smoked cigarettes, played cards, dated girls, and drank whiskey.

Now that he was no longer the "freak" at Beverly Academy, he worked at his uncle's tobacco farm.

He found a role model for normalcy in Tom Andrews, who taught him to play poker and to dance. Outside a dance hall one night, gunfire erupted and Edgar got a bullet to his shoulder. A doctor removed the bullet, cleaned his wound, and bandaged it. Edgar kept his bandage hidden under his coat, keeping his injury secret from his family for a year. That was a big secret for a 16-year-old boy in the throes of discovering his masculinity, but already shouldering a man's responsibility—supporting the Cayce family.

His new lifestyle apparently did not seem so appealing after that, and—if it hadn't ended before—it probably ended when Tom moved away from Hopkinsville.

March 28

The body is only the vehicle ever of that spirit and soul, and wafts itself through all times and ever remains the same.
                                                               5717-2

On this day in 1911, just days after returning home from the Chicago fiasco, Gertrude gave birth to the Cayces' second son, Milton Porter.

He faced several health problems. He was not getting enough nourishment from his mother's milk and he came down with whopping cough and then colitis.

Why Edgar didn't do a reading right away is not positively known, but speculation is that Gertrude objected, as she objected a few months later when she herself had pneumonia.

Edgar didn't do a reading until his son was critically ill and was apparently told it was too late. Milton died on May 17 at 11:15 a.m.

Two family members took the blame.

Edgar blamed himself for not doing a reading sooner when he was sure it would have helped.

Hugh Lynn, thinking he had brought the whooping cough home to his brother, blamed himself. He ran away, but Edgar found him weeping under the front porch steps, assured him he was not to blame, and brought him inside where they comforted each other.

Gertrude stopped eating and spent much time in bed. Before long she would be very sick herself, but she would actually be on her deathbed before she consented to a reading.

March 29

Let thy purposes, thy aims, be kept in the way thou hast chosen that the Lord thy God, through the Christ, be magnified more and more in the hearts and the minds and the souls of those that ye seek to aid day by day. Well hast thou chosen. He will not forsake thee if ye will keep in His ways. 281-23

The day before this in 1931, some seventy Cayce supporters met at the Cayce home on 34th Street in Virginia Beach.

The meeting's purpose was to establish an organization to replace the now defunct Association of National Investigators. Morton Blumenthal had turned the Cayce Hospital into a hotel and the Cayces had been forced to move from the home Morton Blumenthal took back from them. The university, though, was still open.

At the meeting's beginning Edgar told them, "I believe you will say when you have left the meeting that it was an unusual meeting. It is not that we may know how to carry on the work, but...that...we shall carry on the work."

The group decided that the new name for what had been the ANI would be the Association for Research and Enlightenment, known as the A.R.E.

Within a few months, the university was given back to Morton, but not until after President Dr. William Mosely Brown put up a fight. He finally signed papers returning it to the Blumenthals, who kept it open two more semesters before stranding professors and students by closing in the middle of a school year.

March 30

Let thy going in, thy coming out, be acceptable in the Lord. Let thy purposes, thy desires be not thine but as the Lord would use thee day by day.   281-23

On this day in 1940 Edgar gave a reading for Faith Harding, known as the Little Prophetess because of psychic abilities demonstrated from an early age.

Two A.R.E. members enticed her reluctant mother, Virginia Harding—who capitalized on her daughter's psychic talents—to come to Edgar.

The reading said she was "a chosen channel...a vessel through which the Prince of Peace would bring encouragement, assurance, and...messages of hope and of light...." It cautioned her parents that "a normal world" would never be hers, but they should give as typical a childhood as possible.

Again on April 16, 1940, Edgar met Virginia and her outstanding child and was concerned that Virginia was so eager to promote her daughter that she might end up exploiting her. A second reading reminded the parents to "heed those warnings indicated."

In a third reading, the Archangel Michael came through Edgar's voice, accompanied by a wiff of wind and vibrating window panes. "Bow thine heads, ye vile ones of the Earth. Know what has been entrusted to thee!" Virginia *did* exploit her daughter and Faith's father Harry divorced her, won custody of the child, and took Faith's psychic skills out of the headlines. The whole charade destroyed Faith's incredible gift.

March 31

Come, my children, and know in whom thou hast believed, for HE is able to keep thy needs, thine wants, thy desires, in the palm of His hand.   2897-4

On this Sunday afternoon in 1901 Edgar, who had spoken only in a whisper for more than a year, diagnosed his problem under hypnosis and was cured.

Al Layne conducted the hypnosis, father Leslie took notes, and mother Carrie observed as Edgar put himself in a trance—an ability he'd acquired from having been hypnotized so many times.

Layne told him to tell what was wrong with the body of Edgar Cayce, and Edgar said, his condition was "due to partial paralysis of the inferior muscles of the vocal cords, produced by nerve strain. This is a psychological condition producing a physical effect and may be removed by increasing the circulation to the affected parts."

Layne said, "Increase the circulation to the affected parts." Leslie, Carrie, and Layne watched as Edgar's neck reddened and swelled. In twenty-some minutes Edgar told Layne to make the suggestion that the circulation return to normal. Layne did.

When Edgar awakened, he coughed, spat blood into his handkerchief, and spoke in a clear voice.

Leslie's notes made this Edgar's first documented medical advice given in a trance. Having the readings taken in shorthand and transcribed became necessary because his physical readings contained medical information too detailed to be trusted to memory.

April 1

> As has been oft given, each individual must ascertain within his own physical, mental AND soul consciousness the sincerity of purpose of others and of self as related to such associations, or such connections, or such conditions. Then, when this is done, when this is found, the way opens itself for such work, such operations, such endeavors. 311-2

Edgar spoke well with his newly found voice for about a month in 1901. Then he would need another treatment from Layne, who suggested if Edgar could cure himself, he could cure others.

Layne became Edgar's first patient. He put him in a trance and asked what he should do about a longstanding gastrointestinal condition and his inflamed nose and throat.

When Layne showed Edgar the many exercises and medications he'd recommended, they were both amazed at the knowledgeable medical terms that had come out of his mouth. Edgar remembered none of what he'd said in a trance, nor would he ever. His trances would always need to be documented.

Layne knew if Edgar could cure him, he could cure others. He suggested a partnership with Edgar as the diagnostician and Layne as the one administering the recommended treatments.

Edgar would receive no pay, but was earning money as a photographer's apprentice and was happy to be putting his skill to good use.

April 2

Look, then, into self. Answer to self. For, each individual must so live each day that he may look into the face of that he has spoken, that he has lived, and say: "By this I stand to be judged before myself, before my God."
257-123

They set up an office with a cot for Edgar to lie on while Layne hypnotized him to diagnose people's maladies.

As people came to their small office above Layne's wife's millinery shop, news of Edgar's cures spread rapidly. An estimated eighty readings were given in their first year, only occasionally recorded by Miss Addie Pool, a stenographer.

The person wanting a reading didn't need to come to the office. Edgar needed to know only the time and the place to locate that person in his trance and start in his usual way with "Yes, we have the body."

He sometimes commented on a patient's unruly pet, the decor of the patient's room, or a bird fluttering outside the patient's window. Once when he couldn't find the patient at the expected place, he searched and reported finding her in the root cellar.

Somehow, even though his readings were healing people, Edgar became uncomfortable with what he considered experimenting with the readings.

Also, he was concerned that Layne was not a doctor. Plus, he was uncomfortable with the attention he received. He didn't want to misuse his God-given talent.

April 3

> *GROW in grace, in knowledge, IN understanding, that thy ways may be one with the CREATIVE ways, and ye shall know the Truth, and the TRUTH shall MAKE you free!*   2897-4

One cure during this 1901 over-the-hat-shop era was for a local druggist who kept losing too much weight.

Edgar told him to drink onion juice, but he hated onions and refused. As he kept going downhill, his family persuaded him to try it, and he did. Very quickly he started gaining weight.

Another cure was for a doctor's daughter who had trouble breathing. Doctors had been unable to figure out why. Edgar said a button was lodged in her throat and told the exact location in her windpipe. Because the button was celluloid, it hadn't shown up on X-rays.

Another cure had an added element of mystery. Edgar diagnosed a New York man—his first from such a long distance—prescribing clary water for a stomach disorder.

The patient, Bill Andrews, was unable to find clary water, so Edgar went into a second trance and gave him a recipe to make it. The recipe was later confirmed to be the same manufactured and sold by a Parisian manufacturer fifty years earlier.

Edgar came to realize that what was told to him when he was in a trance was always right, but sometimes he needed to ask for additional help, which always came.

April 4

For God is not mocked, and whatsoever a man soweth, that shall he also reap.   1436-1

Because Edgar wanted more out of life than his informal partnership with Layne offered, he broke off the partnership and got a new job in April of 1902.

Edgar started working at Lucian Potter's bookstore in Bowling Green, Kentucky, with the understanding he could have a photo studio on the premises.

Edgar was very happy having his voice back, even though he still got together with Layne once a month to keep his voice in tip-top shape.

He was also happy having a job he loved with a steady income. A drawback, of course, was not having Gertrude with him. Until he could afford for her to join him, he rode the train to Hopkinsville to visit her.

He lived at Hollins Boarding House, sharing a room with Hugh Beazley, a young doctor. Other boarders were a dentist, a secretary, a department store clerk, and sometimes a judge who was a newspaper publisher.

Most were a little younger than 25-year-old Edgar, and he got along well with them all. He kept his psychic abilities low key, if he revealed them at all.

Edgar quickly became a deacon at First Christian Church of Bowling Green and he taught a popular Sunday school class. He was pleased that his photography job gave him a steady income, and he liked Bowling Green well enough that once he and Gertrude were married, he thought they might settle there.

April 5

The sojourn of a soul-entity other than in materiality often influences or bears weight with individuals within the material plane - as an odor, a scent, an emotion, a wave, a wind upon the activities. Such are termed or called by some guardian angels, or influences that would promote activities for weal or for woe. THUS does the association of individuals at times become as an influence in the activities of individuals through particular periods or experiences.   538-59

On this day in 1898. Edgar developed a gratifying relationship with Dwight L. Moody, a well-known, illustrious preacher, who came to Hopkinsville for a week-long revival. He met Moody accidentally as he was searching for the family's missing cow, which he found behind Moody, who was seated along the riverbank.

The two hit it off so well that Edgar met him there every morning and went to his sermons every night until he left town.

Edgar shared things with him that he ordinarily kept to himself. He told him of the little people, the angel, and the voices and was pleased when Moody shared a story of having heard an angelic voice singing one of his favorite hymns—an experience that led to the start of his ministry.

Moody assured Edgar that people who said that his skills were the work of the Devil were wrong. Edgar was gratified with his assurance that it was the Lord who spoke to him. He hated to see his new friend leave town.

April 6

For it is in patience that ye become aware of thy soul, and of its ideals and purposes.   2938-1

Edgar knew he had an unfair advantage playing card games that took concentration because he could read minds and know what the other players held. While living in a Bowling Green boarding house in 1902, he hesitated to play cards with the other tenants.

He wanted a card game that moved so fast he wouldn't have time to key in on his opponent's thoughts.

After a meal when the diners talked about trading in the commodities market, he got the idea to invent a game called *The Pit* or *Board of Trade*.

He came up with a card game about trading wheat, sugar, and coffee, and other options in the commodity market. Each of 64 cards represented different commodities. The object was to get rich by trading options and cornering the market.

He sent a sample to Parker Brothers, a renowned game publisher, and received a check for $6, with thanks for the idea. The company also sent him a dozen decks of the cards manufactured with his idea.

Publicity in two Bowling Green newspapers was the only other profit he received for his originality.

FAST FORWARD: After *The Pit* was distributed nationwide and became a big seller, he wrote asking Parker Brothers for a percentage of the sales. They refused. *The Pit* is still sold today.

April 7

For a kindness, a gentleness to a fellow person brings more harmony into self than some great deed that may be wellspoken of. For this is soon forgotten, but the fruits of the spirit - as may be experienced in thy daily life - become as wells of living water, springing up within thine self to bring that joy, that harmony that comes from walking oft with Him.　　1183-1

Edgar's life was full of examples demonstrating the rewards that come to people who are kind and complimentary to others.

While working alone at Hopper Brothers' Bookstore, Edgar waited on a dignified man who asked about the bestsellers. Edgar told him several titles, but recommended as his personal favorite, *The Jacklins*, by Opie Percival Read.

He gave him the book to look at and then expounded at length on the plot. The customer was happy to listen, and when Edgar had finished, he introduced himself.

He was Opie Percival Read, the author himself. He gave Edgar a free pass to attend his lecture that night in the 2,500-seat Sam Jones Tabernacle. Edgar and the two Hopper Brothers were there that evening when the author bragged about the young store clerk who had surprised him by reciting such a detailed, accurate rendition of his book's plot.

One wonders if Edgar knew all the time who the man was. After all, he was clairvoyant and could read minds.

April 8

How aright then? In that influence as is seen in the influence of the knowledge already obtained by mortal man. Give more of that into the lives, giving the understanding THAT THE WILL MUST BE THE EVER GUIDING FACTOR TO LEAD MAN ON, EVERY UPWARD.   3744-4

Time and again Edgar was called upon to prove his psychic skills to skeptics. In April 1917 Dave Kahn put him to the test, but without letting him know his intent.

When Edgar previously told Kahn he would wear a uniform, he himself had been skeptical. He had no intentions of being a policeman, or fireman, or hotel doorman. But here he was in New York ready to don a U.S. Army uniform, and he had a cough and was losing his voice.

His new friends at the Hotel Girard scoffed at the notion that Edgar could help him, but Kahn thought this wire to Edgar should do the trick: "Please tell me why I am in New York. Advise as to my physical condition and what I should do next."

Edgar's reply stated his exact military status and prescribed "cherry bark from north side of cherry tree, taken three times a day" for his cough and voice.

Kahn had a druggist grind the bark he somehow attained to make a solution he could gargle. He was well in three days.

His skeptical new friends were impressed that a diagnosis came from Selma all the way to New York, and they were skeptics no more.

April 9

> *Realize the influence that is shed even by the careless word that may be spoken; how that the smile makes a day entirely different for those who are burdened with the cares oft; how that the handshake may strengthen those who have in themselves lost hope... In the abilities, then - keep that faith, that ability to coordinate physical, mental and spiritual phases of human experience.*   2560-1

Edgar's readings for David Kahn helped him have a highly successful World War II military career—best of all, without fear. Edgar told him he would serve and come home with honor, and because Kahn had faith, he never hesitated to put himself in danger's way.

The readings said he was to serve the needs of the troops, and Kahn grasped the first opportunity he found, arranging an impromptu show, hoping enough soldiers would take to the stage to make it a treat. The show was so popular he was given the job as director of amusements to put on a show every week.

Kahn felt he was too young to call Edgar by first name, so he called him Judge, as a title of respect. In his memoir he wrote, "Every week or so during this period, I either got a letter from Judge or I wrote him. Often he would respond with a reading."

One gave him the courage to obtain 400 pairs of shoes without written orders and get them to troops who needed them. The General was later furious, but Kahn wasn't punished. Edgar had assured he wouldn't be.

April 10

With each development, that force, known upon the plane as WILL, is given to man over and above all creation; THAT force that may separate itself from its Maker, for with the WILL man may either adhere or contradict the Divine law - those immutable laws, as are set between the Creator and the created.   3744-5

Back in Kentucky after the war, Dave Kahn proposed a partnership to help Edgar build a hospital and to help himself pay off the huge debt he'd inherited with his father's death. Having been stung before by partnerships gone sour, Edgar was wary. But he liked Kahn and met him in April 1919 to discuss Kahn's business ideas.

The two were having their fifth day of discussions when Edgar mentioned a letter he'd received from a Texan wondering if Edgar's psychic powers could locate oil underground. He had dismissed the notion as equal to using his skill to win in poker or at the race track.

Kahn, though, jumped quickly at this possibility. He explained that oil belonged to the person who owned the land above it. Showing him where to find that oil would be making money for the landowner, not cheating like card playing or betting on horses.

He saw nothing wrong with locating oil for a fee, assuring Edgar any landowner would be happy to pay.

Edgar gave a reading for the Texan's property which had been unsuccessfully drilled 3,500 feet. The reading told exactly what to do. Kahn and Edgar, invited to be partners, left for Texas in early July to check it out.

April 11

Ye CANNOT go against thine own conscience and be at peace with thyself, thy home, thy neighbor, thy God! For as ye do it unto the least of thy brethren, ye do it unto thy Maker.   1901-1

On this day in 1932 Edgar and Gertrude lost the only home they'd ever felt was theirs. Morton Blumenthal had certainly led them to believe it was rightfully theirs, but nevertheless, Morton and Edwin sued for possession of the 35th Street property.

In the Princess Anne County Courthouse, Edgar admitted that Morton had paid for the house, and the judge ruled for the Blumenthals.

After the settlement, Morton would not shake Edgar's offered hand, and he never answered letters Edgar wrote asking for a reconciliation.

Edgar had once thought Morton was one of the finest men he'd ever met, but that man's actions threw him into a hard-to-shake gloom. He dug up violets from his beautiful garden to transplant at the 105th Street summer cottage the Cayces could barely afford to rent.

From upstairs they could see the former hospital, now The Cape Henry Hotel.

FAST FORWARD: The hospital would later be the Princess Pat Hotel, then a nightclub, then an officers' club, and then a Masonic Temple. Many years after Edgar's transition, it would be purchased back by the Association for Research and Enlightenment.

April 12

While you each have had your fears, your doubts, your uprisings, your downsittings - yet in giving ye find rest and PEACE and comfort as He alone can give...For He, too, was a man of sorrow and acquainted with grief. He has promised that all tears would be wiped away, and they ARE for those who wholly put their trust in Him... What greater promise, what greater blessing may come to any soul than to know that He cares!...He is mindful of thy petitions, of thy aches, thy pains, thy disappointments, thy sorrows, thy joys, thy exultations. 281-40

On this day in 1917 Edgar's father Leslie died at age 83 after escaping with severe burns from a fire.

He had traveled from Virginia Beach, where he lived with Edgar and his family, to visit his daughters, Annie and Sarah, in Nashville where the fire broke out in an upstairs apartment in Annie's house.

About a week after his Hopkinsville funeral, Gladys heard footsteps in his upstairs bedroom, and Hugh Lynn heard his grandfather's unique breathing. Edgar investigated and reported, "He's back, but he'll only be here for a few days." Edgar explained that his father thought he needed to straighten out some papers, and he would leave when he figured out that all was okay.

Hugh Lynn invited the mailman into the house to see if he could hear anything. Half way up the stairs he heard the heavy breathing, and when Hugh Lynn told him the truth, he whitened and fled. After that the mailman put the mail in the hedge rather than bring it to the door.

April 13

(Q) How may my eyes be strengthened so as to eliminate the necessity of reading glasses? (A) By the head and neck exercise in the open, as ye walk for twenty to thirty minutes each morning. Now, do not undertake it one morning and then say "It rained and I couldn't get out," or "I've got to go somewhere else," and think there aren't these despot conditions that rebel at not having their morning walk!   2533-6

Edgar's Forces recommended the head and neck exercises as helpful for dozens of ailments, but as a very specific cure for myopia.

After working for Edgar only a few months, Gladys asked for a reading for severe headaches and was told they were due to deflected circulation because of bad posture.

The exercise recommended was to stretch the neck up and down, lean sidewise right, lean sidewise left, and then roll the head around slowly in each direction—doing each movement three or four times.

He told her to use a hand-made violet ray machine three times weekly, and to discard her glasses.

She found she didn't need glasses any more, and the effect was instantaneous.

Some patients couldn't throw away their glasses for six months, maybe because they used only the exercise, not the expensive machine which is still available for sale.

Everyone would benefit from selecting a specific time and remembering to do this simple exercise daily.

April 14

For, was not the physical being made from all else that grew? For, of the dust of the earth was the body-physical created. But the WORD, the MIND, is the controlling factor of its shape, its activity, from the source, the spiritual - the spiritual entity. Thus there are within the abilities of each soul that ability to choose that as will keep the body, the mind, the portion of the spirit, attuned to holiness or oneness with him. 263-13

Readings often stressed using the head's brain for positive thinking because thoughts manifest, but they also gave help for the head's problems.

Like so many ailments, migraine headaches begin from congestion in the colon. "First, we would X-ray the colon and find areas in the ascending and transverse colon where there are fecal forces that are as cakes."

Dissolving those cakes requires several full colonic irrigations using a solution of two teaspoons of salt and 1 teaspoon of soda to a gallon of water at body temperature. In the rinse water, use 2 tbsp. Glyco-Thymoline to a quart and a half of water.

With that treatment Edgar also recommended using a radio-active appliance, meditation, and osteopathic adjustments to relax the neck area, the sixth dorsal in the mid-back, and the lumbar axis in the lower back.

For another head problem, the treatment is simpler. To promote new hair growth, eat more shellfish and occasionally massage your head with a few coffee grounds. Maybe good-working bowels would also help.

April 15

Will ye allow self to separate self, the real self, from the living Christ? HE calls ever, "If ye love me, keep my commandments." What are His commandments? "Love one another." Do good, speak gently, even to those that thou in thine darkness of heart feel would do thee an injustice. 254-58

    Edgar certainly practiced the above principle in his daily life, as he certainly taught it repeatedly to his Bible school classes.

    When his employee Harmon Bro socked him in his stomach, he didn't fire him. Instead he kept trying to help the troubled young man with his emotional problems. (See Mar. 15)

    When Morton Blumenthal took away the hospital Edgar had worked for so many years to attain, he didn't get angry. Instead he tried to shake Morton's hand, but Morton wouldn't allow him to do so. (See Feb. 28)

    When Morton sent policewomen to arrest Edgar for fake fortune telling and alerted the press to embarrass him publicly, Edgar only said he wished the man would leave him alone. (See Nov. 10)

    Edgar chose to distance himself from people who did him wrong, people he may have had difficulty loving. When he discovered his partner Dr. Wesley Ketchum was faking readings to get horse racing tips, he simply dissolved the partnership. (See Oct. 12-14)

    Negative emotions were not his, for as many readings said, "Thoughts are deeds." One should keep them pure.

April 16

. . . each soul choosing such a body at the time of its birth into material activity has its physical being controlled much by the environs of the individuals responsible for the physical entrance. Yet, the soul choosing such a body for a manifestation becomes responsible for that temple of the living God, when it has developed in body, in mind, so as to be controlled with intents, purposes and desires of the individual entity or soul.
263-13

Edgar's Forces said all should respect and treat their physical bodies like temples of God.

To get rid of skin sores or actinic keratosis, rub with castor oil in the morning and camphorated oil in the evening. The cure might not be instant, but should happen within six weeks.

Get rid of bad breath by "making better conditions in the eliminations." Put six drops of Glyco-Thymoline in water and drink as an ntestinal antiseptic two or three times a day. Bad breath "is poisons being thrown off into the lungs (into the body forces) from the changing in cellular activity of lymph forces that become fecal."

To help with multiple sclerosis, massage with equal parts of olive oil and peanut oil with some lanolin to nourish weakened tissue. Years after Edgar's demise, massage became standard to maintain the tone of muscles which have lost their usual nerve network, so that the muscle will not atrophy and shorten.

The oil mixture was more complex for advanced cases.

April 17

Happiness...is...Being glad when you are persecuted for His name's sake, being in that attitude of forgiving those who speak unkindly... and not saying under your breath, "Poor saps! I'm the one persecuted but they are the ones that must receive the damnation," for you have turned it then on self.   262-109

On this day in 1944 Edgar gave a reading to a woman who had been present when Jesus taught the lesson of forgiveness.

Discovering that the Master and His disciples were coming to Bethsaida, she rushed to the road with her child, eager to hear the teacher whose reputation had spread since His baptism by John in the wilderness.

Confused by the division between the Samaritans, the orthodox Jews, and the Essenes, she had a happy-go-lucky, what-does-it-matter attitude—faith that "sometime, somewhere, somehow I will know."

Jesus set her child before the disciples and said, "Who is the greatest in the kingdom of heaven?...Unless ye become as a little child, ye shall in no wise enter in. Unless you become as open-minded, unless you can get mad and fight and then forgive and forget. For it is the nature of man to fight, while it is the nature of God to forgive...As ye forgive, so are ye forgiven. As ye treat thy fellow man ye are treating thy Maker." (3395-3)

With that lesson the woman changed entirely from the attitude of "What difference does it make?" for she "knew there was a work to do." Edgar's work was to tell us all.

April 18

No soul may help another except as to that which may aid ...to find its own self and its relation to the Creative influences in that entity's, soul's, experience.   443-3

On this day in 1900 a doctor in Elkton, Kentucky, gave Edgar a white powder for the headaches he had suffered since starting to travel selling insurance.

He took the drug with water at his hotel and went to bed. Ross Rogers, a Cayce family friend, later found him wandering around and acting strangely at the Elkton railroad station. He took him to his parents' home in Hopkinsville.

He was put to bed without any communication with his family, and he slept through the night.

***

On this day in 1934 Ernest Zentgraf, who had lost a $2 million inheritance by bad investments, left home with a pistol and sent his wife Helene a suicide note the next day.

Edgar previously read for Helene to help her find a job to support the family. She asked for a reading now to find her husband.

The reading explained that nothing could force Ernest to come home, saying, "We are helpless. A man's will is supreme."

However, maybe prayer could change a man's will. Edgar came up with a plan to find out.

April 19

> Wilt Thou, O Father, come into the lives and hearts and minds of those, as we pray for them, with them. Move Thou through the spirit of truth their expressions to enjoin in Thy love. 281-23

On this day in 1900 Edgar awakened to find he had no voice. The powder had robbed him of his memory, and he couldn't speak above a whisper.

Hopkinsville's two doctors couldn't determine why. A throat specialist came, diagnosed the problem as aphonia or laryngitis, and said he would soon be all right. But he wasn't.

News of his malady traveled all the way to Louisville, and Margaret paid for a European specialist to examine him—to no avail.

Edgar wondered if his voice had been taken from him because he had decided not to become a preacher.

FLASHBACK: In Louisville, Edgar and Margaret had a strong relationship, but when their liaison threatened his engagement, Edgar stopped seeing her in late 1899.

***

On this day in 1934 the study group began a series of 33 sessions of prayers to bring Ernest Zentgraf back to his wife Helene. As always, they began by opening a psychic channel for receiving advice and sending prayers. They then opened and ended each session with individual prayers assuring Ernest of God's love and his innate worthiness to live. Between prayers, Edgar did a reading for further advice to help Ernest.

April 20

> *Then it behooves EACH soul - here, everywhere - to seek more...for the strength, the direction, the might of that promised in, "If ye will call, I will hear."*   3976-24

On the day before this in 1934 the study group prayed at the meeting's beginning and end to assure Ernest Zentgraf of his worthiness to live and have a good life. Edgar continued going into a trance for clues to help.

By the third reading, Helene had news that Ernest was alive, but still suicidal. The reading warned, "To desecrate the body that is the temple of the living God is to belittle self...Put thy burden on Him, and He will sustain and guide and guard thee."

The fifth reading said that Ernest had a bad cough and was in Philadelphia. Another reading said Helene had received a letter from Ernest, and she had. An April 26 reading said very clearly that Ernest would come home. A May 14 reading showed him amidst greenery.

Two days later Edgar saw Jesus smiling at the study group praying for Ernest. On June 2 Gladys dreamed she saw Ernest sitting with the Cayce family. The last reading on June 11 said: "How beautiful the face of those whom the Lord, the Christ, smiles upon!"

A few days later Ernest returned from Philadelphia and wrote to his wife: "I needed this shock to cleanse my soul. I have confessed my errors to God and I know He has forgiven me, for wonders have happened."

April 21

> *Then cultivate that ability for counsel to those that seek from loneliness, from fear, from the turmoils of their experiences with others, those that feel slighted, those ...disappointed in the experiences of material affairs. Turn their minds rather...to those things that endure forever. For only the spiritual forces for thine soul endure forever.* 1183-1

Edgar needed to find a job that didn't require talking. He certainly could no longer sell insurance policies. Unfortunately, without Edgar's sales, his father Leslie was now spending more money trying to sell insurance than he was making.

The family had to move to a smaller home, and Edgar's sisters Annie and Mary dropped out of school to make hats for the J.H. Anderson Department Store.

Edgar became an apprentice at Hopkinsville's only photo studio with William R. Bowles.

Photography, a fairly new profession, was one of the nation's fastest growing businesses. People flocked to have their pictures taken with the innovative new cameras.

The year of 1900 was not good for the entire Cayce family. Edgar had hoped to be married to Gertrude and starting a family by now, but instead he was once again responsible for supporting his mother, father, and sisters.

The setback was only one of many Edgar would face before he and Gertrude could get married and face an uncertain future together.

April 22

That there has been set a monetary STANDARD by many as to that which is of worth or is success, indicates the vibrations as well as the purpose of such. Not by might nor by power, but by "My Word." Not that man lives by bread alone, but by EVERY WORD that is a promise to that man by or from the Creative Forces, or God. That that a man worships, THAT that man becomes.   2897-4

His friend Joe Dickey was always on the lookout for ways for Edgar to make money. In Bowling Green at a time when he was barely able to pay his bills, he gave a reading on horse races, revealing that only four out of the seven races were not already fixed. He and Dickey bet on them, and Edgar's take got him out of debt.

His new financial boost, though, came at a price. He had used his ability out of sync with its purpose and ideals, and suddenly he could not go into a trance.

Sadly, a reading was needed for Gertrude's brother Hugh Evans, who had tuberculosis. He tried readings for him and two other friends, but failed. He realized he was becoming more like the people requesting readings for personal financial profit.

He closed his studio, left Bowling Green, joined Gertrude back at The Hill, and immersed himself in serious Bible study. For three months, Edgar prayed for forgiveness for straying from the spirit of the readings. Perhaps from the stress of living with his self-loathing and the loss of her brother, Gertrude lost weight, cut off her long beautiful hair, and dressed in black.

April 23

In the Christ Consciousness, then, there is the oneness of self, self's desires, self's abilities, made in at-onement with the forces that may bring to pass that which is sought by an individual entity or soul.   5749-4

On this day in 1924 Edgar began writing a screenplay for actress Gloria Swanson. His screenplay for actress Violet Mesereau had never been produced, and he was still awaiting word about *Why?*, a screenplay about a psychic handyman with skills similar to his own.

Any reluctance he might have had to pursue a path that had so far done nothing to alleviate his usual financial woes was overcome by assurances from two friends.

Tim Brown had met with film producers about using Edgar's abilities to plot stories, and he was still optimistic.

Alf Butler, a Birmingham film distributor, also encouraged Edgar to take on the project.

One of these men told Edgar that Gloria was having trouble finding a story suitable for her talents.

Seven readings begun on this day resulted in *Bride of the Inca*, a 20-page screenplay about how greed changes the lives of an archaeologist and other treasure hunters as they search for gold in the Andes.

Information heard before in life readings made its way into the story. Whether or not Gloria read it is not known. What is known is that it was never produced. However, Gloria and other Hollywood notables admired Edgar and in future times donated to support his work.

April 24

Study to show thyself approved in all good conscience to that thou dost set as thy ideal, and know - as has been indicated - that thy ideal is only in Him who is the keeper, who is thy Brother, who is thy Friend, thy Lord - even the Christ!   1650-1

In the spring of 1921 when Edgar had been home with Gertrude, Hugh Lynn, and Edgar Evans only twice during the last year and a half, he went on the road again. Cayce Petroleum had started drilling Rocky Pasture #1 in March, even without a formal contract, and Edgar arrived in time to see the derrick erected.

Although readings said the well would produce 5,000 barrels a day, they ran into problems in the first 250 feet. At 1,000 feet they reached water, and then tools disappeared, and then a second set also disappeared.

One of the workers dropped a tombstone into the drill hole. At the end of May Edgar took another fundraising trip and sold another 50,000 shares to keep drilling.

Back at the site in December, indications were that the well was within feet of a major strike, but a worker dislodged a coupling, causing their tools to drop into the hole. Competitors who knew Edgar's reputation for finding oil had sabotaged again. Edgar's Force declined to name the perpetrators.

By summer 1922 the lease expired. Another company was already drilling and hitting oil on an adjacent property.

Edgar felt he had misused his God-given gift.

April 25

> All being of one accord, moved to this or that activity! ... in the beginning was the word. The word was God. The word was with God. He MOVED! Hence as He moved, souls -portions of Himself -came into being.   263-13

    Sporadic information about creation is scattered throughout the readings.

    Apparently, no one seeking answers to philosophical questions asked directly about how the earth was formed or how humans came into existence.

    However, through bits and pieces mentioned in readings delving into clients' past lives, a clear picture of creation and the development of humankind can be pieced together.

    To Edgar the word "God" and "Creative Forces" are interchangeable. God is the spirit that permits everything, and in the beginning all our souls came into activity.

    God's moving brought light, and then chaos. In this light the earth was created and came to be matter. Thus, our universe evolved into the heavens, the constellations, and the stars. We were spirit then.

    Best of all, as the above quote points out, we all are portions of God. We all have God in us. All things are possible for us if we attune to those Creative Forces.

    Another quote is also reassuring: "Are ye not all children of God? Are ye not co-creators with Him? Have ye not been with Him from the beginning?" (294-202}

    When our souls return to our spirit bodies, we will remember and be able to answer that question.

April 26

For, as is given in the beginning: God moved and said, "Let there be light," and there was light, not the light of the sun, but rather that of which, through which, in which every soul had, has, and ever has its being. For in truth ye live and love and have thy being in Him. These considerations, then, each in analyzing of self, each has its part in thine own physical consciousness....   5246-1

The creation of light as explained in the readings is different from the usual interpretation of the Bible's creation myth. The general idea has been that the light and darkness were the illumination for the earth, even though the firmament and the waters were not created until the second day.

We must remember "that lesson must ever be that the spirit is the life, the mental is the builder, and the physical or material results are the effects of the application of the knowledge or understanding toward life, light, or the spirit of ANY effort." (262-20)

Along with this enlightenment the souls received the gift of free will. "Then a soul—the offspring of the Creator—entering into a consciousness which becomes a manifestation in any plane or sphere of activity, is given free will for its use of those abilities or qualities of conditions in its experience." (5753-1)

The three phases of the thought process are: the conscious mind which gives directions, the subconscious mind which stores memory, and the superconscious which is the soul mind.

April 27

> ... in the beginning, when all forces were given in the spiritual force ... the morning stars sang together in the glory of the coming of the Lord and the God to make the giving of man's influence and developing in the world's forces.   2497-1

This quote is reminiscent of Job 38:7, in which the Lord speaks from a whirlwind to Job about creation: "When the morning stars sang together, and all the sons of God shouted for joy."

Edgar's readings often have Biblical quotes. He read the Bible from start to finish every year of his life, so we can assume it was thoroughly engrained in his subconscious, whether in a waking state or hypnotic state when he was in touch with the universal consciousness. Readings repeat the story of the morning stars many times.

One client was told he was there "when the forces of the Universe came together, when there was upon the waters the sound of the coming together of the Sons of God, when the morning stars sang together, and over the face of the waters there was the voice of the glory of the coming of the plane for man's dwelling." (341-1)

Many who were told the same then knew their souls were among the first to come to dwell on earth, and "the earth in its form became a place; and afterwards able to be an abode for the creature called man." (341-1)

We were spirits then. Bodies would not come until spirits wanted to enjoy more of the earth's pleasures.

April 28

The first cause was, that the created would be the companion for the Creator; that it, the creature, would - through its manifestations in the activity of that given unto the creature - show itself to be not only worthy of, but companionable to, the Creator.

Hence, every form of life that man sees in a material world is an essence or manifestation of the Creator; not the Creator, but a manifestation of a first cause - and in its own sphere, its own consciousness of its activity in that plane or sphere. 5753-1

Creation took place in spirit before it was manifested in materiality. God, the Creative Forces, imaged the pattern of each creation, and because God is spirit, all God's imaging was spiritual.

Souls were still spirits when we first came to earth, but we would decide we needed material bodies. Even from the beginning, God gave spirits free will. Some spirits chose not to come to earth.

Readings say that only on earth do souls take on matter and become physical. Only in this three-dimensional plane does the transition from one plane to another necessitate birth and death. Between sojourns on earth, souls visit other planets and stay in spirit form.

While visiting earth, though, spirits did not immediately decide to become physical. That transition did not happen until some became obsessed with selfishness. Then we wanted physical bodies.

April 29

Let it be remembered, or not confused, that the EARTH was peopled by ANIMALS before peopled by man! First that of a mass, which there arose the mist, and then the rising of same with light breaking OVER that as it SETTLED itself, as a companion of those in the universe, as it began its NATURAL (or now natural) rotations, with the varied effects UPON the various portions of same, as it slowly - and is slowly - receding or gathering closer to the sun, from which it receives its impetus for the awakening of the elements that give life itself...that gives the SUN as the father OF light in the earth. 344-6

The above explanation of how the earth was formed was accompanied by insight into the Akashic Records, which Edgar often consulted under trance.

The Akashic Records contain memory of any activity that ever happened. Each thing makes a vibration that passes faster than time, attunes itself to particular incidents, and is recorded for all eternity. The record can be contacted by a sense above and beyond our five human senses.

We humans have that sense, but most have not developed it, just as all have the ability to communicate telepathically, but only those who've practiced it have developed and use that skill.

In the forming of the earth, this reading went on to say, "Elements have their attraction and detraction, or those of ANIMOSITY and those of gathering together... The attraction...gives...an impulse to create."

April 30

It is true that the activities so far as in this sphere or Galaxy of activities of the planetary forces within this present solar system, the earth first became as the indwelling of the consciousness of the race or the man in this particular sphere, but sin - the separation - that as caused the separation of souls from the universal consciousness - came not in the sphere of materiality first, but in that of spirit. 1602-3

Readings say the first influx of souls to the Earth was around 4.5 billion years ago. This first root race was primarily spiritual and did not leave physical remains.

The second root race was also non-physical. They were etheric, the medium that transmits radio waves, a rarefied element formerly believed to fill the upper regions of space.

Even before souls manifested into material bodies, we sinned—probably forgetting the reason we had been created: to be companions of God, the Creative Force. Our sin was separating ourselves from the universal consciousness—the one mind that we are all a part of.

Thus began the souls' journey home, knowing that "no one may come except if called by God." That will be when "the activities of the individuals through the various actions or consciousness or awareness in the various spheres of activity BECOME AS a part of the divine plan for the return, only THROUGH...reincarnation...in which choices may be made...to...become one with Him."

May 1

> *Then we must know from whence we came; how, why; and whence we go - and why.*

> *In God's own purpose, Spirit is His presence then. For the Spirit of God moved and that which is in matter came into being, for the opportunities of His associates, His companions, His sons, His daughters. These are ever spoken of as One.*

> *Then there came that as sought for self-indulgence, self-glorification; and there was the beginning of warring among themselves... STILL in Spirit.*   262-114

Souls forgot their oneness with their Source: God, the Creative Forces. We forgot our oneness with each other. Our souls were given free will, but through our misuse of God's gift of free will, our states of consciousness deteriorated.

Our struggle to reconnect with our Source began billions of years ago and continues to this day.

All souls are on the same spiritual journey. "The soul of man is what makes him above the animal, the vegetable, and the mineral kingdoms of the earth.... All souls were created in the beginning, and are finding their way back to whence they came." (3744-5)

"The first cause was, that the created would be the companion for the Creator; that it, the creature, would - through its manifestations in the activity of that given unto the creature - show itself to be not only worthy of, but companionable to, the Creator." (5753-1)

May 2

> *For, of the dust of the earth was the body-physical created. But the WORD, the MIND, is the controlling factor of its shape, its activity, from the source, the spiritual - the spiritual entity.*   263-13

> *In the matter of form, as we find, first there were those as projections from that about the animal kingdom; for the THOUGHT bodies gradually took form, and the various COMBINATIONS (as may be called) of the various forces that called or classified themselves as gods, or rulers over - whether herds, or fowls, or fishes, etc.* 364-11

Spirits pushed themselves into matter. We literally thought ourselves into earthly bodies.

Each soul sought more expression, and as it moved through mental associations in its surrounding environs, it gave out either a selfish reaction of its own ego or became the I AM to be still "at-one" with the great I AM THAT I AM.

Selfishness separated souls from light. We forgot we were traveling on a journey of self-discovery and spiritual growth. "Each soul that enters, then, must have had an impetus from some beginning that is of the Creative Energy, or of a first cause." (5753-1)

"The purpose of the entity in the earth is that it may know itself, also to be itself...fulfilling those purposes for which the entity comes into the earth, accepting, believing, knowing then thy relationship to that Creative Force." (3508-6)

May 3

> *These took on MANY sizes as to stature, from that as may be called the midget to the giants - for there were giants in the earth in those days, men as tall as (what would be termed today) ten to twelve feet in stature, and in proportion -well proportioned throughout.* 364-11

> *. . . there were still those who were physically entangled in the animal kingdom with appendages, with cloven-hooves, with four legs, with portions of trees, with tails, with scales, with those various things that thought forms (or evil) had so indulged in as to separate the purpose of God's creation of man, as man - not as animal but as man.... All these forms, then, took those activities in the physical beings of individuals.* 2072-8

Spirits created grotesque bodies. Many of the weird creatures described in Greek mythology might not be mythological at all.

Souls divided into two groups: the selfish sons of darkness who concerned themselves exclusively with their own creations, and the sons of light who followed the orderly unfolding of the divine plan and who viewed these creatures with great consternation.

In the beginning living souls, still in spirit form, were given the power of choosing for themselves.

Not until the third root race did spirits become individualized and then became what we recognize in one another as individual entities, but all still part of the universal consciousness. Each soul had and has the ability to choose a body, but keep its spirit attuned to holiness—of oneness with the Creative Forces.

May 4

The spirit chose to enter (celestial, not an earth spirit - he hadn't come into the earth yet!), chose to put on, to become a part of that which was as a command not to be done! Then those entering MUST continue through the earth until the body-mind is made perfect for the soul, or the body-celestial again.   262-99

For the soul had understanding before he partook of the flesh in which the choice was to be made.   262-96

Readings say the Lemurians—the third root race—were the first spirits to take on physical bodies. They were a race who inhabited a lost continent of Lemuria, also known as Mu, which was where the Indian and Pacific oceans are now. Edgar says this entry into matter happened 4.5 billion years ago—much earlier than the theosophical version that claims 18 million years ago.

The continent, ruled by women, existed in ancient times and sank beneath the ocean because of a geological or other cataclysmic change, like a pole shift.

Spirits had been hanging around earth and "The Knowledge, the understanding, the comprehending, then necessitated the metering in because it partook of that which WAS in manifestation; and thus the PERFECT body, the celestial body, became an earthly body and thus put on flesh." (262-99)

Earth had all the terrestrial trappings of nature, including animals. Spirits chose whether or not they wanted to be part of it. Some came; some didn't. For a while we could alternate between spirit and body.

May 5

The Creator, in seeking to find or create a being worthy of companionship, realized that such a being would result only from a free will exercising its divine inheritance and through its own efforts find its Maker. Thus, to make the choice really a Divine one caused the existence of states of consciousness, that would indeed tax the free will of a soul; thus light and darkness. Truly, only those tried so as by fire can enter in. 262-56

All souls in the beginning were one with God. The separation, or turning away, brought evil. Then came the self's awareness of being out of accord with, or out of the realm of blessedness. So the Creator caused the existence of states of consciousness that would tax the soul's free will: thus, light and darkness.

"'Let there be light,' then, was that consciousness that Time began to be a factor in the experience of those creatures that had entangled themselves in matter; and became what we know as the Influences in a material plane. And the moving force and the life in each, and the activities in each are from the Spirit." (262-115)

Humanity traditionally has recognized light as good and darkness as evil. Early humans worshipped the sun for it perceived power, and variations of sun worshipping can be found through most of recorded history. But light and darkness are not simply good and evil. Light is mental and spiritual enlightenment—a recognition of where we came from and where we are going. Without knowing, we cannot reach our destination.

May 6

(Q) Is this work to be perpetuated? (A) That is its material force, its universal force...With a body surrounded with those elements...not...in accord with the work attempting to be accomplished, there is not the best given off through the work itself. 3744-4

On this day in 1927 the organization that would oversee the Cayce Hospital received its Virginia state charter to do psychic research and to apply knowledge obtained psychically to hospital patients. The Association of National Investigators was now legally in business. A by-law required prospective patients to join the association, acknowledging psychic research was experimental. Edgar and the ANI could then not be accused of fortune-telling—a misdemeanor in Virginia.

The $65,000 hospital complex would be financed by Morton Blumenthal, who spearheaded fundraising drives that failed to raise the needed cash. As his financial portfolio rose with readings' guidance, he became rich enough to pay for the project on his own.

The main four-level building would have therapy and machines on the ground floor and patients' wards and private rooms on the top two levels. The second floor would have doctors' offices, a library, treatment rooms, and a lecture hall.

To provide for exercise so frequently prescribed in the readings, patients would be able to play tennis, croquet, and shuffleboard, plus bathe at a bath house on the beach, which readings often suggested as a healing aid.

May 7

> The land was among those in which there was the first appearance of those that were as separate entities or souls disentangling themselves from material or that we know as animal associations. For the projections of these had come from those influences that were termed Lemure, or Lemurian, or the land of Mu. 877-10

> in that land that has been termed Zu, or Lemuria, or Mu. This was before the sojourn of peoples in perfect body form; rather when they may be said to have been able to...be in the body or out of the body and act upon materiality. 436-2

The Lemurians were workers in gold, silver, lead, and radium. They were wise enough to practice monogamy and conserve their natural resources. A reading described one as six-fingered and five-toed.

The Lemurians had one big problem: their bodies were not perfect. They were the race of souls projected into trees or animals, resulting in what we today would call monstrosities. However, they must have had good brains, or they wouldn't have been capable of developing such a workable society.

A man came to Edgar because he had a tightness in his head, feeling as if something in his head were broken. One of his past lives was as a Lemurian, and "Hence it may be given in passing, to the entity, that the love of and for a pure body is the most sacred experience in an entity's earth sojourn." (436-2)

May 8

This has nothing to do with Knowledge, or it is too much knowledge for some of you, for you'll stumble over it; but you asked for it and here it is.   262-99

Considereth thou that Spirit hath its manifestations, or does it USE manifestations for its activity? The Spirit of God is aware through activity, and we see it in those things celestial, terrestrial, of the air, of all forms. And ALL of these are merely manifestations! The Knowledge, the understanding, the comprehending, then necessitated the entering in because it partook of that which WAS in manifestation; and thus the PERFECT body, the celestial body, became an earthly body and thus put on flesh.   262-99

    The top quote shows the impatience Edgar's Forces sometimes had with questioners during readings, but it also shows the source had a subtle sense of humor.

    The words coming out of Edgar's mouth were always in the language of the King James Version of the Bible—very unlike Edgar's own manner of Southern speaking, not just in tone but vocabulary. These quotes mainly say because spirits used what was already created, it became necessary for them to take on earthly bodies.

    "Earth became a dwelling place for matter, when gases formed into those things that man sees in nature...then matter began its ascent in the various forms of physical evolution—in the MIND of God!" (262-99)

    Our bodies were thought projections. Now we could feel what we were already using.

May 9

The land under those influences of Mu became as what would be termed in the present as among or the highest state of advancement in material accomplishments for the benefit or conveniences for man's indwelling, or the less combative influence of the elemental or of that man knows as nature - in the raw.   **877-10**

In the spirit or in flesh these made those things...that brought destruction; for the atmospheric pressure in the earth in the period was quite different from that experienced by the physical being of today.   **436-2**

    Lemurians were said to be mainly spiritual peace-loving people, who lived on their 102,000-square-mile continent in the Pacific Ocean from 98,000 BC to 80,000 BC—long before and partially at the same time as Atlantis in the Atlantic Ocean. A cataclysmic event destroyed their continent—either one of their own making or of the Atlanteans, the fourth root race.

    The continent's disappearance had begun before its final destruction. "Then, with that portion, THEN the South Pacific, or Lemuria, began its disappearance - even before Atlantis, for the changes were brought about in the latter portion of that period, or what would be termed ten thousand seven hundred (10,700) light years, or earth years, or present setting of those, as set by Amilius [?] - or Adam." (364-40)

    Amilius and Adam and their contribution to humanity are still to come in this creation story.

May 10

(Q) Did the appearance of what became the five races occur simultaneously? (A) Occurred at once.   364-13

Let these represent the attributes of the physical, or the senses and what forms they take, rather than calling them white, black, yellow, red and green, etc. What do they signify in the SENSING? Sight, vision - white. Feeling - red. Black - gratifying of appetites in the senses. Yellow - mingling in the hearing. What is the law of the peoples that these represent? Their basic thoughts run to those elements!   364-13

The Atlanteans were among the fourth root race, but they did not come to earth alone, as the Lemurians had. Five races occurred simultaneously on this planet.

The White were in the Carpathian region, now considered to be the Garden of Eden, where   Amilius was separated into Adam and Eve. The Brown were in the Andean; the Black in Sudan "or in African"; the Yellow were in "Egypt, Indian, Persia, and Arabic"; and the Red were in Atlantis and "the American."

Earth had a different configuration at that time. The extreme northern portions were then the southern portions, and the polar regions were tropical and semitropical regions.

The Nile entered the Atlantic. The Sahara was inhabited and very fertile.   The Mississippi basin was all ocean.   Parts of Nevada, Utah, and Arizona were the biggest part of the U.S. The oceans were turned about.

Edgar's story of creation follows only the Atlanteans.

May 11

We find the entity was in that land known as the Atlantean, during those periods when there were the questions arising... as to the acknowledgement of the castes in a land where the untouchables are considered as but dogs among the higher castes.   333-2

    The Atlanteans, with physical bodies designed by God and his son Amilius, arrived in a land already populated by monstrosities, the result of earlier souls projecting into animals and objects.

    Creatures with appendages of wings, tails, feathers, claws, and hooves abounded in Atlantis. The sphinx was not a statue then, but a living being.

    These monsters had existed for hundreds of thousands of years. They varied in shapes and sizes, ranging from tiny pygmies to giants twelve feel tall.

    The new Atlanteans came to earth with occult powers originating from their third eye, the pituitary gland in the center of the forehead. They could ascertain what was going on in earth's other four inhabited areas, and they could foresee future events.

    They certainly had the power to control the mixed monsters, who became social outcasts, known as "things," and used for the most menial tasks. These lower class people are referred to in the Bible as "daughters of men" and "giants."

    Two camps within Atlantis became bitterly opposed about mixing their pure lineage with the freakishly abnormal. But animals were an even bigger problem.

May 12

Then...with the change that had come about, began in that period when there were the invasions of this continent by those of the animal kingdoms, that brought about that meeting of the nations of the globe to PREPARE a way and manner of disposing of, else they be disposed of themselves by these forces.

With this coming in, there came then the first of the destructive forces as could be set and then be meted out in its force or power. Hence that as is termed, or its first beginning of, EXPLOSIVES that might be carried about, came with this reign, or this period, when MAN - or MEN, then - began to cope with those of the beast form that OVERRAN the earth in many places. 364-4

When animals became a threat to humanity's existence, a council of wise beings from the world's five nations met to come up with a plan to combat the creatures overrunning the earth.

One can only guess how the individuals communicated the need to get together or transported themselves for their meetings. We *do* know they had great occult and technological powers—maybe enough for interplanetary interaction. They used balloons of elephant hide, filled with gas, as crafts to carry them or cargo around the continent—and perhaps to others.

The 5-nation council must have concluded that eradicating the animals was the key to their own survival. Powerful explosives may have solved the problem, but may have also contributed to Atlantis's final destruction.

May 13

(Q) How long did it take for the division into male and female? (A) That depends upon which, or what branch or LINE is considered. When there was brought into being that as of the projection of that created BY that created, this took a period of evolutionary - or, as would be in the present year, fourscore and six year. That as brought into being as was of the creating OF that that became a portion of, OF that that was already created by the CREATOR, THAT brought into being as WERE those of the forces of nature itself. God said, "Let there be light" and there WAS light! God said, "Let there be life" and there WAS life!

(Q) Were the thought forms that were able to push themselves out of themselves inhabited by souls, or were they of the animal kingdom? (A) That as created by that CREATED, of the animal kingdom. That created as by the Creator, with the soul.   364-7

    Amilius provides an explanation of the Biblical quote: "And God said, let us make man in our image, after our likeness." God's image was spirit, but once souls pushed themselves into matter, a good physical body was needed. He split entities into two sexes, and these twin souls stay together throughout all their reincarnations.

    Many in Atlantis survived the first continental catastrophe around 50,000 BC and were still there to rebuild after the second, the great flood around 28,000 BC. Their technology advanced to great heights.

May 14

Hardly could it be said that they were in the exact form as in the present. For there were more of the influences that might be used when necessary; such as arms or limbs or feet or whatnot.

Their STANDARD was that the soul was given by the Creator or entered from outside sources INTO the projection of the MENTAL and spiritual self at the given periods. THAT was the standard of the Law of One, but was REJECTED by the Sons of Belial.

The Sons of Belial were of one group, or those that sought more the gratifying, the satisfying, the use of material things for self, WITHOUT thought or consideration as to the sources of such nor the hardships in the experiences of others....The other group - those who followed the Law of One - had a standard. The Sons of Belial had no standard, save of self, self-aggrandizement.
877-26

The untouchables remained outcasts until animal influences disappeared around 9000 BC.

The newly split humans—not yet like us—divided into groups. The Sons of Belial used material things for themselves, without considering others. They had no standard of morality.

The other group followed the Law of One, recognizing that eternal truth is eternal love, and eternal love is the consciousness of the God or the Creative Forces. The Law of One group were the laborers, the farmers, the artisans whose individual activities benefited all.

May 15

> ...there crept in those pollutions, of polluting themselves with those mixtures that brought contempt, hatred, bloodshed, and those that build for desires of self WITHOUT respects of OTHERS' freedom, others' wishes - and there began, then, in the latter portion of this period of development, that that brought about those of dissenting and divisions among the peoples in the lands.
>
> Then, with these destructive forces, we find the first turning of the altar fires into that of sacrifice of those that were taken in the various ways, and human sacrifice began.... man brought in the destructive forces as used for the peoples that were to be the rule, that combined with those natural resources of the gases, of the electrical forces, made in nature and natural form the first of the eruptions that awoke from the depth of the slow cooling earth, and that portion now near what would be termed the Sargasso Sea first went into the depths.
> 364-4

Atlanteans entered into mineral and jewel deposits, misusing the earth's spiritual centers through which spiritual forces flow. This misuse would eventually lead to the destruction of their continent.

By 10,700 BC human sacrifice, sun worshipping, and corruption were prevalent.

Sun crystals developed to give them electrical power were used for torture, and low morality, violence, and rebellion were rampant in their land.

May 16

> The use of these influences by the Sons of Belial brought, then, the first of the upheavals; or the turning of the etheric rays' influence FROM the Sun - as used by the Sons of the Law of One - into the facet for the activities of same - produced what we would call a volcanic upheaval; and the separating of the land into SEVERAL islands - five in number.
>
> So, in following or interpreting the Poseidian period - or in Atlantis - let it be understood that this was only ONE of the groups; and the highest or the greater advancement in the earthly sojourning of individual entities or souls at that particular period - or the highest that had been save that which had been a part of the Lemurian age. 877-26

Atlantis was one island, divided into five with the first destruction around 50,000 BC. Poseidia still remained when the second great upheaval around 28,000 BC reduced Atlantis to three major islands. That land shift occurred around 22,000 BC.

The final destruction around 9500 BC was probably caused by light rays harnessed from the sun's energy with huge reflective crystals called Tuaoi stone.

Once the stones generated higher energies, they were called Firestone, or the Great Crystals. They powered ships by remote control and provided electricity to cities.

Many Atlanteans fled before the final destruction, becoming the Mayas in Honduras and Mexico, and the Mound Builders and Iroquois Indians in North America.

May 17

The Atlanteans were those that had reached an advancement, had been entrusted with divine activities in the earth, and - as the entity - forgot from whom, in whom all live and have their being; thus brought about within themselves - that which destroyed the body, but not the soul.

Thus there was prepared the way, even through Him who is now the life, the light, the immortality, the resurrection, the way through which peace and harmony, beauty and love, may be in the experience of each and every soul that seeks and acknowledges Him as thy Lord, as thy Savior. 2794-3

Readings for reincarnated Atlanteans—and many are on earth today—warned not to repeat past mistakes.

"This, then, is the purpose of the entity in the earth: to be a channel of blessing to someone today, now; to be a living example of that He gave, 'Come unto me, all that are weak and have laden—take my Cross upon you and learn of me.' These are thy purposes in the earth. These ye will manifest beautifully, or make a miserable failure again as ye did in Atlantis, as many another soul in this particular era is doing. Which will it be?" (2794-3) The same reading says we can be sure "no leader in any country or clime—whether friend or foe of what the entity believes—is other than Atlantean."

The same mindset that destroyed that great civilization runs our world now. We face a key testing period for the survival of our planet and way of life.

May 18

Take this thou hast in hand and make and mold it into the present plane's development, that thyself and others may know that God is God, and demands of His creatures that of the knowledge of self, that they may better serve their fellows, and .... present themselves as the ever giving force, bringing to others to the knowledge of Him.   294-8

On this day in 1921 Edgar made an agreement for Cayce Petroleum to drill for oil in San Saba County, Texas, making the owner William Barrow a major stockholder and company officer.

In return for Barrow's mineral rights, Cayce Petroleum would finance the venture.

The company had money because of Edgar's trip to New York when he met Houdini and other men of prominence and wealth.

The trip had netted $100,000 in promissory notes and some cash—assuming Edgar charged for them—from the more than a hundred readings Edgar gave. All too often, he gave his service free of charge.

Some of the company's $50,000 in cash came from Gertrude's relatives and people who became Edgar's supporter after seeing him in action.

A reading had placed oil at a point where Big Rocky Pasture connected with Little Rocky Pasture.

The company's first oil well was called Rocky Pasture #1. Prospects for success with oil were very promising. Prospects for a hospital—the purpose of this pursuit—were promising, too.

May 19

> ...spirit sought projecting; chose to enter that as had been the creation of the Father as manifestations, that still is as manifestations; and thus enters, leaves, enters, leaves, or incarnates through the lessons gained in each experience. For each experience in the earth is as a schooling, is as an experience for the soul. For how gave He? He is the vine and ye are the branches, or He IS the source and ye are the trees. As the tree falls so does it lie. THERE it begins when it has assimilated, when it has applied in SPIRITUAL reaction that it has gained. 262-99

The projection of beings simultaneously in five different places represented the physical senses that need to be conquered before spiritual perfection can be attained—sight, feeling, hearing, smell, and taste.

Souls know, before we're born again on earth, what lessons we need to learn. We each have that soul memory attainable to us if we become accomplished meditators.

Our souls came into being when God moved, putting a part of God in each of us. Our capabilities exceed what we are aware of in this three-dimensional world.

Whether aware of it or not, all humans are on the same journey to bliss in companionship with the Creative Forces. We make it, or come back to try again.

Even Amilius, who was divided into Adam and Eve, became subjected to that universal law. For him to live a life worthy to become God's companion took several reincarnations until he perfected himself as Jesus.

May 20

> . . there lived in this land of Atlantis one Amilius, who had first NOTED that of the separations of the beings as inhabited that portion of the earth's sphere or plane of those peoples into male and female as separate entities, or individuals. As to...forms in the physical sense, these were much RATHER of the nature of THOUGHT FORMS, or able to push out OF THEMSELVES in that direction in which its development took shape in thought….. 364-3

Summarizing information given about creation in life readings, we find that Amilius was the first soul created for God's companionship and present when all souls—a part of God—came into existence for the same reason. All were spirits then and were given free will.

Spirits used their free will to stray from God's purpose, launching the fall from divinity. They had free reign of all planets and were attracted to earth, where some thought projected themselves into animals, plants, and other objects. They became monstrosities known as sons and daughters of men. Those mingled with animals could reproduce, and their appendages receded by 9000 BC.

Another influx of 133 million souls came in five races in five different places at the same time, but they were not good keepers of the earth. Amilius came to help them and divided the androgynous beings into two sexes. That bunch was the last created by Creative Forces, for humans were then capable of reproduction.

All had the same earthly journey—to return to God.

May 21

> When seeking for that as may be the means to an end, seek not from without but from within. For to have and to hold the correct attitude to Creative Forces or the God-self in self is to rely upon same. It is not IN the expression in another save as a hope for clarification, *but it...is PERSONAL!* 440-20

In 1890, Edgar won a bet his father made with Congressman Jim McKenzie, Leslie's boyhood friend.

Over drinks to celebrate Jim's recent appointment as ambassador to Peru, McKenzie scoffed at Leslie's bragging about his son's unique ability to memorize a book by sleeping on it. So Leslie bet him that Edgar could memorize the entire 110-page speech McKenzie planned to deliver the next night in Hopkinsville.

Edgar came through with flying colors at a well-attended school event the next night, delighting Leslie, but giving the audience the fidgets during his long harangue.

His remarkable feat was reported in the *Kentucky New Era,* and Leslie won his bet. Chances are he celebrated by treating his friend to drinks at a local pub before he took off for Peru.

Leslie was a paradoxical father, loving one moment and tyrannical the next. His heavy drinking caused much distress in the Cayce household and contributed to his ongoing inability to provide adequate support for his family. He couldn't live up even to his own expectations.

May 22

> (Q) What is the law of love? (A) Giving. As is given in this injunction, "Love Thy Neighbor as Thyself." As is given in the injunction, "Love the Lord Thy God with all Thine Heart, Thine Soul and Thine Body." In this, as in many, we see upon the physical or earth or material plane the manifestations of that law, without the law itself. With any condition we find ... the manifestation of the opposite from law of love. The gift, the giving, with hope of reward or pay is direct opposition of the law of love. 3744-5

Variations of the need to put others first appear throughout the majority of Edgar's readings. Even the physical readings, which certainly gave material advice for curing, did not lack spiritual advice.

"One can get so in the habit of just being cross until he alone doesn't think there's anything wrong - everyone else knows there is." (849-75)

"Thus you can take a bad cold from getting mad. You can get a bad cold from [cursing] blessing out someone else, even if it is your wife." (849-75)

"And use that thou hast in hand today, so that TOMORROW He may give thee the better the greater blessings." (1595-1)

"Faint not at waiting, for in patience ye become aware of thy soul." (2144-1)

"First, know self. Continuous study of self is the greater study of others. Do not become egotistical. Do care for the health." (2938-1)

May 23

> *Hence we find these as those things that should be in the form of omens about the body; not as good luck charms, but they may be termed so by many; for these are from those activities and sojourns that will make for variations in the VIBRATIONS about the entity, hence bringing much more of harmony into the experience of the entity in the present activity.* 694-2

Readings often recommended particular stones be worn next to the skin to give the body good vibrations. A stone's mineral content and color both affect the wearer.

One woman with relationship problems was told that she should wear rose coral, "not red, not white, but rose coral...this is made up of nature's activity attempting to manifest, so...it is the little things in the association one with another that build those that prove to be the real experiences of the life. A word, a look, a sign, may make, may undo, all of the thoughts of many." (2154-1)

The reading further explained, "The vibrations of same, from same, may aid in the mental as well as vibratory urge to make those influences less of a disturbing nature which might otherwise become disturbing." (2154-1)

The red and blue coral are good for most. "Hence the red, the deep red coral, upon thine flesh, will bring quietness in those turmoils that have arisen within the inner self; as also will the pigments of blue to the body bring the air, the fragrance of love, mercy, truth and justice that is within self." (694-2)

May 24

> *Cherish those that are creative, or that remind the entity of such, and of its relationship to the creative forces in the experience. Look not upon, nor entertain, in mind or purpose, those only that arouse emotions that may be gratified in self-indulgence.*   951-4

If the above quote sounds like you, the pearl might contain the vibrations best for your further creative development.

That reading continued, "The pearl should be worn upon the body, or against the flesh of the body; for its vibrations are healing, as well as creative - because of the very irritation as produced same, as a defence in the mollusk that produced same."

If you happen to have a bad temper, "do wear the amethyst as a pendant about the neck, as a part of the jewelry. This will also work with the colors to control temperament." (3806-1)

The amethyst is also like the chrysolite: "For they will bring as an atturement the quieting, and the entity will find that whenever there is a feeling of physical depression, physical reactions that are as dis-ease in the body, the colors in any of these natures or forms will bring quietness to the body; as in having about the body the chrysolite or the amethyst color, in cloth, in drapery, in hangings." (1626-1)

The amethyst is light purple or dark lavender. The chrysolite, or peridot, ranges from chartreuse green to pale olive. Think twice before redecorating your abode.

May 25

> (Q) Describe in more detail the lapis stone suggested for the body to wear. (A) As understood, and may be found by the investigating of same, there is a blue-green stone, that is a fusion in copper deposits, that has the same vibration as the body; and thus is a helpful influence, not merely as an omen or good luck charm, but as the vibratory helpful force for health, for strength, for the ability through the mental self to act upon things, conditions, decisions and activities. 1651-2

The vibratory forces of lapis lazuli are good for health and also help their wearer with difficult mental tasks. Readings identified the stone's blue color with spiritual growth.

This stone, unlike most others, should not be worn touching the skin, and the recommendation was to have a piece of glass between the lapis and skin.

Edgar's Source compares the lapis to the ornamental agate and the beryl, which includes emerald and aquamarine and "carry an incense to the finer self that makes for an awakening, an opening of the inner self for the RECEPTIVENESS. And attunement is made through such vibrations, just as...those vibrations from stones as given, with metals such as come in the lapis lazuli, make for the raising of the attunement in self through meditation.

"But know these, my child, are but means - and are NOT the God-Force, NOT the Spirit, but the MANIFESTATIONS of same." (707-1)

May 26

When ye enter into the inner self and approach the throne of grace, mercy, love, hope, is there within self that which would hinder from offering the best or seeking the best from that throne of grace? Doesn't it then become necessary that such hindrances be...laid aside?
257-123

On this day in 1924 Edgar began a series of readings to take static out of radio tubes.

These readings were suggested by Tim Brown, the one who persuaded him to write screenplays and who still searched for ways to use Edgar's talents profitably.

These static eliminator readings continued through September and gave amazingly detailed instructions on how to build static-proof radio tubes.

Rather than market the design to an existing radio company, Brown unsuccessfully tried to build prototypes himself, but was unable to meet the readings' difficult specifications.

Years after he gave up, Mitchell Hastings, an electrical engineer and IBM consultant, succeeded with the prototype Brown had needed, but too late. Radio had by then advanced behind tubes, and Edgar's designs were obsolete.

FAST FORWARD: In 1934 Edgar and Mitchell Hastings, who was also psychic, traveled together for the sun and dry air of Arizona, and shared many visions on their way through Texas, New Mexico, and Mexico. Hastings later pioneered FM radio and held many innovative patents.

May 27

Each phase of self, then, must find in the Creative Forces a reflection of that which it may choose for its direct-ing light at EVERY stage of the experiences in material plane.   2427-1

On this day in 1880 when Edgar was three years old, he fell from a fence and landed on a board with a nail that went deep into his head. His father Leslie and mother Carrie poured turpentine into the open wound before bandaging it. It was said to have punctured his cranium and entered his brain cavity.

Also at age three, he almost drowned when he lost his footing in shallow water while catching fish in his hands. His grandfather's former slave saved him.

At age six a playground accident changed his docile personality to that of a belligerent bully. He got his old demeanor back by prescribing his own cure in a dream.

Around sixteen or seventeen he was shot in his arm and concealed it for a year.

As an adult he damaged his feet and body running with heavy loads in both hands trying to catch a train.

He didn't choose the above physical maladies, just as he didn't choose the gift that enabled him to help so many others with their physical deficiencies.

Edgar Cayce himself was the chosen one, and he lived his life trying to live up to the omnipotent trust placed in him. He died trying to do the same thing, refusing to give up readings for others in order to take care of his own ailing physical body.

May 28

For if ye would have life, give life! If ye would have friends, BE friendly! If ye would have loved ones, love others, do good to them though they may despitefully use you;...In the application of self in the fields of activity, draw nigh unto that which is good and it will draw nigh unto thee. 1362-1

Readings repeatedly stress the law of reciprocity, the need to put others' interests before our own selfish ones and to see our Creator in every person on earth.

"Remember, then, that all is ONE, and look into SELF if ye would understand thy neighbor, thy friend, yea thy foe. For that ye do TO thy friend, thy neighbor, yea thy foe, is a reflection of what THOU THINKEST of thy Creator!" (257-123)

We are encouraged to never slack in being nice to others: "...be not WEARY IN well-doing; rather let it be said of thee as of David of old, 'Though He slay me, yet will I serve Him the better; though He forsake me, yet will I draw the closer.' As one does THOSE things to his neighbor, to his wife, to his friend, to his foe, may the knowledge, the understanding, the BLESSING of life flow in." (99-8)

Kindness is an essential virtue on our journey back to our source. "If ye would know God ye must be godlike to some poor soul. If ye would have friends, be a friend to a friendless one. If ye would know peace and harmony, BRING peace and harmony to the experience of another soul." (262-88) How great our world would be if all did!

May 29

For selfishness is the real sin, and as we become less and less conscious of self and more aware of being at an onement with Him, greater may be the possibilities and blessings in the material earth, as well as in the beautiful heavenly rest.   5265-1

The same selfishness that caused the original disconnect from God is the trait most apt to keep us from successfully completing our earthly journey.

The following quote reminds us that all others we meet are on the same spiritual journey.

"For, self must become selfless, and the spirit must become magnified in the relationships of the individual's activity in its meeting with the fellow man; whether this is in relationship to seeking to know how the response of spirit or spirituality in the experience of another soul acts upon it in its environ, in its surrounding, in its journey back to its Creator, or what not." (440-4)

We gain in this incarnation when we help others. "And he that saves a soul has experienced…that realm of joy, peace, solace, understanding, that may only come to those who have experienced in saving, in directing, in blessing, a soul. For, the soul of self, as the soul of thine brother, is seeking its way, its journey, to its Maker.

"The birthright of every soul, as given by its Creator is coming into a material plane, is the same as for self; that it may experience the fruits of the spirit that may be manifested in a manifestation of life in a material… plane." (440-4) When we do, our karmic dues are paid.

May 30

That that one metes must be met again. That one applies will be applied again and again until that one-ness, time, space, force, or the own individual is one with the whole, not the whole with such a portion of the whole as to be equal with the whole. With it keep first and foremost that continuity of purposes with its self that it must be the servant of all to be the greatest among all and that in applying self, there comes first that knowledge of self and as has oft been given, my son, seek first that knowledge or that kingdom...for the silver and gold is mine, saith the Lord of Hosts and the cattle on one thousand hills and those that make themselves a channel for those blessings or natural consequences of same... 4341-1

On this day in 1944 a Washington, D.C., visitor, later described as "one of the higher ups," met with Edgar behind closed doors in Virginia Beach.

Edgar did not tell anyone about this visit, but he did mention it in a letter to Edgar Evans, writing that his visitor was an advisor to authorities that would "formulate the patterns about the inter-relations" of other countries after the war.

This incident was not the only time he'd been approached by someone from Washington, D.C. A call came from the office of Harry Truman, who would be sworn in as vice president in January of the next year.

Edgar never revealed details of that call. Both events happened while Edgar's health was seriously threatened, but he still kept his usual rigorous schedule.

May 31

So, in self, in self's experience, in self's application of the spirituality of self, know that He gives His angels charge concerning thee, and that they will bear thee up in the experiences that ye have in a material plane - if ye will but keep the heart, the mind, the soul, SINGING the praises of a RISEN Lord.   440-4

Angels know to care for us, and they will definitely help those who try to lead righteous lives.

"He has given His angels charge concerning thee. Then, lest thou dash thy foot against a stone, lest thou unheeding turn into those directions...that will bring thee ...consternation.For, whom He hath called, him also hath He glorified and WILL glorify, through his activities...or... callings to those that seek to do His biddings." (338-3)

Angels make their presence known in a variety of ways. "The sojourn of a soul-entity other than in materiality often influences or bears weight with individuals within the material plane - as an odor, a scent, an emotion, a wave, a wind upon the activities.

"Such are termed or called by some guardian angels, or influences that would promote activities for weal or for woe. THUS does the association of individuals at times become as an influence in the activities of individuals through particular periods or experiences." (538-59)

Edgar reminds us that better than angels, "know the Master's touch, the Master's voice; for He may walk and talk with thee. HE is the Way; there is no other." (5749-4)

June 1

Keep the self well-balanced. Keep the mental and spiritual coordinating, with the advancements that are to come in the material and the physical things of the experience...doubt not; for with the doubting comes the destructive thoughts that make for the hardships which must be met somewhere along the way. With constructive thought the building is made. With destructive thought hardships must ensue in some association...or relation.   2136-1

Sometime in June 1900 Edgar, now twenty-three years old and able to speak only in a whisper, had little hope for his and Gertrude's future.

His attempt to sell insurance with his father had failed—not because he couldn't sell, but because he couldn't cope with the company's racist attitude.

Thankfully, Gertrude refused to consider breaking their engagement, as he begged her to do.

He needed a job that didn't require talking, and an apprenticeship with photographer William B. Bowles became his temporary profession.

He went back to Louisville to study photography at Bryant and Stratton Business College in Louisville, but he lacked enthusiasm for his new venture.

Relatively new, photography was becoming a fast growing business, and Edgar quickly began receiving recognition for his photos.

Best of all, he had a steady income and was in Hopkinsville near Gertrude.

June 2

> ...happy may he be that is able to say they have been spoken to through the dream or vision.   294-15

> As in dreams, those forces of the subconscious, when taken or correlated into those forms that relate to the various phases of the individual, give to that individual the better understanding of self, when correctly interpreted, or when correctly answered.   3744-5

In the summer of 1937 the Cayces were so near broke Edgar feared he would not be able to make mortgage payments.

He had a dream that he and Jesus had shared champagne at a Paris cafe with the Duke of Windsor and Mrs. Simpson, who left before the bill arrived.

When Edgar expressed sorrow at being unable to pay the $13.75 bill, Jesus laughingly paid and said, "Don't worry. On the wedding day of the two who have just left us, your troubles will be over."

On June 2, 1937, a stranger came to Edgar with an envelope given to her on a recent trip to Paris by a woman who told her about a reading Edgar had given her in New York. The envelope contained $1,375—the exact amount Edgar owed the bank on his mortgage.

The day was not only a wonderful one for Edgar, but also for the Duke of Windsor and Mrs. Simpson. It was their wedding day.

Occurrences such as this happened so often in Edgar's life, he probably wasn't even surprised. But he certainly was always grateful.

June 3

Blessed, then, are they that make their wills one in accord with Him, as they seek to know, "Lord, what would thou have me do!" Not Lord, may I do this or that! Show forth, ye all, the Lord's death - DEATH - till He come again, in the lightening of the way for those that seek, those that seek to know His way. 254-68

On this day in 1924 Edgar wrote two letters that expressed his optimism about forming the Cayce Institute to enable more readings and their study to help others.

To a doctor interested in his work, Edgar wrote that his work for others had grown to such a degree that he felt his entire time should be devoted to it.

To his cousin Fannie, he wrote, "I am building for myself, and for the generations to come, the foundation for a more perfect knowledge of the Laws of Heaven and of God as relating to humanity. I do not mean to infer from this that I am trying to establish some new kind of religion but a more perfect understanding of how to live rather than [only] profess Christ's principles."

The Cayce Institute never happened, and Edgar would soon leave Dayton and start pursuing an even bigger dream.

Rather than have an institute to study the readings for sharing, why not have a hospital with doctors on staff to carry out the readings' instructions for cures?

Such an arrangement would allow for the ultimate use of his psychic skills. He would devote many years pursuing the finances to make this dream come true.

June 4

Let thy prayer, thy meditation be, "Here am I, O Lord, use me as thou seest fit. Thou knowest the needs, Thou knowest the purposes, Thou knowest the desires. Make them pure indeed in me, that I may be the greater channel of blessings to others."   281-23

By early June in 1909 Edgar, now age 32, was still indulging in his personal pity party because he could no longer go into a trance.

He wanted to do good. He wanted to help people. Why had he allowed financial woes to let him stray from the straight and narrow? He had to put his life as a psychic diagnostician behind him and earn money to support his family.

Time had come for him to leave The Hill, where he, Gertrude, and 2-year-old Hugh Lynn were crowded in with too many other relatives, and Gertrude's stress showed in her pale face and underweight body.

Edgar wrote letters to people he knew in Texas and Alabama, asking about employment possibilities and eventually was offered a job by a photographer named Harding in Gadsden, Alabama.

He went to Gadsden in early June and roved between towns taking classroom pictures. Before long he had an offer for a higher paying job that required a move to Anniston, Alabama, to work at the Russell Brothers Studio. The higher salary wasn't the best thing. The best thing was that he could once again go into a deep trance. His prayers had been answered.

June 5

Hence there cannot be a complete expression of self in the activities and in the body of self unless the attitudes are kept in a constructive way and manner so as to justify the adding of material benefits.   658-15

Information about Edgar's subliminal messages came through a reading for Arthur Lammers in June 1923. The two men met in March, and now Lammers wanted to establish an organization to study Edgar's powers.

Edgar's Source said he should be asked only questions never detrimental to anyone, but in accord with spiritual laws. The information given would be correct if the conductor giving suggestions was also in accord. Maybe when Edgar ended a reading by saying, "We are through," the subconscious connection had been compromised.

Using readings for something other than helping someone was acceptable if used for unselfish purposes. Then information "may be, should be, used and given to the world." The divine law is "Love is Law, Law is Love. God is Love. Love is God." A person's free will—a gift from God—ultimately shaped that person's life.

This reading said unequivocally that all can do what Edgar does—with development. Edgar gave good trance advice because of eight generations of soul development—a reading's first hint of reincarnation. The new idea was basically ignored because what followed was Edgar's true passion: Yes, now was the time to start an institution for "the work." He could then share insights given to him with humankind.

June 6

> *But go that the self may be aware of those very effects as has been given, that Life is continuous, that there IS divinity in the soul of man, that the training of the spiritual consciousness of the mind is as necessary as the training of the physical consciousness to enjoy even the conveniences of the day.*   1298-1

"*Do not* leave out spirituality in thy dealings with others." (2599-1) Edgar said, "Practice!"

Practice giving others something to live for "within as well as without themselves. For he that contributes only to his own welfare soon finds little to work for. He that contributes only to the welfare of others soon finds too much for others and has lost the appreciation of self or of its ideals. "(3478-2)

As in all life's areas, balance is key—"not being an extremist in any direction—whether in diet, exercise, spirituality or morality—but in all let there be a coordinant influence. For, every phase...physical, mental and spiritual...is dependent upon the other." (2533-3)

Spirituality in our daily lives will be a given if we live by the ideal we've established for ourselves.

"Know thy ideals - spiritually, mentally, materially... And we will find that it will bring harmony, contentment, and sufficient of EVERY worldly, spiritual, material thing necessary for thy soul development. Then what thy destiny is depends upon what ye will do with thyself in relationship to thy ideal." (257-249)

"Spirituality grows, as love...being given out." (920-9)

June 7

Each soul meets CONSTANTLY itself; not alone in what is called at times karma or karmic influences. For remember Life is God; that which is constructive grows; that which is destructive deteriorates.   1436-1

On this day in 1927 Edgar gave a reading for Tom Sugrue, who came to Virginia Beach to expose Edgar as a fake psychic.

Tom and Hugh Lynn were classmates at Washington and Lee University, and he could not believe the wild stories Hugh Lynn told him about his father.

An ardent Catholic, he turned his nose up at the idea of reincarnation and the stories not in the Bible that Edgar had learned about Jesus.

Hugh Lynn's motive for inviting him home was to prove Edgar's legitimacy. Tom's motive for accepting the invitation was to make a name for himself as a writer by destroying this fake in print.

When his life reading tied a previous incarnation to Hugh Lynn at a time when Tom as a priest rebelled against Hugh Lynn as Egypt's Pharaoh, he became interested in pursuing the idea further. Could that be an underlying reason for his and Hugh Lynn's constant arguing that often led to fistfights?

Studying the readings, he began to believe.

FAST FORWARD: He became a convert when a reading told things about himself that no living person knew. He would write *There Is a River,* Edgar's first biography.

June 8

Mind...is the factor governing the contention, or the interlaying space, if you please, between the physical to the soul, and the soul to the spirit forces within the individual or animate forces.   3744-2

On this day in 1881 when Edgar was four years old, he saw his grandfather Tom Cayce have an accident that killed him.

Tom had just let Edgar off to catch minnows while he watered his horse, when the horse—startled by something—plunged into the water and swam to the other side. Tom held on while the horse failed at jumping a fence, but when the horse stumbled, he fell off and was thrown into the water.

Edgar watched as the horse stomped its hooves into his beloved grandfather's chest. When a neighbor passed by, Edgar showed him where his grandfather sank in the water.

A nearby doctor was summoned to help, but Tom was dead. Edgar had not only lost his paternal grandfather, but his best friend.

After his death Edgar often spent time in the tobacco barn, which had been his favorite place to spend time with his grandfather. Now, he was heard talking with the man he loved so much.

The Cayces kept little Edgar's conversations secret, probably not even suspecting that he might have psychic skills.

June 9

(Q) Is the psychic phenomena an inherited trait? (A) Not necessarily so unless the spirit or soul of the forces of those directly connected are transplanted in the one. The law of attraction is positive and remains with one. The material attraction is to be to those of the same form, as to whether the phenomena is produced by heredity is far from being correct. 3744-2

The day before this in 1893 was the anniversary of Grandfather Tom's death. On that day Edgar visited his bedridden Grandmother Sarah, who helped him accept that because of his special power, he could never be like other people.

She helped him realize that he was like his grandfather, who had a green thumb, could find water, and could make tables, chairs, and brooms dance.

About his skill she said, "Don't be afraid of it, and don't misuse it." She advised him to compare the voices he heard in his head to what Jesus would say, and to act accordingly.

Like his grandfather, Edgar didn't like entertaining people with his skill. He made a commitment to use it only to help others.

He confided to his grandmother his desire to be a minister, and she was pleased. She asked him to promise through his lifetime to look not at others as antagonists, but as, like him, children of God.

She probably realized that Edgar would meet many who'd consider him a freak, as his young classmates had.

June 10

For, as seen, the mental body, the physical body, with its mental activities, and the soul or spiritual body often war one with another through those two influences that may be designated as will and desire. These are, then, the contending influences in the experiences of every soul, whether these activities are in the direction of that ...held by the soul as its ideal, makes for either that retardment or development in each experience. 443-3

On this day in 1911 Gertrude was throwing up blood and had absolutely no strength. She had caught pneumonia from her brother Hugh while she was trying to nurse him back to health.

Edgar immediately wanted to do a reading, but Gertrude would not allow him to go into a trance for her. She still wasn't comfortable with Edgar's psychic side. She liked having him home in Hopkinsville, but she preferred he would be simply a photographer, not a psychic diagnostician.

She also objected to the many who had tried to use Edgar for get-rich-quick schemes. Refusing a reading for herself was her way of registering her opposition to the cramp Edgar's gift had put on their lifestyle.

Her health continued going downhill, and she would not consent to a reading until almost two months later when she surely was on the verge of death.

The reading's advice saved her life and changed her attitude toward Edgar's desire to pursue his psychic calling. She became his staunchest supporter.

June 11

it is not from without, but it is within thyself that ye may meet Him. For thy body is indeed the temple of the living God. There He has promised to meet thee, just as sincerely as ye seek; though knowledge without understanding may become sin.   2795-1

After a long, debilitating illness, Gertrude agreed finally to let Edgar give her a reading.

For 45 minutes the Forces analyzed her body's condition and spewed out an extensive list of recommendations. They included having osteopathic adjustments, inhaling spirits, taking powerful drugs—including heroin and three others mixed with water in a capsule. The spirits needed to be app e brandy fumes inhaled from a charred oak keg.

She was also to eat a high-iron diet and have laxatives injected into her colon.

Gertrude's doctor and the specialist he called to help would not sign a prescription for the drugs, so Edgar asked for help from Dr. Wesley Ketchum, the osteopathic doctor who gave treatments to Edgar's clients.

Ketchum prescribed the drugs, and Gertrude stopped hemorrhaging after the first capsule. After the second day, her fever disappeared. Very slowly she gained strength, falling time and again in relapse.

Edgar kept giving readings and new recommendations were followed until she got well. Her faith in him never wavered after that.

June 12

> *In sleep all things become possible, as one finds self flying through space, lifting, or being chased, or what not, by those very things that make for a comparison of that which has been builded by the very soul of the body itself. What, then, is the sixth sense?*   5754-2

While sleeping, our souls take stock of what we've done since the last time we slept. Our dreams are making comparisons of whether we've experienced the fruits of the Spirit, or just the opposite—"hate, harsh words, unkind thoughts, oppressions and the like."

"When the physical consciousness is at rest, the other self communes with the SOUL of the body, see? or it goes OUT into that realm of experience in the relationships of all experiences of that entity that may have been throughout the EONS of time, or in correlating WITH that as it, that entity, HAS accepted as its criterion or standard of judgments, or justice, within its sphere of activity."

"Sleep is a shadow of, that intermission in earth's experiences of, that state called death; for the physical consciousness becomes unaware of existent conditions, save as are determined by the attributes of the physical that partake of the attributes of the imaginative or the subconscious and unconscious forces of that same body."

We need to know that "there is a DEFINITE connection between that we have chosen to term the sixth sense, or acting through the auditory forces of the body-physical, and the other self within self." (5754-1)

June 13

The activity, or this sixth sense activity, is the activating power or force of the other self. What other self? That which has been builded by the entity or body, or soul, through its experiences as a whole in the material and cosmic world, see? or is as a faculty of the soul-body itself. 5754-2

During sleep the subconscious makes us aware of conflicting actions or thoughts we may have had.

We discover "some action on the part of self or another that is in disagreement with that which has been builded by that other self, then THIS is the warring of conditions or emotions within an individual."

If we go to bed sad and awaken happy, sleep has shown us that our emotions are not conflicted. If we go to bed happy and awaken sad, our emotions are at war.

"There has been, and ever when the physical consciousness is at rest, the other self communes with the SOUL of the body...or it goes OUT into that realm of experience in the relationships of all experiences of that entity that may have been throughout the EONS of time, or in correlating WITH that as it, that entity, HAS accepted as its criterion or standard of judgments, or justice, within its sphere of activity." (5754-2)

"What, then, is the sixth sense? Not the soul, not the conscious mind, not the subconscious mind, not intuition alone, not any of those cosmic forces - but the very force or activity of the soul in its experience through WHATEVER has been the experience of that soul itself." (5754-1)

June 14

Each soul is a portion of the divine. Motivating that soul-body is the spirit of divinity. The soul is a companion of, a motivative influence in, the activities of an entity throughout its experiences in whatever sphere of consciousness it may attain perception. 1096-4

On this day in 1932 Edgar spontaneously viewed the Last Supper as it was happening. He had just finished a woman's reading and did not respond to three suggestions to wake up. (5749-1)

Jesus, wearing a pearl-gray robe, weighed about 170 pounds with hair "most red, inclined to be curly in portions, yet not feminine or weak—STRONG, with heavy piercing eyes that are blue or steel-gray."

Edgar gave shorter descriptions of the disciples, saying, "The better looking of the twelve, of course, was Judas." Their meal was "boiled fish, rice, with leeks, wine, and loaf." A pitcher's handle and lip were broken. The atmosphere was one of merriment and joking.

After Judas departs, Jesus gives "the wine and loaf, with which he gives the emblems that should be so dear to every follower of Him." Peter refuses when He kneels with the wooden basin, "Then the dissertation as to 'he that would be the greatest would be servant of all.'" Jesus plays a harp as they sing Psalm 91, and then they leave for the garden.

Edgar told the woman that this vision came because "It became so close to the part of the entity's experience for He with His Teachings is to all men HELPFULNESS."

June 15

Should the Maker use a gnome, a fairy, an angel, a developing entity FOR a guide, alright - for a specific direction; for He hath...given His angels charge concerning thee. Then, lest thou dash thy foot against a stone, lest thou unheeding turn into those directions or channels that will bring thee rather consternation. For, whom He hath called, him also hath He glorified - and WILL glorify, through his activities or experiences, or through His callings to those that seek to do His biddings.
338-3

Sometime in 1889 Edgar built a crude retreat where he could be alone to read his Bible, pray, and enjoy nature. The Cayces had moved to a cottage which father Leslie and his brothers had built in the woods. One day Edgar was at his secluded spot under a willow tree, pondering how he could best serve God.

That night an angel came to him and said, "Thy prayers are heard. You will have your wish. Remain faithful. Be true to yourself. Help the sick, the afflicted."

Those words guided him the rest of his life. When he discovered the extent of his psychic gift, he came to think that it was given to him to do what the angel said. Whenever he used his skill for anything else, he wondered if the Forces would approve. Whenever he faced a setback—and he had many—he feared he had betrayed his calling.

But this night he was only astounded. For many years he told no one about this angelic visit.

June 16

So in the body they are one; body, mind, soul. Body is temporal, mind is partially temporal and partially holy... So the soul is that which is eternal. Thus does there come in the experience of each soul those problems in a material world of the constant warring of material or changing things, or earthly experience, with mental and spiritual or soul forces.   2600-2

In the summer of 1893 the tobacco market dropped, and Leslie came home from auction $18,000 in debt. The family lost everything, including their horse and buggy. They had to move from their their cottage back to Mother Carrie's girlhood home with her alcohol-abusing father and her mentally disturbed mother.

Edgar's four sisters hated being in that big red brick house with their maternal grandparents and their inexplicable emotional bouts.

Edgar didn't have to contend with those problems because he still worked and lived at his uncle's farm. His salary was more of a necessity than ever now that father Leslie did little but pamper the pain of his venereal disease and try to dream up get-rich schemes.

His problem, though, was a serious one. He was now the family's sole breadwinner, a giant responsibility for a 16-year-old farm boy. Had he not already dropped out of school after eighth grade, he would have had to at this time anyway.

Self-educating continued with his daily Bible reading, and even at this age he was teaching Sunday school and amazing the elders with his Biblical knowledge.

June 17

So we have LOVE is LAW, LAW IS LOVE. GOD IS LOVE. LOVE IS GOD. In that we see the law manifested, not the law itself. Unto the individual, as we have given then, that gets the understanding of self, becomes a part of this. As is found, which come in one, so we have manifestations of the one-ness, of the all-ness in love. Now, if we, as individuals, upon the earth plane, have all of the other elementary forces that make to the bettering of life, and have not love we are as nothing - nothing. 3744-5

On this day in 1903 Edgar, age 26, and Gertrude, age 23, were married at The Hill with all of their family and probably most of the 300 invited guests.

Gertrude was lovely in her white traveling dress with a white rose in her bonnet.

After an elaborate reception on the lawn, the happy couple took a carriage to board the 8:55 p.m. train for Bowling Green, where Edgar had lived and worked since April 1902. More than a hundred of Edgar's church friends met them with a shower of rice as they stepped off the train at 10:15 p.m. in Bowling Green.

They moved into a boardinghouse across the street from the Hollins House, where Edgar had lived and which was restricted to singles only.

Gertrude came to the marriage with a dowry of gold coins worth $100, a gift from her mother.

After a very long engagement, they were ecstatically happy and ready for a life together in Bowling Green.

June 18

Hence no hate, no dishonor; but patience, longsuffering, brotherly love, kindness, gentleness; not exalting of self but rather abasement of self that there may be the closer union, the closer walk with that I AM THAT I AM…. Not saying nor acting unkind things. No harsh words. None of these are a part of the soul, that seeks for soul or psychic development.   1376-1

The day after their wedding, as the newlyweds had their first Sunday dinner at the Hollis House with boarders Edgar had previously lived with, Al Layne arrived.

The boarders took this opportunity to ask him about his monthly visits with Edgar, and Layne told them about Edgar's voice therapy.

When Judge Roup made disparaging remarks about his correspondence degree, Layne was provoked into bragging about the many cures he had accomplished with Edgar as a psychic diagnostician.

Gertrude burst into tears and left the room, but Edgar stayed and defended the value of the healing work he and Layne had accomplished.

Persuaded to give readings for several patients, Edgar astounded all with detailed diagnoses and medical treatments only a doctor should know.

Back at the couple's boarding house, Edgar found Gertrude packing to leave him. Somehow he convinced her that he came as a husband with the baggage of his psychic skills. She unpacked her hope chest and stayed.

June 19

Seeking, knowing - as ye measure, as ye act in thought, in mind, in heart, in body, and the imaginations of thine self become MATERIALIZED in others' actions.   281-2

An unfounded rumor that raised Gertrude's suspicions resulted in a family friend hurting himself and disrupting progress on Rocky Pasture #1.

With Edgar spending so much of 1922 and 1923 in Texas with his oil venture, rumors that he was having an affair circulated around Hopkinsville.

Gertrude became concerned when Edgar broke his promise to send $100 per month. She had received a few smaller checks, but then none at all arrived in the mail. The Selma photo studio, poorly handled by Edgar's father Leslie, didn't generate the expected income, and now Leslie was bedridden with back injuries.

Here she was, stuck in Hopkinsville raising a 16-year old and a 4-year-old alone while Edgar was off chasing pipe dreams and maybe chasing another woman.

Because she had to know the truth, she sent Thomas House to sleuth around and find out. He tried to light his pipe on the drilling platform, causing an explosion that blew him and others off the platform.

Edgar accompanied him back to Hopkinsville in June, but soon left for Selma, spending July and August in trying to save the Cayce Art Company from its monetary mess.

Although House's written report to Gertrude made no mention of another woman in Edgar's life, she didn't go with him to Selma. She stayed in Hopkinsville.

June 20

> ...but know, only they that are able to suffer are able to know glory, to know peace, to know harmony. These may sound at first only as idealistic sayings, but if ye turn within and ask of thy better self ye will find the answer there.   1362-1

Alone in Selma in 1923 Edgar made one last effort to save Penn-Tenn's oil venture, but gave up when Tex Rice was indicted for defrauding investors. (See March 20)

He was now age 46, overweight, and in worse shape financially than when he set out to expand "the work" by striking it rich with oil. However, he now realized his true life's mission was to help others with his unique gift from God. He would never again sway from that mission.

He knew "the work" deserved his highest and best efforts, and the readings deserved to be preserved.

He converted a room in his studio for their transcripts to be stored and for him to have a couch to lie on to go into a trance for readings.

While at the oil rig in Texas, a young woman named Fay Autry had recorded the readings, and Hopkinsville gossipers had spread false rumors about his relationship with Fay. Even though their friend whom Gertrude sent to spy on him didn't mention the woman's name, Gertrude surely would have confronted him. Surely that's why she didn't accompany him to Selma.

Now he wrote to her with hope in his heart: "I'm home to stay. Please come back." And so she did.

June 21

Then with the breaking up, producing more of the nature of large islands, with the intervening canals or ravines, gulfs, bays or streams, as came from the various ELEMENTAL forces that were set in motion by this CHARGING - as it were - OF the forces that were collected as the basis for those elements that would produce destructive forces, as might be placed in various quarters or gathering places of those beasts, or the periods when the larger animals roved the earth - WITH that period of man's indwelling. Let it be remembered, or not confused, that the EARTH was peopled by ANIMALS before peopled by man!   364-6

Edgar had an unusual affinity with animals. Once after a day working in the field on his uncle's farm, he rode a mule back to the farmhouse.

A worker yelled at him. "Get down! That mule will kill you!"

Edgar may have been perplexed, but he dismounted.

"She's never been ridden," the man said. "Won't let anyone get on her."

Another said, "She's too tired to fuss now. Good time to break her in."

A third man mounted the mule, which immediately and roughly threw him off.

Edgar was sick at heart. He certainly knew by this point in his life—he was seventeen—that he was different. He wanted his difference to help people, not hurt them.

June 22

For He hath given His angels charge concerning thee, that ye faint not by the way. For He stands - STANDS - at the door and knocks, and if ye will open He will come and sup with thee. For He IS life and light and immortality; and the way is good.   1436-1

Sometime in June 1894 when Edgar was age seventeen, he was visited just after he'd had lunch by the same angel who had come into his bedroom years ago. He was repairing a broken plow when he heard a pleasant humming that rushed through him like soothing music does. Then the voice he recognized—one he'd never forget, the one which set his course for life. "Leave the farm," the angel said. "Go to your mother. Everything will be all right."

He didn't hesitate to follow the instruction. He led his mules to pasture, packed his few possessions and—ignoring his uncle's protests—started the seven-mile walk to Hopkinsville.

He recently had a dream about walking with a veiled woman and wondered if she might be the woman he would marry. Might he find her in the city?

Life might possibly be getting better for the Cayce family. They had just moved to a log home with a barn in the back, and his aunt had given them a cow. All this was possible because of money Leslie inherited from his mother's estate.

Edgar felt sorry for his mother whose affluent lifestyle of her youth disappeared when she married Leslie.

June 23

An entity, or soul, is a spark - or a portion - of the Whole, the First Cause; and thus is a co-worker with that First Cause, or Purpose, which is the creative influence or force that is manifested in materiality...Thus, whether the activities or consciousnesses are in the material expression or in the universal cosmic expression in the spirit, these are ever a part of the entity's expression - for either development or retardment. 2079-1

How we conduct our lives in this incarnation results in either returning to our Creator or coming back to earth for another chance to do better.

The above reading also states: "Each entity, each soul, is endowed with self-will; that which is the force that makes it able, or gives it the capacity, to be the law, and yet complying with a universal purpose."

Everything we do in our lives matters. "If it is for self-expression, self-indulgence, self-glorification, self-gratification, the inclinations become in a direction away from, and not toward an at-onement with, the Whole. Yet, being of the Whole, and with the Creative Forces...

"For, indeed each entty, each soul, is in the process of evolution towards the First Cause. Much becomes evolution - much may become involution." (2079-1)

God is inside us. "Clear thyself of confusion. Know it is within thee. Failure or success, right and wrong, good and evil; yet He meeteth thee in thine own tabernacle, in thine own holy of holies...in thine own tabernacle." (1210-1)

June 24

> As ye would that others would forgive you, even so must you forgive - if you would find that peace, that harmony within self. And thus may ye help those; not condoning, no - but not condemning either. For, to condemn is to become as a party to such. And with what measure ye condemn others, ye are guilty... 293-3

Just one week after Edgar and Gertrude moved into the boarding house on their wedding night, the manager told them they would have to move out.

The reason was a *Bowling Green Times Journal* front-page story written by the judge and newspaper publisher who had occasionally stayed at the singles-only boarding house where Edgar had previously lived.

The story detailed Edgar's unusual childhood and the Aime Dietrich case (Aug. 9), also naming Edgar's job location and his church in Bowling Green. The next day the same story was published in papers throughout Kentucky and Tennessee.

Mr. Potter, although he didn't immediately fire Edgar from his bookstore job, told him to find another job. He would also have to move his photo studio.

First Christian Church authorities, citing his psychic healing as the work of the Devil, asked him to leave the church.

The newlyweds' marital bliss was definitely amiss. The blessed new life he and Gertrude had planned to start in Bowling Green had come to a screeching halt.

June 25

The spirit of all that have passed from the physical plane remain about the plane until their development carry them onward or are returned for their development here. When they are in the plane of communication or remain within this sphere, any may be communicated with. There are thousands about us here at present. 3744-1

On this day in 1933 Edgar had a stint as a ghostbuster. Florence Edmonds, a study group member, called him to her home which had suddenly become haunted.

She was frightened by strange sounds, doors unexpectedly creaking open, and an unearthly presence she sometimes felt around her. Even in her dreams she felt haunted by these unwelcome spirits.

Edgar's reading revealed that she herself had psychic powers which had magnified with her work in the study group. That psychic gift gave her an awareness of metaphysical things that would elude most people.

Maybe knowing this reality diminished the problem because all the weird happenings stopped.

Edgar's one visit to her home not only ended the haunting, but started her on the path to becoming a legitimate healer, just as two other study group members would do.

Many people would come to Florence to be cured by her laying on of hands. The work was expanding.

June 26

Its functioning, then, is as that, of that, which makes for - or known as - the impulse or imaginative body. Hence one that may be called demented by others, who has hallucinations from a pressure in some portions, may be visioning that which to him is as real (though others may call him crazy) as to those who are supposed to have an even balance of their senses; which [such visioning?] has been formed by the circulation, or the activity of the gland - as it is called - in its incipiency, until it becomes - or is - as a mass without apparent functioning. If the imaginative body, or the trained body (as is called in a material world) is, trained constantly away FROM the activities of same, it - in natural consequence of things in physical being - draws, as it were, within self. Hence senility sets in. Keep the pineal gland operating and you won't grow old - you will always be young! 294-141

The top recommendation for keeping the pineal gland active—with its promise above of perpetual youth—is to meditate daily, preceded by chanting "Ar-r-r-r-r-AR-aum," with tongue behind the upper teeth.

Gentle forehead tapping has also been advised to wake up the pineal, as has the yogic child's pose. Kneel and lower the bottom to the legs. Lean forward and touch forehead to the floor.

"Thy God-consciousness, thy soul, either condemns, rejects or falters before conditions that exist in the experience of the mental and material self. Mind ever is the Builder." (1436-1) Remembering this helps.

June 27

Study well, then, the influence ye have upon those ye meet day by day. For, again, with what measure ye mete, with what judgment ye act, so comes it back to thee. For, to have love one must manifest and show love in one's life and one's dealings with others. To have friends one just show self friendly. 2560-1

Late June 1894 and now living with his parents in Hopkinsville, Edgar went downtown looking for a job.

He was amazed at the quantity of books when he visited his first bookstore, Hopper Brothers—the same one whose now deceased owner had given Edgar his Bible six years ago.

Edgar asked Will Hopper for a job, but was told he and Harry needed no more employees.

He proceeded to R.C. Hardwick's Jewelry Store and was turned down for a job.

Continuing through the town, he perused Garner's Drug Store, Wall's Clothing Store, Hoosier's Tailor Shop, the bank, and several other stores, ending up back at Hopper Brothers.

He offered to work there for no salary for a month, and if Will and Harry didn't want him after that, he would leave. They agreed.

After a month they bought him a suit. After two months they gave him $15 and promised the same each month. This was the first but not the last job he attained in an ingenious way.

June 28

Let mercy and judgment and honor be as one in thy dealing with thy fellow man. For he that showeth mercy may obtain mercy, he that brings Happiness into the lives of others will know Happiness. And only by the sowing of the seed of that nature that ye desire the full activity of in thy life may ye accomplish or accede to such an experience. For what you ARE speaks so loud, few hear what you say. 262-109

Actions speak louder than words, and though Edgar never said so in such simple language, he often repeated that simple truth.

"Keep thy heart singing, for there is music and joy in the Happiness of knowing that you may be - and are - at a oneness with Him. Though there may come disturbances, shadows, turmoils, these must pass in the light of patience, persistence, loving kind-ness." (262-109)

As long as we are aware of our oneness with God we have no danger of mistreating others. If we slip, "God is still mindful of the children of men; that though they may have wandered far afield, though they may come to those crossroads in all phases of their experience, He is ready to answer when they call." (1472-12)

"Ye must forgive as ye would be forgiven... Know that ye live and move and have thy being in Him, who is the way, the truth, the light. As ye have seen, as ye experience in thy circle of admonition to others - ask not others to do that ye would not do in thine own experience." (3299-1)

June 29

Remember then as this: There are promises made by the Creative Forces or God to the children of men, that "If ye will be my daughter, my son, my child, I will indeed be thy God.   1436-1

On this day in 1932 the A.R.E.'s first annual Congress was held at the first home Edgar and Gertrude actually owned. A reading told Edgar to buy it when he had less than $100 in the bank, not enough for the $500 down payment.

On the very day he needed it, a grateful client's check for $250 arrived along with another from new members to pay for life readings they'd already had.

The Arctic Crescent house was big enough for an A.R.E. meeting and also an upstairs A.R.E. office with three desks. Four bedrooms upstairs housed the Cayces' books, father Leslie, Edgar and Gertrude, and Gladys with her cousin Mildred. Edgar had an office downstairs with more than sixty framed pictures displayed on the walls.

Eighty people in attendance at this first Congress were privileged to listen as Edgar gave readings on subjects they chose.

***

On this day in 1943 Edgar's second grandchild Edgar Evans Jr. was born. A reading predicted he would be short and accident-prone from age two to five. He *was* short and before his fourth birthday severed an artery with a broken milk bottle.

June 30

Self must open the door that He may enter in. Self will work at that job of bringing that consciousness, that awareness of His presence in the material and mental affairs of life, knowing that lesson must ever be that the spirit is the life, the mental is the builder, and the physical or material results are the effects of the application of the knowledge or understanding toward life, light, or the spirit of ANY effort.   262-28

Edgar was introduced to the love of his life, Gertrude Evans, by Ethel Duke, a frequent customer at Hopper Brothers bookstore where Edgar worked.

Ethel, a teacher, had heard Edgar deliver the long McKenzie speech some five years ago. On a previous visit to the bookstore, she invited him to come to a moonlight at The Hill, and Edgar immediately accepted the invitation. Leslie, however, was not so enthusiastic and forbade him to go.

This day she asked Edgar to come outside, and she introduced him to Gertrude, who was waiting in a buggy.

Edgar was immediately struck by her beauty and was very pleased to be invited to a party at her Grandfather Salters' house called The Hill in a part of Hopkinsville's high society area.

He was about to be introduced to a lifestyle of luxury and a love of enlightenment to which he had never before been exposed. He later confessed that his first experience at The Hill made him feel "uncouth and uneducated."

July 1

> Arguments will seldom change the aspects or the views of any. And truth itself needs no champion, for it is of itself champion of champions - and needs no defense; only for self to live according to that which IS the truth! 1669-1

Arguments are useless and should be avoided, and criticizing another is taboo. If tempted to criticize another, remember "what one says of another will usually be one's own state also - in one form or another. Hence such criticisms..only create barriers, animosities, hates, disputes, corruptions - and these are never in THEIR reaping very beautiful to behold!" (1669-1)

Do not show temper or harbor resentments. "No one has a right to hold any grudge. Would you ask the Father to hold a grudge against thee, or do you ask forgiveness daily?" (3299-1)

Know your own ideals and stick with them. "One may be free indeed in thought, though the body may be bound in chains; and be much more free than those who are chained by their own consciousness in those things which are in keeping with the ideals in the material as well as mental and spiritual life.

"These understandings the entity must gain through the abilities to curb self, in being too quickly outspoken when little resentments arise...." (1669-1)

There is no virtue in either arguing or criticizing. "There are faults, there are virtues. We would mini-mize the faults, we would magnify the virtues." (3299-1)

July 2

Do not confuse self, nor consider or feel that the spiritual and mental life is different from the material things. For, one is the shadow or the reflection of the other. If ye live in the light, the shadows fall behind. If the face is turned from the light, there can be nothing in the life - in the mental or material things - BUT shadow. TURN to the LIGHT! 257-123

Edgar had never seen such a palatial home as the one Gertrude's family called The Hill.

Upon his arrival Ethel Duke introduced him to many dignitaries, family members, and guests. The family patriarch was Samuel Salter, Gertrude's grandfather, who —with his wife Sara—had given all five of their children college educations.

Lizzie, his first child, Gertrude's mother, lost her husband when their three children were very young and then built a small house adjacent to The Hill. Gertrude and her brothers Hugh and Lynn spent as much time at The Hill as at their own home.

Edgar was impressed with the many young males vying for the attention of Gertrude's 21-year-old Aunt Carrie and was equally impressed by the caliber of guests—clergymen, engineers, and many college students.

Finally he and Gertrude had some moments alone as they took a walk around the home's lush gardens. Edgar always remembered how beautiful Gertrude was that night with a rose in her lovely brunette hair. In his lifetime he never planted a garden without a rose bush.

July 3

(Q) Are there any bodies still reposing in the wreck and if so should an effort be made to recover them? (A) To be sure, recover them - and there are hundreds!

(Q) Can the divers expect sympathy or antagonism from the souls of those who lost their lives when the ship sank? (A) Sympathy and help, as has been indicated. For the many hundreds are anxious, and would aid and would direct. 1395-1

The above Q & A happened on this day in 1937, as Edgar gave John D. Craig—renowned deep-sea diver and underwater photographer—a vicarious tour of the *Lusitania,* which had lain on the ocean floor since a German torpedo sunk it on May 7, 1915.

Edgar pinpointed the position of the wreck off the South Irish Coast, the visibility of the torpedo hole, and the positions of purser's safe (containing $2,800,000) and measure compartments (containing "more millions there than in the purser's!")

The best time to enter the wreck, Edgar said, would be "the harvest moon of August or May or June...As the moon's influence upon the waters is the greater at those periods indicated, and especially in these portions of the sea, these individuals - the souls of those whose bodies are here confined - work with same; for their release to many is just as important as on the day torpedoed."

This was not the first reading to speak of souls of the deceased communicating with the living. Unfortunately, World War II kept Craig from diving to the *Lusitania.*

July 4

(Q) Where do I vibrate best (that is, in what locality)?
(A) Where thou ART! For the vibrations should be from WITHIN, rather than from WITHOUT! And so create within thine inner self those closer relationships that where thy body is, THERE may be found succor and aid and help and love for others.   1183-1

On this holiday in 1910 Edgar moved with his father to Jacksonville, Alabama, to open a branch studio for Russell Brothers Studio, the company he had worked for in Anniston.

In Anniston Leslie wanted Edgar to try to give a reading for 21-month-old Gordon Putnam, who was unable to move his legs. He would be Edgar's first subject since he regained his ability to go into a trance.

Dr. Posey implemented the reading's recommended treatments, which worked. After that Dr. Posey sent a woman blind from glaucoma, and she was cured. The doctor urged other doctors to try Edgar for their difficult cases.

During this period when he had just regained his ability, five readings were done to determine how he could best be of service to humankind. The verdict was: not in Kentucky or Alabama, but in Dayton, Ohio. But his ultimate good for others would happen in Virginia Beach.

This was the first of many times readings pointed to Virginia Beach, the small fishing village where he would eventually treat patients in a hospital specializing in carrying out treatments from his psychic diagnoses.

July 5

As there are the beginnings of those of science, of philosophy, to seek for the knowledge of the true relationships to the soul, then in those activities that may aid those seekers - whether they be the laymen or whether they be the great or those that would be great but aren't. Aid them in their seeking; remaining free in self as in the advice to those, not becoming hidebound or so set in a line that the knowledge of those things that are making for fear in the experiences of those about you is lost sight of. In such a field may the greatest help, the greatest blessings to self and the greater help to others come.   1210-1

On this day in 1937 Edgar gave a reading to locate Amelia Earhart, a pilot who disappeared flying near Hawaii on July 2, 1937.

Her husband George Putnam asked for Edgar's help.

The reading found the condition for Amelia and her companion "rather serious," as lack of fuel had caused them to crash on a coral reef some ninety miles northwest of Howland Island.

The reading stressed a sense of urgency for rescuers, who eventually gave up their search on July 18. Another reading later revealed that Amelia died on July 21.

Years later a plane wreckage around Edgar's specified location was found. Anthropologists concluded from bones that the two at the crash site had survived for some time. Controversy still exists about whether or not the bones were of Amelia and her companion.

July 6

> ...first analyze self, self's desires, self's purpose. Put away from the mind, the heart, the experience, those things that make afraid. Know that the true spirit of creative influences, of God influence, of that which will succeed in every phase of the experience, is within the abilities of self WITHIN. And when this is done, then BUILD upon same in a creative way and manner. 1579-1

On this day in 1938 a 46-year-old male afflicted with Parkinson's disease returned to Edgar for a second visit. He had followed recommendations and was much improved after only one month.

Physically he was healing, but he could do even better with an attitude change. "Is the body to be saved from physical disturbance that the real self or soul is to be purged into greater depths of disappointment and disdain? Then let the physical and the mental and the spiritual coordinate, cooperate. Make the life more worth while, more purposeful. Arouse the activities of the mental and physical self to the better influence in a spiritual way and manner. Not that the entity...should become as one goody-goody, or sanctimonious...but... use consistency.

"What is thy ideal? What is the outlook upon the experiences in the associations with others? Is it only for the gratifying of appetites, only for the self-indulgence for the moment? Can these do anything but weaken the physical as well as the better self?" (1555-2)

Edgar's advice to one so often applies to so many.

July 7

One loving the beautiful; attracted to same in every form, whether that of the physical, spiritual, or plain material, and to the entity - even the toad, the serpent, the cabbage or the flower, may be beautiful, dependent upon the attitude, by antics or action of such in its relation to that attempted this entity to illustrate in the life's action of individuals….One that is high minded, in that character and action are ever studied by the entity - and whether one of low estate, origin, or in social life, the BEAUTY and the purity of the life is ever the appealing factor to the ENTITY.   345-1

In 1895 when Edgar was 18 years old, he decided not to be a minister.

His reasoning was very logical. He would need to go back to school and take three more years to graduate from high school. He would be almost 22 before entering college. By that time he should be married and at least starting to have a family.

He decided that a true preacher would be a missionary and own nothing but his Bible.

All those reasons changed his mind about spending his future in the pulpit. Maybe the financially lean years of his youth left him with a yearning for more possessions than a Bible.

Maybe—most probably—he wanted to marry that beautiful young girl he'd been seeing ever since going to a party on The Hill. He was very much in love with Gertrude.

July 8

Death - as commonly spoken of - is only passing through God's other door. That there is continued consciousness is evidenced, ever, by the associations of influences, the abilities of entities to project or to make those impressions upon the consciousness of sensitives or the like. As to how long - many an individual has remained in that called death for what ye call YEARS without realizing it was dead! 1472-2

On this day in 1895, Edgar was holding Grandmother Sarah's hand when she passed into the next realm. At the very end she whispered, "I see your grandfather coming for me."

In 1851 Edgar's grandparents married and had thirty years together before Thomas Cayce's death. His grand-mother was Tom's cousin from Piney Fork, Tennessee. They had seven sons and one daughter. One of the sons was Edgar's father Leslie.

Some time after Tom's death, Sarah was injured when the family home's top floor caught fire, and she lived in Edgar's bedroom so that his mother Carrie could take care of her. Edgar stayed with his aunt and uncle.

Over the years she had observed Tom's water-witching skills and his psycho-kinetic powers—the ability to telepathically move objects. Of Edgar's powers, she told him, "Don't be afraid, and don't be proud."

On her deathbed she advised him to look upon every person as someone like himself, searching for their place in God's kingdom. Edgar was so glad Tom came for her.

July 9

Each and every soul leaves the body as it rests in sleep. As to how this may be used constructively - this would be like answering how could one use one's voice for constructive purposes. It is of a same or of a similar import, you see; that is, it is a faculty, it is an experience, it is a development of the self as related to spiritual things, material things, mental things.   853-8

Edgar was the major supporter of the Cayce family when they were living in a rental home on Seventh Street.

He invited an old school friend to spend the night with him and became very angry when he found the house full of Cayce relatives who had arrived uninvited and unexpected.

Edgar's bed was already occupied, and there was no place for either Edgar or his friend to sleep. Edgar uncharacteristically lost his temper, and he and Leslie had a verbal fighting match.

His friend had just returned home from a Sam Jones revival, and Edgar was distraught when he left the house during the father-son harangue.

Edgar finally fell asleep on the living room sofa, which in the middle of the night suddenly burst into flames. He ran outside and rolled in the snow, then pulled the sofa outside, too.

The fire, which seemed to have started in Edgar's clothes, had no definitive explanation. Was his anger hot enough to start the fire? He must have wondered.

July 10

Study to show thyself approved unto God, a workman not ashamed, rightly dividing the words of truth and keeping from condemnation of self as well as others. 5322-1

So may we, in our OWN little sphere, take upon ourselves the burdens of the world. The JOY, the peace, the happiness, that may be ours is in DOING for the OTHER fellow. 262-3

In the summer of 1895 Edgar was devastated when he lost his job at Hopper Brothers. Because the brothers were taking on a new partner, they no longer needed him.

He immediately got a job as a sales clerk in a dry goods store, but by fall he was unsuccessfully applying for other jobs.

Once again he went downtown to hunt for a new job and followed a huge crowd entering Richard's Department store, which was having a sale. At the shoe department, a man asked him for help, and instead of telling him that he didn't work there, Edgar sold him a pair of shoes, and then helped another customer. The department manager noticed and must have thought he looked like an honest guy because he sent him to the bank for change.

When he returned, the manager let him work the rest of the day. Edgar showed up the next day and sold shoes for the next year. He must have been hired sometime.

July 11

Now when we speak of the mental, know that it is as a channel; that is, it is both material and spiritual, and hence is the builder. For when there is an excess of energies used in any direction, without the supplying in each of its phases the material and the spiritual, it becomes unbalanced and incoordinant - not cooperation or coordination. 1436-1

In 1895 Gertrude and her family at The Hill came to realize more and more that unexplained things sometimes happened when Edgar was around. Books fell off shelves. Papers flew with no breeze.

Gertrude's family was intrigued by Edgar who shared stories of seeing auras and correctly guessed the numbers on cards without turning them over. Edgar worked up the nerve to ask her what she thought of his abilities, and she said, "I don't like it."

One Sunday night Edgar, sitting in an armchair, was drowsily nodding off, and Gertrude told him he should just go to sleep.

He certainly did because nothing done by her or anyone in the family could wake him up. The next day after more attempts to shake him awake, Gertrude ordered him, "Wake up!"

He opened his eyes and didn't realize until told that he had spent the night in that armchair.

Years later Gertrude was the conductor who put him in and ordered him out of trances.

July 12

For, in every association and connection, to those that would approach such an association or such a connection with work that may be accomplished through Cayce, there first must be within self that which does convince self of the plausibility, the reasonableness, and of the aid that may come to another through such.
323-1

A Texas visit in July 1919 resulted in Edgar giving readings and locating oil for several speculators, finding many gushers. All were tremendously impressed with the geological knowledge that spewed from Edgar's mouth while in a trance, and tremendously pleased with their potential profits.

Edgar was probably not paid for these readings, and he certainly was not given any of the profits. He and Dave Kahn were testing the possibility that going into the oil business could raise money for Edgar's hospital and to pay off Dave's huge inherited debts.

A reading suggested that Kahn become a partner in the Sam Davis Company, whose profits could skyrocket with 99-year leases in Desdemona.

When the company's well—with Edgar's explicit directions—gushed oil in January 1920, they were ecstatic. That success was all Kahn needed to persuade investors to back him as a partner.

The company ignored the advice to get 99-year leases, and sometimes ignored other advice considered not to be cost-effective. Those decisions would backfire.

July 13

But life is earnest, life is true - and that which each soul experiences is a part of that necessary, if it will be used as such and not looked upon as a drudge or as a hindrance. Whom the Lord loveth He cherisheth, whom the Lord loveth He chastiseth, whom the Lord loveth He raiseth up to opportunities. 1463-2

In the summer of 1920 Edgar and Dave Kahn were on site daily at the Desdemona oil well that was expected to make them a fortune.

Edgar was an oddity around oilmen, although the Texas boomtowns had many who claimed to be oil smellers or oil witches, dousing with a tree branch.

A cowboy, testing Edgar, asked him after several days of drought when it would rain. Edgar immediately said, "Four o'clock on Friday." Nature proved him right to the minute.

Their well experienced expensive delays. Parts disappeared. Cables broke. After their rig worked and they were drilling, pipes supplying the drilling water broke. It became obvious someone was sabotaging them until their lease ran out.

By September 1920 the well still hadn't come in. Partners accused Kahn of trying to delay Desdemona until the lease expired when he could own his own company and drill it himself.

They demanded a reading, and Edgar went into a trance *before* Kahn gave him the suggestion. He said nothing. Had the Forces decided not to speak?

July 14

Hence man in his search has given the Godhead a three-dimensional expression; thus meeting each phase of each soul's experience. Thus the way is opened continuously; that they who seek may find, that they who believe that He is may know Him and thus pattern their lives - physically, mentally, spiritually - according to the pattern which has been set for each soul. 2021-1

In a reading for his own health in 1933, Edgar received advice for curing toxemia affecting his body's organs. The advice included massage, special additions to his diet, a certain syrup, and electrical treatments with a violet ray machine.

Edgar then asked the Forces to give any mental or spiritual advice that would be helpful.

The answer was: "Any that may be added to that to which the body ministers itself, would be: That life in its activity is the expression of the divine influences in a material world. And individuals in the application of that that comes in their ken of activity may, through the drawing wholly, solely, upon the Creative Forces within, CHANGE their own surroundings, their OWN vibrations, within their bodies!…Keep sweet; keep hopeful; KNOW that the Redeemer liveth." (404-3)

The message about creative powers within all of us, waiting to bring divine influence into our lives, came through time and time again in many readings.

July 15

...without that whole-hearted cooperation and oneness of mind and purpose, irrespective of position, condition, relation one with another, there may not be expected the result desired; any more than of a mis-directed mind attempting to understand a spiritual law through a purely physical application, or a physical law by spiritual application; for the spiritual is the LIFE; the mental is the BUILDER; the physical is the RESULT.   254-52

In this month in 1928 the Archangel Michael interrupted a reading exploring formation of the Association of National Investigators and the building of the hospital in Virginia Beach.

Edgar's Infinite Intelligence had already given the above warning and had said the new hospital's cornerstone should read Cayce Hospital - Research and Enlightenment - founded by (the next stone) Association of National Investigators, Inc., 1927.

Then Edgar said, "HARK! There comes the voice of one who would speak to those gathered here: I AM MICHAEL, LORD OF THE WAY! BEND THY HEAD, OH YE CHILDREN OF MEN. GIVE HEED UNTO THE WAY AS IS SET BEFORE YOU IN THAT SERMON ON THE MOUNT...."

All present—including Morton, Gertrude, Gladys, and Thomas House—were aware of the vibrational change, window panes shaking, and the sensation of wind gushing across the room—sensations later described by Gladys, whose trembling fingers nevertheless recorded the shocking event.

July 16

> *For you grow to heaven, you don't go to heaven. It is within thine own conscience that ye grow there. For there first must come peace and harmony within thy purpose, thy ideal, thy hopes, thy desires. Thy wishes must be in harmony with thy ideal if you would make the experience in the earth of value to thee.* 3409-1

A soul's reason for coming to earth is to earn the blessing of eternal bliss as the Creator's companion.

"No soul enters by chance, but that it may fill that it has sought and does seek as its ideal." (3051-2)

Doing so requires "putting proper emphasis in the proper places, and do not become sidetracked by things that would pertain to material or spiritual alone, or things of the body or things of the heavenly force." (3409-1)

Edgar's Forces direct us to understand immutable, unchangeable laws:

"Seek and ye shall find; ask and it will be given thee - IF ye have chosen aright.

"The manner in which ye treat thy fellow man is the manner ye are treating thy ideal.

"All of the divine ye may know in the material plane ye CAN, ye MUST, manifest in thy dealings with thy fellow man." (3051-2)

By consistently living up to the expectations set by our ideal "we would keep the constructive SPIRITUAL attitude and atmosphere about the entity. Not as goody-goody, but good for something." (416-13)

Who wouldn't like to be good for something?

July 17

No one mind may conceive all that may be done through the power of the Master Musician; for it may bud as the rose, it may be the song of the frog - or of any - even those that would be to SELF as those that would be GRATING vibrations; for the cricket on the hearth to self is obnoxious! but to some would bring harmony and peace, as home!   281-8

On this day in 1935 Edgar used a visit to Egypt's Temple Beautiful around 10,500 BC to show the Glad Helpers how music could help with spiritual healing.

The service there was to purify and prepare initiates for understanding the spiritual powers in their material bodies.

"Do not, my children, confuse thine bodies of today with those attributes of same, with the conditions existent in the Temple Beautiful."

"The individuals having cleansed themselves of those appendages that hindered, came not merely for the symbolic understanding." No, they needed to learn how to remain spiritual beings after having taken on material bodies.

They were taught to chant Ar-r-r-r-r-AR-aum, "which makes for the losing...the association of the body with that save the VIBRATIONS of which the body was then composed; yea now is, though encased in a much more hardened matter, as to materiality...." (281-25)

What was good for early humanity s good for us today. Chanting raises vibrations and returns us to spirituality.

July 18

> *Whether stringed instruments, whether unusual types, do attempt to bring greater harmonies into the experience through the practice and through the application of self in making music. Even though it may be only on a comb or on glasses or on bells, on a harp, violin or a piano, MAKE MUSIC!*   5201-1

Music creates emotions and can and should be used both for healing, lifting spirits, or for putting people into a proper somber mood.

The same musicians who can't keep tears from streaming down their cheeks while playing Tomaso Albinoni's *Adagio* will be bouncing with joy while playing *Beer Barrel Polka*.

For a 22-year-old highly intelligent, but mentally ill, young woman, Edgar prescribed: "Keep about the body the colors of purple and lavender, and all things bright; music that is of harmony - as of the Spring Song, the Blue Danube and that character of music, with either the stringed instruments or the organ.

"These are the vibrations that will set again near normalcy - yea, normalcy, mentally and physically, may be brought to this body, if these influences will be consistently kept about this body." (2712-1)

For an instant mood changer, "Think, for a moment, of the music of the waves upon the shore, of the morning as it breaks with the music of nature, of the night as it falls with the hum of the insect, of all the kingdoms as they unite in their song of appreciation.... " (2581-2) Relax!

July 19

Keep thine heart pure, thine body strong, thine mind open. Attune thine inner man to the harps and the chords of the universe, and harken to the love that brings service - service - to all. 1735-2

Edgar frequently compared service to others with the harmony of music.

He said any kind of service "can be done in the nature of harmony in a musical vibration; whether it is in the ministering to the needs of others... or as an aid or helpfulness to smaller groups, or children, or adults, through harmony, through music." (5201-1)

We will not only be a "helpful influence of force in the minds of others," but we ourselves will gain "greater abilities" by approaching service with songs in our hearts.

"If the activities of a soul-mind are in that direction of manifesting the love of the Father to others, then it - the activity - must be glorious in the essence of that causing, producing or making for such an activity.... Hence, be glorious in thine activity - joyous in thy service." (262-59)

"For ye have been called unto a purpose, as into the service of the Son of man. Make known to Him thy desire, in HIS will, and - thy will one with His - there will come to thee many blessings, physically, mentally, spiritually." (262-58)

"Then as ye pattern thy life by His, ye will mete the fruits of the Spirit to thy fellowmen day by day, in whatever field of service is chosen." (1650-1)

July 20

> (Q) How can I obtain relief from resentment and bitterness? (A) As ye forgive, ye are forgiven. As ye love, so are ye loved. As ye resent, so are ye resented. This is LAW - physical, mental and SPIRITUAL! Then, chuck it out of thy life. Let the love of God so fill thy mind, thy body, that there is NO resentment. As to how - though ye may not of thyself, put the burden on Him and it becomes light. But ACT in the manner as He did, not resenting any. 2600-2

Forgiveness, patience, and tolerance are necessary ingredients for our souls' spiritual development.

"Hence the injunction to be mindful of judgments and to be just as patient with others as you want others to be with you. Be as forgiving to others as you want others to be forgiving to you." (3409-1)

If someone hurts us, we should never consider attempting to get revenge. "In thine experience, have you found ever that to 'get even' with anyone made thee happy? To forgive them is divine and brings Happiness to all. THESE things SOW in the lives, in the hearts, in the minds of others. Grace and mercy, Lord, not sacrifice - nor judgment." (262-109)

"For unless you would forgive thy brother, that you see and know in the flesh, how may ye expect thy heavenly Father to forgive...unless ye prepare the way here and now. Then, do things not to be seen of men but to be seen and judged of God. For His judgment and His justice is right." (3409-1)

July 21

Do not, then, merely have a verbal or vocal ideal. Do write what is thy ideal. Begin with that under these three headings: Spiritual, Mental, Material. And write what is thine own ideal. As ye may find, these may change from time to time. For, each soul grows in grace, in knowledge, in understanding. Just as the awareness, the unfoldments come to the self AS the entity applies that it has chosen and does choose from day to day. 3051-2

A successful sojourn on earth depends upon our living up to an ideal we've set for ourselves, and it must be an ideal that puts others before ourselves.

Edgar's Forces expressed optimism about those of us having our material existence during his era, and let's hope the same cheery outlook is applicable today.

"Individuals are becoming more and more aware that the greater blessings, the greater experiences, the more worth while things in their lives are those not bought with money, nor by patting the other fellow upon the back only; but with love, patience, hope, brotherly love - just being kind one to another!" (1472-12)

The Forces gave an example of good action. "For instance - the entity may speak to those who open the door of a morning - whether it be to the cage or to the street - in such a manner that the whole day is brighter because of a kindness expressed.

"Would that men, then, EVERYWHERE, would learn such a lesson!" (1472-12)

July 22

For mind is the builder. This keep ever before thee - the attitude of mind. If you expect to make a failure who else is going to expect you to succeed? It must be within yourself. For as has been indicated, think not who will come from heaven or who will come from over the seas to tell you, but know it is within thine own heart, thine own conscience. For thy body is indeed the temple of the living God. And if ye choose Him, His Son as thy companion, as thy ideal - if He be with thee, who can be against thee? What does it matter if they are! They are naught! 3409-1

Our thoughts are things, our thoughts are deeds, our thoughts are what we manifest in our lives. That truth is one the readings repeatedly stress. We need to practice thought stopping. When a negative thought pops into our minds, we need to say "Stop!"

Right thinking helps everything, even dieting. "Urges arise, then, not only from what one eats but from what one thinks; and from what one does about what one thinks and eats! as well as what one digests mentally and spiritually!" (2533-6)

We should always expect the best. "Such things as the black days and the bright days exist most for those who THINK they exist!...So does poison gas exist, but if we keep away from it or if we control it in our experience it may cause little trouble!" (440-2)

"Remember, the mental is the builder, the spiritual is the guide (or the life), the conditions builded in material things are the results." (257-123)

July 23

(Q) Is it proper for us to study the effects of the planets on our lives in order to better understand our tendencies and inclinations, as influenced by the planets? (A) When studied aright, very, very, very much so. How aright then? In that influence as is seen in the influence of the knowledge already obtained by mortal man. Give more of that into the lives, giving the understanding THAT THE WILL MUST BE THE EVER GUIDING FACTOR TO LEAD MAN ON, EVER UPWARD.
3744-4

A reading defines astrology as "that position in space about our own earth that is under the control of the forces that are within the sphere of that control, and all other spheres without that control. That is astrology, the study of those conditions." (3744-4)

Asked if the planets have an effect every individual's life, Edgar answered, "They have. Just as this earth's forces were set in motion...those forces that govern the elements, elementary so, of the earth's sphere or plane, and as each comes under the influence of those conditions, the influence is to the individual without regards to the will...the developing factor of man." (3744-4)

"BUT LET IT BE UNDERSTOOD HERE, NO ACTION OF ANY PLANET OR THE PHASES OF THE SUN, THE MOON OR ANY OF THE HEAVENLY BODIES SURPASS THE RULE OF MAN'S WILL POWER, THE power given by the Creator of man, in the beginning, when he became a living soul, with the power of choosing for himself." (3744-4)

July 24

> *For do not consider for a moment (for this might be carried on to an indefinite end) that an individual soul-entity passing from an earth plane as a Catholic, a Methodist, an Episcopalian, is something else because he is dead! He's only a dead Episcopalian, Catholic or Methodist. And such personalities and their attempts are the same; only that IDEAL! For all are under the law of God equal, and how did He say even as respecting the home? "They are neither married nor given in marriage in the HEAVENLY home but are ONE!"* 254-92

On this day in 1904 Edgar and his new partner Frank Potter purchased a photography studio in Bowling Green. It had belonged to Edgar's competitor when he had his studio at Potter Bookstore. His new partner was a distant cousin of his former employer.

Edgar's share of this purchase was financed by a mortgage on The Hill. Early in July 1903 Edgar and Gertrude had returned to The Hill, despondent that unwanted publicity about Edgar's psychic healing ability had disrupted their new marriage.

Gertrude's family persuaded the couple to return to Bowling Green, where Edgar had been successful until the unwanted notoriety.

Potter organized the studio while Edgar learned modern photography techniques in an eight-week course in Tennessee. The studio was quickly a financial success.

Life became even better when Edgar was welcomed back to church after a friend pleaded his case and won.

July 25

First, know self. Continuous study of self is the greater study of others. Do not become egotistical. Do care for the health.   2938-1

In July 1905 Edgar won first prize in *Ladies' Home Journal*'s mother and son photo contest. By this time he had earned a reputation for being especially good at getting hyperactive children to hold poses quietly.

Sometime during this year he made the longest trip he'd ever taken—a train trip to St. Louis to display photos in the National Association of Photographers competition. He won three honorable mentions.

His expertise attracted so many customers to the Cayce Studio in Bowling Green that his competitor offered to sell his larger studio to him. Two new partners, one being Gertrude's brother, helped finance the acquisition.

Gertrude joined the business as an artist hand-tinting photographs. Perhaps she should have been manager to keep Edgar from giving away photos and too easily forgiving debts owed to the studio.

He was inclined to do both, just as he had never charged for the physical readings he gave to help Al Layne's patients or the cure he facilitated for little Aime. He had little concern about money, saying any time times were tough, things would work out, and they did.

FAST FORWARD: In 1906 Edgar took first place with a portrait photo he called *A Kentucky Belle*. Possibly Gertrude was the model?

July 26

> *There is the physical body, there is the mental body, there is the soul body. They are One, as the Trinity; yet these may find a manner of expression that is individual unto themselves.* 281-24

As late as 1905 when Edgar had a successful photo business in Bowling Green, he still needed hypnotic treatments to keep his vocal chords speaking properly.

He went monthly to Franklin, Kentucky, where Al Layne attended medical school. Eventually he decided a Bowling Green hypnotist could do what Layne was doing.

He and Layne wrote down a complete list of instructions, and Edgar gave them to Dr. John Blackburn, who boarded at Hollis House, where Edgar lived while single. His giving the suggestions worked, and Blackburn assembled a team of doctors to study Edgar's abilities.

Edgar suggested that he demonstrate "mind is the builder." They chose one of the doctor's sons, a perfectly healthy person, and each, when they met him that day, told him he didn't look good.

The unsuspecting subject assured the first few he was fine, but after a few more, he was feeling a little achy, and after more, his shoulders ached, his back hurt, and his stomach felt heavy. He asked his doctor father to examine him, and sure enough—he was sick. He was coming down with the flu.

Thoughts are things, and this day Edgar proved it.

July 27

Yet, as we find, if there is the turning of every man and woman to the thought of God, then we may solve every problem. For it is not by mere thought, not by any activity other than the moving force within each entity, each body; and when more of patience, more tolerance, more thought of others is advanced and kept in the heart of the individual, this lends that power, that influence, that force for good.   3976-24

By the summer of 1898, Edgar realized how improbable good job opportunities were for him in Hopkinsville. He decided to follow Gertrude's Aunt Carrie's suggestion to look for a job in Louisville, the state's largest city.

He decided to apply to work for J.P. Morton Company, a wholesale book distributor with an inventory much larger than Hopper Brothers, where he had previously worked in Hopkinsville.

He barraged J.P. Morton Company with letters of recommendations solicited from every political officer, judge, doctor, lawyer, and businessmen he knew.

When told there were no openings, he put more recommendations in every mail. Three days later he received a welcome telegram saying, "Quit sending recommendations. Report for work August 1."

He was twenty-one years old and had been engaged to Gertrude for more than a year. He needed to earn enough money to marry her and have her join him wherever that job took him. He was elated.

July 28

(Q) In the physical plane, do the thoughts of a person of another affect the other person either mentally or physically? (A) Depending upon the development of the individual to whom the thought may be directed. The possibilities of the developing of thought transference is first being shown, evolution, you see. The individuals from this plane will and are developing this as the senses were and are developed.   **3744-1**

One day Edgar decided to experiment with mental telepathy. He knew he could read people's minds, but he didn't know if he could will someone to follow his telepathic suggestion.

He asked his receptionist to name two Bowling Green people who would not be expected to visit the photography studio. He then concentrated, trying to entice them to come to him.

The first man came the same day and admitted to the receptionist he didn't know why he had come. The second arrived the next morning.

After helping other people become skillful with using mental telepathy, Edgar decided everyone had this ability. Unlike him, they weren't born with it, but with practice could develop it.

He cautioned that to use it to control another would be morally wrong and destructive to anyone using it in such a sinful way. He called it "dangerous business."

July 29

The mind, through anger, may make the body do that which is contrary to the better influences of same; it may make for a change in its environ, its surrounding, contrary to the laws of environment or hereditary forces that are a portion of the *elan vitale* of each manifested body, with the spirit or the soul of the individual. Then... one may be dispossessed of the mind; thus ye say rightly he is "out of his mind." 281-24

Edgar solved a murder that occurred in the Canadian hometown of a professor at Bowling Green Business College. The victim, who lived alone with her sister, was shot walking down their home's interior staircase.

Edgar told them the other sister was the murderer, and she had thrown the pistol she used out the window. He told them where it could be found after it slid from a gutter down a drainpipe.

He even told where the gun had been purchased—in Roanoke, Virginia; how many empty chambers it had; and its name, make, and serial number.

Canadian officials requested a second reading to determine the sister's motive for the killing. The sister she killed had hidden a letter containing a marriage proposal from the man she loved.

She had gone through life thinking he deserted her, while he received no answer to his proposal and disappeared. When the betrayed sister found the letter, she took deadly revenge. After being confronted, the sister confessed and was imprisoned.

July 30

Lord, thou who art holy, keep and preserve thou my every effort, that I may bring to the experience of others and to myself the awareness of thy presence abiding with them. 281-23

On this Saturday in 1898 Edgar took a nine-hour train ride from Hopkinsville to Louisville to start his new job at the J.P. Morton bookstore. He had borrowed cash to buy a suit and to pay $2.59 for the nine-hour train trip.

He had to pay $5 in advance for a month of room and board at Hollis House on Second Street, and by then he was almost broke.

He was happy to find that other boarders included a medical student, a government worker, a musician, a journalist, a railroad clerk, and an artist.

A man who was both a judge and a publisher had a room which he used the few nights a week he was in the city.

Edgar expected his fellow tenants would open his country-boy mind to many unfamiliar topics.

At dinner that evening he was gratified to find they all seemed to be lively conversationalists and as well versed in many topics as the people at The Hill. He didn't mind that some of their stories were as suggestive and off-color as those he'd sometimes overheard around his uncle's farm workers.

He was in a man's world again, but already wishing Gertrude could be with him.

July 31

> As the consciousness of the Christ presence comes nearer and nearer to thee, may ye be endowed with that of shedding HIS joy, HIS love into the life of others. The more knowledge, the more responsibility. The more love, the more ability. Keep thou the way open; for as He has chosen thee, so must ye choose His ways. For as He gave, "If ye love me, keep my commandments." 281-23

On this Sunday in 1898 Edgar for the first time saw women wearing makeup on their faces. He saw them at First Christian Church of Louisville—a church so huge both of his previous churches would have fit inside it several times.

He knew the minister Dr. Edward Lindsay Powell, who had briefly preached at First Christian Church in Hopkinsville. After the service Dr. Powell invited Edgar not only to meet at a weekly Bible study, but to teach a Sunday school class.

This proposal, coming from a minister of Powell's high esteem, must have been very flattering to Edgar. Since becoming minister at this church, Powell had almost doubled its membership, and the local paper often published his entire sermons.

But Edgar's reputation as a Biblical scholar had preceded him, even though he was now only age 21. He immediately accepted the assignment.

Powell would soon stir Edgar's interest in the Christian Endeavor, a fast-growing movement for young people of many Christian denominations.

August 1

> As ye sow, so shall ye reap - this again becomes the foundation of what self, as well as others, may expect. If ye would have friends, show thyself friendly; if ye would have love, love ye one another. These are unchangeable. They do not alter. Man alters them only in the application, as to whether it is to satisfy the ego or the animal, or the flesh, or the mind.   2174-2

On this morning in 1898 Edgar reported for his first day at J.P. Morton bookstore in Louisville. The manager Mr. Griswold and all the other employees were eager to meet him because of all his superb recommendations.

Edgar did not disappoint them. He had memorized the store's entire catalog, and he recited every book with its author and price. His regular salary was $5 a month, with a $1.50 per week rooming allowance.

Because this salary was not enough for him to save money to marry Gertrude, he moonlighted at an art gallery introduced to him by a roomer at his boarding house. Another roomer, a railroad clerk, arranged for him to take tickets on a night shift in exchange for free railroad passes.

He quickly earned respect among his co-workers for help he gave them locating books and also for his contributions in preparing the company's new catalog.

He trained back to Hopkinsville to see Gertrude on long weekends and holidays, and—because of moonlighting as a ticket clerk—he didn't even have to pay for the long round trip.

August 2

Be patient. Be gentle. Be kind. Be longsuffering. For, these are the fruits of the spirit, and these will conceive - in self's own giving out - to such an extent as to commend in the life such activities as to make self known more and more; be needed, be in demand, in this, that and the other place. So does one build within self that personality that is at such a high demand in the affairs of men today. But with the building, give the credit to the influence within the inner self, and not to self alone - but to thine Maker.   430-2

One of his early customers was Margaret, who was rich enough to buy several hundred of dollars' worth of merchandise, and she did. The day after Edgar made the big sale to Margaret, J.P. Morton landed her family's account—one Griswold had tried to entice for many years.

That same day Edgar and Morton were also invited to Margaret's house for dinner. Edgar said he had nothing appropriate to wear, so Morton arranged with a tailor for a new suit that very afternoon.

Griswold raised Edgar's salary to $10 a month.

FAST FORWARD: A few weeks after the dinner an expansion and renovation of the bookstore was paid for by Margaret's father, who had made a fortune in dark tobacco. Edgar's salary was raised to an unbelievably high $40 a month.

August 3

Then, to know to do good and not to do it is sin. To know the truth and not give expression is fault-finding in self. Yet know, until an individual entity - in time or space, or in acquaintanceship or in the friendship of an individual - sees in every other entity that he would worship in his Maker, he has not begun to have the proper concept of universal consciousness.... 1747-5

Edgar and Margaret had many mutual friends because of both being involved with the Christian Endeavor movement. They began attending activities together, seeing each other every Sunday.

At a vaudeville show Herman the Great, who—unlike Hart the Laugh King—hypnotized Edgar very easily. Edgar followed all of Herman's suggestions, highly entertaining Margaret and the audience.

Back home in Hopkinsville, Gertrude wasn't laughing. She wasn't receiving many letters from Edgar, and those that came didn't mention any savings for their marriage.

She dropped out of college, and she lost too many pounds from her already tiny body. She walked with a slump and spent much too much time in bed. She was like widow in mourning.

FAST FORWARD: When he went home for Christmas, 1899, Edgar found an unhealthy, 75-pound Gertrude, barely a wisp of her former self. Although he made several trips back to Louisville, he never saw Margaret again.

August 4

Then, let not discouragement, let not disappointments cause thee to falter in the ways thou hast chosen to serve thy fellow man; but give GOD the praise, and never threaten another by thy own might, nor by thy position. For, know, each soul merits that condition, that position it TODAY occupies! But be not THOU the judge. Rather OPEN the way that new hope, new light, new joy, new aspirations may be in the hearts and minds of those ye would serve. 262-121

On this day in 1928 Hugh Lynn invited all Association of National Investigators members to a meeting to brainstorm more plans for the hospital. He stressed the need for cooperation, warning that many had problems with each other in previous incarnations.

Three who had problems with each other in previous lives were present this day: Morton Blumenthal, Dave Kahn, and Franklin Bradley.

The meeting started happily with lots of hugs and good cheer, but before long Morton and Franklin were into a shouting match about whether a tin or shingle roof was preferable for the 12-car garage behind the hospital. Their disagreements escalated throughout the meeting.

Those at the reading a few weeks ago when the Archangel Michael warned that the hospital venture was to be treated as an opportunity to serve God must have been forlorn. Was the petty bickering an omen of problems to come?

August 5

> *The Law is ONE, the Source is ONE! and those that seek other than that find tribulation, turmoils, confusion. Though there may be many approaches, cooperation in the activities - as in the Universe - brings the harmony of the universal activity; as does cooperation in human experience bring harmony and peace; while egotism and self-assertion and self-exaltation and self-indulgence bring inharmonious experiences, and the activity of turmoils, wars, strifes.* 1297-1

Cooperation was Lesson One for Edgar's study group that developed the *Search for God* literature that has changed many lives for the better.

The Forces said, "If the beings builded in self mentally have been anxiety, fear, trembling, hate, and those things that are founded in fear, then indeed there must be turmoil within thyself. For thy spiritual self, thy soul, rebels against disorder, inharmony....

"There is set before thee good and evil, life and death - CHOOSE THOU! For with the will, that is the heritage of each soul, thou choosest that which is to bring, or will and does bring harmony or peace, or destructive forces with their attributes of every nature." (1297-10)

"Beware that the temper does not overcome the better self...For, this is as the warning: Keep thine own JUDGEMENTS, yes. He that hath no temper is of little value, but he that controls not his temper is worse than though he had none at all!" (524-1)

Cooperation beats carping every time.

August 6

Then there are those visions of the character to be sought, rather than rejected; as the experiences of the unconscious self or subconscious self that may come as warnings or as helpful experiences, or of that through which those influences acting about self become a part of self. 1472-10

Edgar first demonstrated precognition in a reading for a Southern Railroad superintendent who wanted to know how an accident had happened.

Edgar named the responsible person and said he should be fired. Skeptical executives balked, saying they had no way of proving the person's responsibility.

Edgar warned that if this person remained in service, before December he would cause the death of the one who refused this information, and his death would happen in Virginia and West Virginia.

The information from this reading surely was not taken seriously, for the man was not fired. Perhaps grasping the idea of someone dying in two states boggled the minds of the officials in charge.

This incident gave evidence that the future could be altered, that it was not preordained.

Nine months later the guilty employee once again failed to throw the switch to change tracks and caused another tragic accident.

The executive who hadn't acted upon Edgar's information was in the train as it smashed into a private car in one state and pushed it over into the other.

He died as Edgar had predicted—in two states.

August 7

Analyze thyself, thy purposes, thy desires. Know that others have opinions also, and those that are workable. Yet study to show thyself - in thy activities, in thy thoughts - approved unto that thou hast chosen, or may choose, as thy ideal.   2144-1

On this date in 1926 a reading confirmed that Dr. Thomas House would be a good doctor to guide the proposed hospital into the future.

Dr. House had arrived in Virginia Beach with his wife Carrie and offered his service as the chief doctor.

They had admired Edgar's work from the time many years ago when he had done for Thomas House Jr. what three doctors had been unable to do. Their premature baby, weak and on the verge of death, was suffering convulsions every twenty minutes.

At Carrie's request Edgar came from Bowling Green to do a reading for him. He diagnosed an epileptic condition causing the convulsions and prescribed belladonna orally, and a hot peach tree bark poultice around his body.

Doctors said the belladonna—a poison—would kill the baby, but Carrie insisted they give the dosage directed. Edgar himself climbed a peach tree for the bark.

Thomas Jr. had his first good night's sleep since birth, and he never had another convulsion.

Now many years later his father said he wanted to dedicate his life to Edgar's work in the hospital Edgar had sought for so many years. He was a good person to help make the dream come true.

August 8

The mind is not the spirit, it is a companion to the spirit; it builds a pattern. And this is the beginning of how self may raise that expectancy of its period of activity in the earth. And this is the beginning of thy ideal. Of what? Of that the soul should, does, will, can, must, accomplish in this experience!   2533-6

Edgar met several notable people during his years in Bowling Green from 1905 to 1907. Professor Joe Dickey, an ardent supporter of Edgar's work, flooded the mail asking prominent people to come to the city to see Edgar in action.

Two such people, Thomas Edison and Nikola Tesla, came for another reason: to attend a lecture series on modern scientific discoveries at Bowling Green Business School. Edgar met them, but if this meeting resulted in readings, the records were destroyed in later studio fires.

Tesla claimed to have been inspired by his higher self and was interested in possible connections between electricity and psychic phenomena, and Edison's interest in the same is well documented.

Records do exist of readings for an engineer who helped found Delco and an IBM engineer who pioneered FM radio at NBC. Edgar said, "Electricity is at the heart of all life.... Electricity is life."

He told both that devices could be invented to measure thought form, just as meters measured volts and amperage. This prophecy has been fulfilled.

August 9

Just as we have in the diagnosis is for the betterment or advancement of the individual, just as the subconscious that communicates to the physical, for with the physical submerged, a universal condition. It may be obtained from all or in part...as for the individual.   3744-3

In early August 1902 Al Layne—still in Hopkinsville—volunteered Edgar—living in Bowling Green—to give a reading to Aime Dietrich, a six-year-old whose brain stopped developing after she had diphtheria as a toddler.

Edgar agreed to arrive by train the next morning. He and Layne walked through alleys to the Dietrichs' back door to keep Edgar's visit a secret, as Aime's father had requested.

In a trance Edgar said her problem started before she caught diphtheria. Her spine had been injured when she fell getting out of a carriage. Germs settled in the damaged area, which thickened and kept blood from circulating correctly to her brain.

He recommended osteopathic adjustments to soften the membrane and said she would recover. Layne did the first adjustment that night and another the next morning.

Edgar stayed two more days for readings to assure that Layne's adjustments were as recommended.

Within three months Aime was a normal six-year-old.

Edgar never again had to sneak through the back alley to visit their home.

August 10

(Q) Why do so many people ridicule the idea of good being obtained through Psychic Readings? (A) Lack of understanding of law governing so called Psychic force, or powers. The lack of understanding is lack of consciousness being brought to the individual of potential powers that are manifest in and through psychic or occult forces. Many are caused by the lack of the proper usage of the knowledge or understanding obtained through such force, for the incorrect use of such knowledge may and would bring destructive elements.
3744-2

Edgar's cure for Aime Dietrich was the talk of Hopkinsville, bringing Edgar much publicity that horrified Gertrude.

She loved Edgar, but she didn't like the psychic side of him. Having waited five years now to get married, she wanted a normal life style when marriage finally happened.

Naturally, Mrs. Dietrich was elated! Her Aime who had been a retarded little girl destined for a dreary life was now a vibrant happy child with high hopes for a happy future.

She exuberantly spread the word about Edgar's accomplishment and was responsible for the *Hopkinsville Kentuckian* praising him in print.

FAST FORWARD: Strong and healthy, Aime graduated from college at the top of her class.

August 11

> Best that EVERY individual ...budget its time. Set so much time for study, so much time for relaxation, so much time for labor mentally, so much time for activity of the phys-ical body, so much time for reading, so much time for social activities. And while this does not mean to become merely a body of rote, it does mean that each of these changes and each of these activities make for the creat-ing of a better balance - that not only facilitates the indiv-idual's activities but gives the ability to CONCENTRATE when desiring on WHATEVER the activity may be! 440-2

All three aspects of our beings—mental, physical, and spiritual—need to be exercised. Variety is the key to a well-balanced life.

"Budget the time, so that the spiritual and mental has its periods of recreation. Budget so that the mental has those relaxations, those periods of stimulation, those periods of social activity that are ever creative. These keep a balance." (257-252)

"At regular periods have thy rest, have thy labors, do feed the mind; do feed the soul just as it is necessary to feed the physical man and these will declare just as much dividend as does that necessity of feeding the body. Without that to be masticated, and without its mastication, it is indigestion and suffering. So with the food for the mind and the soul, it must be masticated and put to use, and these will bring much more harmo-nious experience." (5246-1)

August 12

Take time to be holy, but take time to play also. Take time to rest, time to recuperate; for thy Master, even in the pattern in the earth, took time to rest, took time to be apart from others, took time to meditate and pray, took time to attend a wedding, to give time to attend a funeral; took time to attend those awakenings from death and took time to minister to all.   5246-1

If we're not having any fun, we should make an effort to find ways to do so.

"Cultivate the ability to see the ridiculous, and to retain the ability to laugh. For, know - only in those that God hath favored is there the ability to laugh, even when clouds of doubt arise, or when every form of disturbance arises. For, remember, the Master smiled - and laughed, oft - even on the way to Gethsemane." (2984-1)

We should find activities that make us happy. "Study that which is the prompting for thy activities; not merely from the material angle, but as to why there is this or that urge.

"And know that same is in keeping with that which is the ideal. For, each soul, each entity, latently or manifestedly, has his ideal - spiritually, mentally and materially. Coordinate these, and know in what ye believe - also who is the author of same; and that the author may be that One to whom ye may trust thy soul, thy body, thy mind.

"In this way and manner ye will find harmony. But do keep that ability to see the FUN in life also." (2984-1)

August 13

The planning of other planets began the ruling of the destiny of all matters as created, just as the division of waters...is ruled by the Moon in its path about the earth; just so as the higher creation...is ruled by its action in conjunction with the planets about the earth. 3744-4

Around this time in 1924 Edgar envisioned the Cayce Institute existing for the purpose of studying the readings and sharing their wisdom with more people.

The Institute would need a manager, and all of the many possibilities suggested to him sounded capable. When he had time, he would need to do a reading on the subject, as he always did with difficult decisions.

Edgar's time in Dayton was getting better and better. But it was also busier and busier. Times had been tough at first when Arthur Lammers, who lured him here with promises of help, had not come through with any financial assistance.

For a while Edgar had so few clients that he had plenty of time to give life readings to all of his immediate family, find out about past lives, and corroborate the findings with library's history books.

Then Hugh Lynn's scholarship at a prestigious school put the family in contact with wealthy, distinguished people such as Orville Wright, a judge for the school's debating club. This connection resulted in the many readings that now caused him to need a manager.

He wanted the Institute to help him share the readings' new knowledge that he previously had disavowed—that about reincarnation and astrology.

August 14

When thou prayest, enter into thy closet - that is, within self; not shutting oneself away from the world, but closing self within God's presence, and pray in secret. And the reward will be in the open.   254-3

Edgar was five years old when he first saw a person praying—his mother Carrie.

She had fallen into a depression when her baby Thomas left the planet after only ten days, and her distraught mind led to a weakened body. Frailty and asthma sometimes confined her to bed for days at a time, and certainly caused Edgar much dismay.

One day when the two of them were alone in the kitchen, Carrie burst into tears and fell to her knees. As he patted her back to comfort her, she pulled him down and—holding his hands in hers—started to pray.

Because the Cayce family did not attend church, Edgar hadn't the faintest notion what was going on, and he never forgot this moment. As his mother asked for the Lord's blessing and help in her time of need, Edgar heard music. Recalling the incident in later years, he said, "Her prayers were like musical notes."

In speeches after he became a popular lecturer, he often compared a single person's prayer to a musical note rising toward heaven. According to the number of people praying together, the note could become a chord, a holy harmony, or even a sacred symphony.

Carrie got better, and Edgar never doubted that the Master Musician enjoyed and responded to prayers.

August 15

What then is the mental attitude to be? In keeping with that which has been given, "Lo, Lord, I am thine - to be directed as THOU - not my fellow man, but THOU - would direct." 1436-1

On this day in 1924 Morton Blumenthal was suggested in a reading as the most suitable among those under consideration to be Edgar's manager.

Edgar had never met Morton, a 29-year-old New York Jewish stockbroker and a friend of David Kahn, who described him as well-educated, financially savvy, and very respected.

Perhaps Edgar was most impressed that Blumenthal reportedly yearned to understand cosmic secrets. Now that life readings revealed enigmas of other dimensions, Edgar shared that yearning.

Because a close friend claimed he was visited by a ghost, Morton had researched spirit communications over the centuries. Though Jewish, he believed Jesus to be an important prophet and a son of God.

Back in June, Kahn suggested Morton obtain a physical reading for his girlfriend, Miriam Miller, a Broadway chorus girl. Edgar would soon do that reading.

Morton and his brother Edwin were very impressed with the results, and Kahn was impressed with their wealth and influence. He arranged readings for Morton. The first addressed a tonsil problem, the second addressed his ear problem. Edgar soon spent ten days meeting with him in New York.

August 16

There is the ability within self to contact as high a soul as is sought, by will, by desire, by the use of that attained for THIS soul, for THIS entity to reach into the cosmic or the universal sources for its supply, for its needs, for its desires. For, with the title clear - as given - that the name is WRITTEN there, and the forces of good, of those that would teach. 443-3

Edgar was a marvel with a Ouija board, and Gertrude kept right up with him. They were enticed into trying one by Edwin Williamson—the man with dreams of the Hollywood fame that Edgar might help him attain.

In later years Hugh Lynn still vividly recalled the night in 1916 when Gertrude and Edgar put their hands on a Ouija board for the one and only time in their lives.

The object was to get the movable indicator to receive messages by pointing to letters, numbers, and other signs on the board. The pointer went crazy, leaping about with a frenzy as it brought forth messages.

One message located an insurance payment Edgar had forgotten to make. Another came from a teenager who had drowned in an Ohio pond and his body was caught in barbed wire under the water. He wanted his parents to know he had not run away from home.

Williamson notified the family, and they later gratefully responded that they had found him. Although good came from this one experience, Edgar felt the negative outweighed the positive and could disturb users.

August 17

Few may even show forth that which is felt in the heart, if the liver is bad! For twice does the blood pass through the liver, to once in the heart. The liver is the clearing house for the blood, both in and out of the heart and lungs. So, in the conduct of thy life and thy study, think twice before you speak once - for there's only one tongue, but two eyes. There is only one heart, but seven lobes in the liver. And as for thy hands, use what thou hast and thine eye will be single in service, thy tongue will be loosened in the right direction.   341-32

One can't have a heart full of anger and still have a healthy body. "No one can hate his neighbor and not have stomach or liver trouble. No one can be jealous and allow the anger of same and not have upset digestion or heart disorders." (4021-1).

"Anger can destroy the brain as well as any disease. For it is itself a disease of the mind." (3510-1)

"Don't get mad and don't cuss a body out mentally or in voice. This brings more poisons than may be created by even taking foods that aren't good." (470-37)

Edgar explains why anger affects the body in such a derogatory manner. "When there is the ruffling of your disposition when there is any anger, it prepares the system so that it blocks the flow of the circulation to the eliminating channels. Thus you can take a bad cold from getting mad. You can get a bad cold from [cursing] bless-ing out someone else, even if it is your wife." (849-75)

August 18

So, in conducting thine own life: make the physical corrections necessary, yes; but also make thy mind and thy body, thy going in and thy coming out, thy activities day by day, consistent. The reward will be an exemplary life, a goodly body, an open mind, a loving spirit. 341-32

A healthy attitude helps the healing process. Edgar told one woman about her ailment, "There will be little to be gained by making physical applications without there being a change in the mental attitude and spiritual purport of many of those conditions about the body.

"Do not be so pessimistic about self, conditions, or others. Do not give expression to nor hold to, nor entertain malice, injustice, self-righteousness, or those things that cause such great amounts of anxieties through the body." (3194-1)

Perhaps before we go to a doctor, we should try thinking ourselves well with a dose of good will toward others and contentment with ourselves.

"Change the attitude towards life...Of course, the change of the general conditions of the body will have much to do with the attitude," Edgar told a man with a constant pain in the alimentary canal. Edgar made it clear that it wasn't good that "the body appears rather peeved with most everything." (4064-1).

He told another, "Become more OPTIMISTIC in the outlook upon conditions surrounding the body" (592-1) and still another, "No healing is perfected without some psychic force exerted." (3744-2)

August 19

> *Let the body enter within self, for in the quiet alone and in this way commune with the Father in Spirit. The way, the how, the manner, will be opened for the body - not to excess, but to that sufficient to meet the needs of the hour, and the way will open for the understanding of the powers that be!* 39-4

Answers to all dilemmas will come to us via prayer or meditation.

About problem solving Edgar said, "Then, in thine own mind, decide as to whether this or that direction is right. Then pray on it, and leave it alone. Then suddenly ye will have the answer, yes or no. Then, with that Yes or No, take it again to Him in prayer, 'Show me the way.' And yes or No will again direct thee from deep within. THAT is practical direction." (3250-1)

He reminds us that if what we want and what we have are different, we need to change our wants to be in keeping with what our Creator wants for us. "Not the prayer, 'Lord, do this - do that - for I am thine!' Rather let thy prayer be, 'Here am I, Thy servant, Thy handmaid - USE ME in the fields of service, in the fields of activity where THOU seest, O God, I may be the greater service to my fellow man!'" (1472-6)

"Let thy prayer, thy meditation be, "Here am I, O Lord, use me as thou seest fit. Thou knowest the needs, Thou knowest the purposes, Thou knowest the desires. Make them pure indeed in me, that I may be the greater channel of blessings to others." (281-23)

August 20

First find self and self's relation, and what is desired to be done! Enter close oft into communion, into meditation with the consciousness within thyself of thy relationship to thy Creator; and then - as this is aroused, and you make application of the material things for the physical relief to give expression of same becomes naturally a part of the self. 658-15

Humans have channels within our bodies that have atrophied—or at least become dormant—in most of us.

"Why? Non-usage, non-activity! because only the desires of the appetite, self-indulgences and such, have so glossed over or used up the abilities in these directions that they become only wastes as it were in the spiritual life of an individual who has so abused or misused those abilities that have been given him for the greater activity. Then, purify thy mind if ye would meditate." (281-41)

The method of meditation depends upon the individual. Edgar advised one who loved exotic odors to burn incense. Music lovers can listen to calming sounds. Others fare better with silence.

"By closing the eyes and meditating from within, so that there arises...that necessary elements that makes along the PINEAL...that will quiet the whole nerve forces, making for that - as has been given - as the TRUE bread, the true strength of life itself. Quiet, meditation, for a half to a minute, will bring strength...PHYSICALLY the flowing out to quiet self, whether walking, standing still, or resting." (311-4)

August 21

Keep the heart SINGING! Keep the mind clear! Keep the face toward the LIGHT! the shadows then are BEHIND! Keep the way open, and be ready to meet the needs, rather than GIVING UP before the work is well begun! While the entity and body-mind is considered rather of the dreamy nature, yet the ABILITY to meet the needs is within the entity's own hands, will the body but apply that as is PRESENT AT HAND! See?   39-4

The Force's consistent message was that we each have all we need to do whatever we want, and whatever is going on in our lives at the present time is what's best for our spiritual growth.

We have a higher power on our side if our pursuits are in keeping with a worthy ideal. "Then seek not worldly fame, worldly recognition, you that are sowing the seeds of truth in your lessons, in your meditations. Because this day or this generation seeks not that as you may understand. KNOW that you cannot do but sow. God giveth the increase. But CULTIVATE that you sow in your daily experiences." (262-115)

"Let the body enter within self, for in the quiet alone and in this way commune with the Father in Spirit. The way, the how, the manner, will be opened for the body - not to excess, but to that sufficient to meet the needs of the hour, and the way will open for the understanding of the powers that be!" (39-4)

Edgar assured us the growth of the mind-spiritual, mind-mental, and body-physical will open the way for us.

August 22

(Q) Should Jesus be described as the soul who first went through the cycle of earthly lives to attain perfection, including perfection in the planetary lives also? (A) He should be. This is as the man, see?

Q) Should this be described as a voluntary mission One Who was already perfected and returned to God, having accomplished His Oneness in other planes and systems? (A) Correct.

(Q) Should the Christ-Consciousness be described as the awareness within each soul, imprinted in pattern on the mind and waiting to be awakened by the will, of the soul's oneness with God? (A) Correct. That's the idea exactly! 5749-14

The reading above was given in 1941 for Tom Sugrue, who requested this reading for clarification of issues he was facing while writing Edgar's first biography, *There Is a River*.

As conductor, Edgar's oldest son Hugh Lynn asked the questions, and was very specific about what information Tom needed. "The entity is now ready to describe the philosophical concepts which have been given through this source, and wishes to parallel and align them with known religious tenets, especially those of Christian theology....

"But the entity wishes to answer those questions which will naturally arise in the mind of the reader, and many of the questions which are being asked by all people in the world today."

August 23

(Q) Please list the names of the incarnations of the Christ, and of Jesus, indicating where the development of the man Jesus began. (A) First, in the beginning, of course; and then as Enoch, Melchizedek, in the perfection. Then...Joseph, Joshua, Jeshua, Jesus.

(Q) Should mind, the builder, be described as the last development because it should not unfold until it has a foundation of emotional virtues? (A) This might be answered Yes and No, both. But if it is presented in that there is kept, willfully, see, that desire to be in the atonement, then it is necessary for that attainment before it recognizes mind as the way.

(Q) Is Gnosticism the closest type of Christianity to that which is given through this source? (A) This is a parallel, and was the commonly accepted one until there began to be set rules in which there were the attempts to take short cuts. And there are none in Christianity!

(Q) What action of the early church, or council, can be mentioned as that which ruled reincarnation from Christian theology? (A) Just as indicated - the attempts of individuals to accept or take advantage of, because of this knowledge, see?

(Q) Is there any other advice which may be given to this entity at this time in the preparation of these chapters? (A) Hold fast to that ideal, and using Him ever as the Ideal. And hold up that NECESSITY for each to meet the same problems. And DO NOT attempt to shed or to surpass or go around the Cross.   5749-14

August 24

> First - there is the consciousness to the body of there being a physical body, a mental body, and the hope or desire for and the knowledge of a spiritual body. These are one - just as the entity finds in the material plane, or the earth-consciousness, that it is of three-dimensional natures. Also...there are three phases of man's relationship or man's comprehension. Hence in the earth there is, in reason, only the three-dimensional attitude. Yet there are the experiences of the entity, as well as of others, of more than three-dimensional concepts.
> 1747-5

If our bodies, minds, and souls become as one in this sojourn, we will find our way home to our Creator.

First, we need a conscious awareness of the difference within our trinities. "Personality is that ye wish others to think and see. Individuality is that your soul prays, your soul hopes for, desires.

"They need not necessarily be one, but their purpose must be one, even as the Father, the Son and the Holy Spirit are one. So must body, mind and soul be one in purpose and in aim, and as ye ask, believing, so is it done unto thee." (5246-1)

We are cautioned not to become so engrossed in our material existence that we forget why we came to this earth. "For, the very fact of an individual having a physical consciousness, no matter his state or status in the material plane, is an indication of the awareness that God is mindful of that soul, by giving it an opportunity to express in the material plane." (1747-5)

August 25

> Let thy meditation, thy prayer ever be: "Father, God! In that Thou hast given to me the Christ Consciousness, may I - in my daily walks before my fellow man - manifest the spirit of the Christ; in humbleness, in love, in patience, in longsuffering; that I indeed may manifest the spirit of the Christ Consciousness."   262-118

The Christ Consciousness is already within us, and if we are practicing faith, hope, patience, longsuffering, kindness, gentleness, and brotherly love we are using it.

If not, we need to activate it. "Then let that thou knowest in the heart of God - mercy, justice, peace and love - be thine in thy EVERY walk; yea, in thy every activity. For the Lord hath called thee to service, and will direct thee - if ye will keep His ways. For the Christ Consciousness awakens, arouses thy consciousness to a greater and greater service to others." (262-116)

The Christ Consciousness, not just for Christians, is the same—perhaps with another name—for followers of Judaism, Buddhism, Platoism, Mohammedanism.

"Little by little does ONE come to the understanding of the PURPOSE for which they came into the earth... that GIVEN in the beginning, and as souls seek the Father, in that companionship that one may have through communion with Him - and communion with Him means DOING; not shutting self away from thine brother, from thine neighbor, even from thine self - rather APPLYING self to the duties material, mental AND spiritual, as IS known." (99-8)

August 26

For what is Destiny? The destiny of every soul is in HIM who gave the soul, that the entity, the individual, might know, might be one with that Creative Force we call God. And how, the manner in which the entity, the individual, uses the opportunities makes for whether there comes the consternation, the turmoils, the strifes that arise from self-exaltation, or just the opposite. For how hast thy God meted to thee judgements? Not other than in mercy as thou showest mercy, as thou art a portion of that.   849-11

Destiny is in our own hands, definitely not preordained, but definitely capable of receiving divine guidance and assistance.

"Then...there is GIVEN the knowledge, the understanding as to the bigger things, the greater things...to make whole men out of pieces, so make then out of thine own self a whole, well-rounded individual, one seeking, one applying that that is KNOWN, and as THAT is applied, so is strength, grace, knowledge, understanding given as to HOW the GREATER things that are visioned by the soul from one experience to another is, and may be accomplished." (99-8)

We can lose the divine help through "the exaltation of self and self's abilities and self's powers and self's own indulgences - these ye must lose in gentleness, in patience. For in patience, as He has given thee, ye become aware of thy soul; thy individuality lost in Him... motivated by thy Master! Thus does the Destiny of the individual lie within self." (849-11)

August 27

> *(Q) Why is it difficult for me to remember? (A) It isn't difficult! It's rather trained in self to FORGET! See the differentiation between forgetting and remembering, is - MEMORY is the exercising of the inner self as related to thought. To acknowledge that the memory is poor, is to say you don't think much! The forgetting is to say that the thought becomes self-centered, for memory is thought - even as thought is memory, brought to the forefront by the association of ideas.* 69-2

Memory problems may develop from lack of use or lack of caring. Here's what Edgar said to a man complaining that his memory was so poor he could no longer develop original ideas.

"Have ye used thy memory as a creative thing? Only that which is creative grows. Thy memory, remember is as the Way has given: 'if ye apply thyself, I will bring to thy remembrance all things since the foundation of the world.' What is lacking?

"It is thine own coordinating of thy mind, thy body, thy soul-purpose to the first cause, the first principle, love. For God so loved the world that He gave His own, His own Son that ye, as an individual, might have access to the Father." (4083-1)

Thus, memory loss can be simply one of many problems caused when we stray from our ideal. Edgar told one boy, "Mostly when individuals forget it is because something within... their inner consciousness, has rebelled—and they prepare to forget." (5022-l)

August 28

They, the physical are under subjugation of the subconscious or soul forces. As we see in the body we have the Trinity for an entity. We have as this: The physical forces and mental mind; we have the spirit or soul force with the superconscience [superconscious?] or soul mind; then we have the spirit, that is, the mind of the soul force, just as the soul occupies the body in its same form and manner. 3744-1

The body is a trinity, with each of the three parts dependent upon each other. The Forces described this three-dimensional concept as "the mind, the physical mind and its associations; the spiritual mind and its hopes and desires. Then there is the soul body also....it is as the spiritual three-dimensional concept of the Godhead; Father, Son, Holy Spirit.

"These, then, in self are a shadow of the spirit of the Creative Force. Thus as the Father is as the body, the mind is as the Son, the Soul is as the Holy Spirit. For it is eternal. It has ever been and ever will be, and it is the soul made in the image of the Creator...." (5246-1)

Our bodies are patterned after the Holy Trinity. "As is understood, then - Father-God is as the body, or the whole. Mind is as the Christ, which is the way. The Holy Spirit is as the soul, or - in material interpretation - purposes, hopes, desires.

"Then, each phase of these has its part to play...in the activities of the entity...These are not then merely ideals, but...working, practical, everyday experiences." (1747-5)

August 29

For, the very fact of an individual having a physical consciousness, no matter his state or status in the material plane, is an indication of the awareness that God is mindful of that soul, by giving it an opportunity to express in the material plane.   1747-5

    On this day in 1943 Edgar's reading helped Bill Starling plan a book about his being a secret service man who protected U.S. presidents from Theodore Roosevelt to Franklin Roosevelt. He was retiring because of concern that the stress of his job would kill him.

    Edgar told him the book should be a strong, impartial story and should be ready by spring. Their mutual friend Dave Kahn should finance the book, Simon and Schuster should publish it, Tom Sugrue should write it, and at least 100,000 people would buy and read it. He proceeded to outline the book and give its theme: "the service of a servant to a nation."

    A few days later in New York, Kahn—who brought Starling to Virginia Beach for the reading—offered to share a taxi with a stranger, who turned out to be the publisher Max Schuster. Kahn told him he was glad to meet him because he was going to publish Bill Starling's book. Schuster was stunned. Starling had made him a Senate page boy when he was an adolescent, and he was eager to see and publish his book. So that's why Edgar's Forces chose him! The next spring Starling was pleased that the book was about to come out, but sadly he died three weeks before its publication.

August 30

Then, as ye show forth the fruits of the spirit. What are these? Faith, hope, patience, longsuffering, kindness, gentleness, brotherly love - these be those over which so many stumble; yet they are the very voices, yea the very morning sun's light in which the entity has caught that vision of the NEW AGE, the new understanding, the new seeking for the relationships of a Creative Force to the sons of men. 1436-1

On this date in 1941 a reading Edgar was giving for a Virginia Beach labor leader was interrupted with an unusual vision. Readings usually stayed focused on the client's concern, but this vision was way off subject.

Edgar saw armored men—one on a white horse, one on a red horse—leading hordes of people who clashed and battled. The warriors following the white horse had weapons, many more than those behind the red horse. Still, the red gang rode right through the white gang, and millions were killed.

Edgar had been predicting a catastrophic war since 1934 when he dreamed about warriors on opposite sides of a stream. One side in white was led by an angel and the other in browns and blacks was led by the Devil.

They were primed to fight. Edgar had been sent to deliver a message before the battle, but the bat-winged Devil wouldn't let him. After the dream he couldn't remember the message.

The war-related vision on this day came more than three months before the Japanese bombed Pearl Harbor.

August 31

...each and every development in the physical, in the social, in the mental plane has its place, each and every reverse, each and every mount surmounted, each difficulty has its place and the body, mentally...or materially, must use each for its own development...Then, do not count any condition lost. Rather make each the steppingstone to higher things, remembering God does not allow one to be tempted beyond that they are able to bear and comprehend, will they but make their will one with His. 900-44

By this time in August 1944 Edgar and Gertrude were at Meadow View Inn so that Edgar could be under the care of Dr. Harry Semones, who owned the Inn. Earlier in the month Edgar had suffered a stroke which partially paralyzed his right side and left him unable to write or type.

Though he would have been the last to admit it, he was also suffering from exhaustion. He had been giving many too many readings, ignoring the Force's advice to slow down and ignoring both Gertrude's and Gladys's pleas to take time for rest and relaxation.

Gladys had the unpleasant task of canceling appointments for people who had scheduled a year in advance. She also had to make ends meet with no income, having to dismiss the extra staff hired to help with the huge bags of letters and constantly ringing phone. She quit paying rent and moved back to the Cayces' home. The office's heyday was over and, unless Edgar recovered, would never be the same.

September 1

There is rather a combination of conditions, attitudes, mental conditions and physical reactions through the body... There is no cure-all except being in attune with the Infinite.   658-15

On this day in 1925 Edgar and his family vacated their Dayton apartment and started toward their final destination of Virginia Beach—the sleepy fishing village repeated readings recommended as the best place for "the work."

Life had gone downhill for them since Edgar and Gertrude started having physical problems.

Edgar needed bed recovery after exhausting himself and damaging his feet running a mile with a suitcase and another heavy object to make a train connection. Gertrude fell down the basement steps, bruising her cheek, and injuring her eye.

Both were ready to leave Dayton, where lack of finances had plagued them until Edgar's practice grew and Morton Blumenthal became their benefactor.

Morton now increased both Edgar's and Gladys's salaries and gave them $1,000 for their travels to Virginia Beach, where he had already rented them a house.

The first stop on their trip was Hopkinsville, where Edgar's mother was bedridden with painful colitis and asthma and his father was bedridden with a severe cold.

Edgar used the travel money to pay their medical bills, and they arrived at Norfolk, close to Virginia Beach, on September 15.

September 2

Study to show thyself approved unto God, a workman not ashamed of that you think, of that you do, or of your acts; keeping self unspotted from your own consciousness of your ideal; having the courage to dare to do that you know is in keeping with God's will. 853-8

Sometime in September 1883, 6-year-old Edgar became a first grader at the one-room Beverly School. He couldn't concentrate, was a slow learner, and was considered strange.

He spent much time in the dunce's chair. His classmates recognized that he was different from them and gave him a nickname he detested—Freak.

He was a student at this school when he was kept after class for misspelling a word and was forced to fill the blackboard with his chalk-written "cabin."

That night he put his head on the spelling book, slept for a few minutes, and awoke knowing how to spell every word in the book.

***

Sometime in September 1889 Edgar had to change schools. The Beverly School closed, and students were transferred to the new Beverly Academy—still only one room, but big enough to hold twice as many students.

The teacher whipped Edgar often for not paying attention in class. He had a reputation among his classmates as a weird boy who talked to ghosts.

He was only interested in reading and didn't like participating in games at recess.

September 3

The first law in every life is self-preservation of the life, and [if] will the basis of the fountain head from which life itself gains its impetus be that upon which the ENTITY depends, BEAUTIFUL indeed will be this life - which astrologically has SO MANY BEAUTIFUL conditions in same.   376-2

    In September 1907 another fire (see Dec. 22) engulfed Edgar's new Bowling Green studio, destroying a negative that hadn't yet been sent to receive the prize for a national Kodak contest Edgar had won.

    The photography partners were not hit as badly by this fire as the first one because their insurance paid better than before, but nevertheless, at this time partner Frank Potter wanted to call it quits.

    The Salters mortgaged The Hill again to buy Potter's interest, and Dr. and Mrs. Thomas House became Edgar's new partners. Dr. House would be both manager and conductor of the readings.

    Reconstruction was rapid, and the studio reopened in two weeks. To save money, Gertrude and baby Hugh Lynn moved back to The Hill, and Edgar slept on a mattress in the studio. Readings addressing money were made because of Edgar's dire financial status and his need to repay the Salters for their loan. Edgar may have had time for these personal readings because of few clients.

    Perhaps people desiring pictures and those wanting physical readings had not yet found his new location.

September 4

Not that man lives by bread alone, but by EVERY WORD that is a promise to that man by or from the Creative Forces, or God. That that a man worships, THAT that man becomes. He that looketh upon the monetary conditions as success looketh in vain!   2897-4

Readings to help raise money revealed a complete story about gold hidden by a Confederate soldier with troops on the way to occupy. But there would be no gold for Edgar to find. The reading told of two men who came after the war and dug up the treasure, even telling that one of the two was killed.

A reading about thousands of dollars worth of stolen bonds told the truth about who had them, and Edgar's father Leslie received the offered reward, but gave nothing to Edgar himself.

Leslie then came up with a scheme—with a few business associates—to make money on the commodities stock market by using Edgar's psychic information. Edgar agreed with the stipulation that a portion of any earnings would go toward reducing his huge debts.

After making money two weeks in a row, the investors moved to Chicago for closer trading, but were certain Edgar was wrong predicting that the wheat market was going to be cornered and then take a huge drop. Not following that tip caused them to lose all of their syndicate's money.

That was the end of Edgar's connection with the commodities market.

September 5

First, know in self that which is the ideal; not for the material standpoint first, but as the IDEAL in the spiritual; and then set the MENTAL self to seeking in the material to give expressions of that in its various relationships and manners in the material plane.   797-1

In 1908 Edgar got involved in a money-making scheme he would later regret.

His friend Joe Dickey believed a New Yorker named Paul Cooksey could raise capital for investing in stocks. To persuade Cooksey of Edgar's readings' accuracy, Edgar— in a trance—followed the New Yorker's movements for a day. When Cooksey received the transcript, he was sold.

Then Edgar had second thoughts, feeling readings for money were not the right way to use his gift.

Cooksey came to town and kept bugging him with requests that sounded more like threats. Finally, Edgar relented and agreed to one reading only if Cooksey would go back to New York and leave him alone.

Leslie conducted the reading which made some $20,000 on tips and paid off one of Edgar's bank loans.

Dickey then became the one bugging Edgar. He put up the front money and finally talked a reluctant Edgar into giving a reading on a horse race.

Edgar's share got him out of debt, but he paid a high price.   He could no longer go into a trance, and he knew he was being punished for using his abilities for material rather than spiritual good.

September 6

> ...peace must begin within self before there may be the activity or the application of self in such a manner as to bring peace in thine own household, in thine own heart, in thine own vicinity, in thine own state or nation.... only one agreement: Worship God in a manner that is in keeping with the dictates of thy conscience.
> 3976-28

On this month's first day in 1925, the Cayces put their belongings in transit to Virginia Beach and went to The Hill for ten days.

Edgar's mother Carrie looked as they expected from a reading which predicted she would never recover from colitis and asthma. Recommendations from the same reading were already being used to reduce her pain.

His father Leslie was in bed with a severe cold on the verge of pneumonia. Their condition cast a pall upon the Cayces' excitement about their generous benefactor and the prospects of Edgar's work expanding to help many more people.

Morton Blumenthal had increased Edgar's retainer and Gladys's salary and provided $1,000 to get them to Virginia Beach, where he had rented them a house.

Edgar's dream of a Cayce Institute for more readings to be studied had expanded. He dreamed now of a Cayce Hospital where doctors would administer treatments prescribed in his readings to patients whom other doctors had been unable to help.

How wonderful that Blumenthal shared that dream!

September 7

Whether in Buddhism, Mohammedanism, Confucianism, Platoism, or what - these have been added to much from that as was given by Jesus in His walk in Galilee and Judea. In all of these, then, there is that same impelling spirit. 364-9

Most religions profess the Christ Consciousness, though called by another name. Most affirm the advisability of turning aside our own immediate needs in the material plane in favor of "the universal conscious-ness of the Father Spirit." (5749-4)

Buddhists call this teaching *Dharma*, and they are called to follow it as their ideal, just as Christians are called to follow the Christ Consciousness.

All should strive to apply "those tenets or truths that become a part of the entity's experience - if they are held to the Law of One as manifested in the man Jesus, as signified in the Christ-Consciousness. (Please gain the difference of these!)" (1010-12) Those same truths were manifested in the Buddha.

Whenever tempted to waver from that ideal, remember "None of such urges, to be sure, surpass the will; but they are expressed...by the sages of old, 'Today there is before thee life and death, good and evil - choose thou!'

"Then, in every experience, in the activity of every individual...the expression or manifestation or result in the life of the individual depends upon the choice between those two factors." (1010-12)

September 8

Enter close oft into communion, into meditation with the consciousness within thyself of thy relationship to thy Creator; and then - as this is aroused, and you make application of the material things for the physical relief to give expression of same becomes naturally a part of the self. 658-15

Meditation is focusing the mind on a particular thing —a game, a television program, a tree, a thought, or any activity. We constantly meditate and can train ourselves to communicate with our Creator.

"For, ye must learn to meditate - just as ye have learned to walk, to talk, to do any of the physical attributes of thy mind as compared to the relationships with the facts, the attitudes, the conditions, the environs of thy daily surroundings." (281-41)

Some meditators know how to empty their minds, others repeatedly think of a mantra, others think of everything at once, boggling the mind so much it has to relax. Meditation "is not musing, not daydreaming; but as ye find your bodies made up of the physical, mental and spiritual, it is the attuning of the mental body and the physical body to its spiritual source." (281-41)

Regular meditation can result in changing lives. "For it is in the practice of peace within self, of love made manifest in self, that you make same manifest in your relationships to others. Not as a goody-goody individual, but as one good FOR something; bringing peace, joy, gladness, hope." (3165-1)

September 9

Don't become cranky - you have almost lost hold of yourself at times in feeling sorry for yourself. You have nothing to feel sorry for! God is just as mindful of you, though you have made a wreck of some people's lives - and you'll have to meet it. But that ye are alive, that ye are conscious, and that ye have the opportunity in this period to apply self in the reconstruction of what man is to look forward to, should encourage thee to know that God is mindful of each soul. 3689-1

Because God is mindful of each soul, no matter how much we've messed up our lives, we have a second chance—and chances ad infinitum.

Hypocrites not only destroy their spiritual journey, their material journey is not as good as they'd like. The client addressed in the above quote was told: "It is well to be subtle, but don't fool yourself - and you know you're not fooling yourself, even when you fool others."

Edgar kept hammering at the client's shortcomings. "But ye used this too good account for the material gains. Did ye use it as well for the spiritual gains? 'Not by might and power, but by my spirit, sayeth the Lord.' This learn in all of thy undertakings."

Of course, he gave him advice to redeem himself. "Study to show thyself approved unto God, a workman never ashamed. Do that in body, in mind, in purpose, which you will not be ashamed to present to thy Maker; rightly stressing the various phases of the experience in the earth." That's wonderful advice for us all.

September 10

Then open thyself more to the possibilities and the probabilities that are about thee day by day, and ye will find greater blessings may come to thee.   3246-1

On this day in 1923, Edgar hired Gladys Davis, age eighteen, to take notes of his readings and transcribe and file them. She applied for the job because she was bored with making lists of nuts, bolts, and nails at her hardware store job.

Eleven females were already at desks and card tables prepared to take shorthand while Edgar gave a reading when she arrived at his Selma office. She sat on an empty chair, and Edgar placed a small table in front of her.

In a trance Edgar said many unfamiliar words, but she did the best she could with phrases like "the Abrahms cycloclast with 37 ohms," not realizing that Edgar himself had never heard such terms in a waking state.

She tried very hard to be accurate, knowing the words coming out of his mouth might save the life of a little boy who had been afflicted since birth—Miss Graham's nephew.

When Edgar chose her transcribed notes as the best and told her she had the job, he said, "No more nuts and bolts."

If she didn't realize then that he could read minds, she would certainly find out in the next 21 years she worked with him.

September 11

The body physically is made up of many atomic units, yet when one is not in accord with another trouble ensues, and when murmurings or dissensions arise from within, dis-ease - and finally DISEASE - sets in. When a body of individuals (with the mind the builder again) sets forth to gain from that same Universal Energy, or Forces that build, and in the physical, the material, the mental, the spiritual plane, are in accord in mind and in action, the WORLD may be TURNED AROUND, see? for, as it has been given, faith may remove the mountain, see? 996-11

Mental dis-ease can lead to physical disease, and it can prevent healing.

Organs need the cooperation of every other portion of the body to reproduce themselves. "When these suffer from mental or physical disorders that make for repressions in any portion of the system, then first dis-ease and distress arise. If heed is not taken as to the warnings sent forth along the nervous systems of the body indicating that certain organs or portions of the system are in distress, or the S.O.S. call that goes out is not heeded, then DISEASE sets in." (531-2)

Disturbances "coming as dis-ease to a portion of a functioning system, then assuming the greater distresses as diseased portions through that of the gradual building up of conditions as are created by misdirected energies in system." (202-1) Dis-ease might be a signal that steps should be taken to prevent an actual physical disease.

September 12

Let not thy heart be troubled. Let it not be afraid. For ye believe in God. Then, as His children - for thy sake, for thy Lord's sake - act like it!   294-202

Late in the summer of 1922 Edgar turned down the opportunity to be a turbaned, white-costumed, rock-star-type psychic, paid $1,000 a day and driven around in a chauffeured limousine.

He was incensed at the offer which was given him by Frederick Gilmer Bonfils, owner and publisher of the *Denver Post.* To earn that exorbitant salary and live that extravagant lifestyle, he would need to do only two readings a day—one for Bonfils himself.

Bonfils heard about Edgar from Dave Kahn, who had been working for an attorney in Denver since leaving Cayce Petroleum. When Edgar accepted an expense-paid trip to demonstrate a reading for Bonfils and a team of doctors, he surely thought he might open the door to interest more doctors in using his skills for diagnoses, and perhaps find a reason to stay and open a photographic studio with space for him to be a psychic diagnostician.

The Rocky Pasture #1 oil well venture had failed, and he was looking for someplace for a fresh start.

Instead he was broke and stranded in Denver with his friend Frank Mohr, who had accompanied him, and his father Leslie who had mistakenly arrived. Luckily, a Birmingham, Alabama, women's club paid in advance for Edgar to come there to give a speech, and he bought train tickets for all three.

September 13

WONDERS may be accomplished, my friend, in thine application of that thou hast here gained, in how thou hast used thine self and thine Lord and thine peoples - yea, help will come by seeking from within to know the ways thou may be guided the better. 699-1

On this evening in 1925 the Cayces arrived at Norfolk, Virginia—only an overnight away from Virginia Beach, a tiny fishing village pinpointed in several readings as the best place for Edgar's psychic work.

The next day Edgar and Hugh Lynn paid a nickel each for the twenty-minute train ride to Virginia Beach, finding many boarded-up cottages and businesses silent after the summer tourist season.

They caught a trolley along Pacific Avenue past Princess Anne Hotel, a children's hospital, and more deserted cottages.

At 35th Street they disembarked and found their new home almost three blocks from Pacific Avenue—a sad two-story white frame cottage surrounded by weeds almost as high as the porch's cement steps.

They stayed only 20 minutes because of a storm brewing in the east. They returned to Norfolk where they sat out a three-day storm in the hotel with Gladys, Edgar Evans, Gertrude, and Gertrude's cousin Stella, who had accompanied them to help with their move.

By October 19 they had all their possessions in place and, in spite of no central heating and an exorbitant $35 monthly rent, they felt good about their very first house.

September 14

Not my will but Thine, or lord, be done in and through me. Let me ever be a channel of blessings, today, to those that I contact, in EVERY way. Let my going in, mine coming out be in accord with that THOU would have me do, and as the call comes, "Here am I, send me, use me!" 262-3

On this day in 1931 Edgar met with the group that would soon become the Norfolk Study Group.

In August he had received a letter from Edith Edmonds asking how she and others who frequently met together could be of help to him and his work. Her group was aware of Edgar's poor health and the change in his financial status caused by the closing of the hospital.

Edgar was pleased with the group's desire to help, and as he always did when needing a question answered, he decided to ask the Forces at this meeting in Minnie Barrett's living room.

The voice within Edgar told the group they could give "light to the waiting world" if they were committed to each others' spiritual development, warning, "First, learn cooperation!"

A reading on October 4 (262-3) said, "Let thy prayer be continually" the prayer at the top of this page.

The informal study group and the existing Glad Helpers Prayer Group started meeting together regularly as the Norfolk Study Group, trying in their daily lives to perfect the lessons Edgar learned while in a trance.

September 15

Use that you have in hand today, NOW, and when your abilities and activities are such that you may be entrusted with other faculties, other developments, other experiences, they are a part of self. 853-8

On this day in 1922 Edgar went to Birmingham with a train ticket financed by a woman's club that wanted Edgar to speak. After having his oil venture sabotaged, he was broke and ready for a fresh start in a new location.

Wow—was he successful! For the first time ever, his sole income was from either giving readings or talking about them, and people flocked to see him at the Tutweiler Hotel, where he stayed for four months.

By January 1923 he liked practicing in Birmingham well enough to invite Gertrude and the children to come there to stay. He might never have left if city authorities hadn't asked him to get a medical license.

Although supportive doctors talked his way out of that requirement, the temporary thought of a setback may have been what prompted him to give a reading.

He asked his psychic sources for the best location for the hospital he so desperately wanted to have doctors close at hand to administer the recommendations given by his inner voice.

The reading said absolutely *not* in Birmingham. The very best location would be the small fishing village of Virginia Beach. Gertrude never came to Birmingham, but he went back to Hopkinsville to visit with his family and pursue their future.

September 16

Be not overcome of thine self, nor of those things that would make thee weak in those that are the besetting influences in thy experience. Know that the strength to overcome is in Him. Conform thine mind and thine body to the things of the spirit, rather than to the things of the flesh. While in flesh we may make manifested those forces in spirit. But abide in His time. Listen to the voice within thee. For, His spirit will bear witness with thy spirit and guide thee in the way that thou shouldst go. 262-59

On this day in 1941 Edgar was a sick man. A reading he did for himself said, "Conditions are NOT good, and unless measures are taken for corrections, they will be much worse." (294-205)

HIs doctor ordered a colonic to treat his intestinal obstruction and cholecystitis. He had it this morning, but it made him feel worse.

He did not feel like doing two readings scheduled for that afternoon, so he lay down and was resting until he heard a voice inside him saying, "GET UP AND GET THAT READING—IF YOU EVER EXPECT TO DO ANY MORE!" He didn't hesitate to follow the order, and he immediately felt well. He did a reading for a child about her bowel problems and then one for a return patient he diagnosed as improved, but still needing massage and wheat germ oil.

That night his Bible group probably never suspected he had been sick, and the next day he was still his old self. This cure was only one of many he did for himself.

September 17

He hath given His angels charge concerning thee. And that being guided by those influences and forces, they become - by application - stepping-stones for greater beauties, and the abilities for greater service.   1463-2

On this day in 1923 Arthur Lammers came to Selma and proposed that he and Edgar form the Cayce Institute for Psychic Research.

The institute would have two purposes: to pursue both oil ventures and the construction of a hospital and publishing company. Lammers owned a large printing and engraving company in Dayton.

On September 20 Edgar and Lammers went to Texas to meet a potential partner, and they ended up forming the Plan of Protected Investment Company with four other partners.

They issued 10,000 shares of preferred stock for $100 per share to be used as an endowment for the hospital and 30,000 shares of common stock to be divided 20,000 for oil ventures and 10,000 for the Institute for Psychic Research.

Even though he'd just hired Gladys as secretary to record readings, Edgar went on a fundraising trip and made a decision to move to Dayton.

Lammers wanted him there for readings to explore mysteries of the universe, and Edgar wanted whatever new knowledge the Forces might give.

September 18

For, while mind is the builder, it is the purpose, the intent with which an individual applies self mentally, that brings those physical results into materiality. And these should be kept coordinant one with another. For, as has been given, there must be those meetings of self in material manifestation of the ideals and purposes of the spiritual and mental aspirations of an individual. And be not deceived, God is not mocked; whatsoever a man soweth, that must he also reap. And with what measure ye mete, it will be measured to thee again.   257-252

The day before this day in 1944 Edgar gave his last reading, and it was for himself. Dr. Harry Semones at Meadow View Inn had been guiding his recuperation based on readings' recommendations, and this time he invited Dr. Henry George as a consultant.

A previous reading on August 28 had told Edgar to stay "Until you are well or dead one!" (294-211) This reading gave twenty-five paragraphs of needed treatments and said nothing about the probability of recovery.

Still at the Inn he wrote a letter to the A.R.E. Board of Trustees about their upcoming meeting, dictating to Gladys in a whisper, "God in His wisdom has seen fit that I not be present. Yet you know I am with you in spirit and purpose, when that purpose is to serve our fellow man—in love, patience, long-suffering, bearing one another's burdens."

He suffered a second stroke on September 24.

September 19

Then why, as has been said, is God mindful of an individual soul? SPIRIT! For our spirit that is a portion of His Spirit.... 262-115

Many times fate seemed to intervene to keep Edgar from doing something foolish.

When he was going through his short-lived macho phase in the fall of 1885, he entered a saloon, sat down at the bar, and ordered a drink. The bartender, a fellow church member, reportedly told him he would not be responsible for giving him his first drink. Edgar probably took that as a sign that the higher power he honored so much did not want him to drink.

Another time Edgar was riding his favorite pony from Beverly to Hopkinsville to visit the John Robinson Circus when another Liberty Chrisitian Church member tried to interfere with his plans.

When A.L. Carter found out where Edgar was going, he gave him a lengthy lecture on the evils of associating with people attracted to that kind of entertainment. He actually begged Edgar not to go, telling him he was too good a boy, trying to scare him about making such a trip alone at night.

When he saw that Edgar wasn't deterred, Carter offered him a dollar if he'd change his mind. Edgar declined and urged his pony on. Very soon the pony balked and refused Edgar's attempts to move it forward. A rock had lodged under its horseshoe. Edgar went back, and Carter gave him a dollar and a prayer. Saved again!

September 20

In the material it must be not what you would want others to do for you, but the ideal manner and way in which ye must meet those influences, those associations, those affiliations with thy fellowman. For, in as much, and in the manner as ye do unto the least of thy brethren, ye do unto they Maker.   2021-1

On this day in 1920 Edgar and Dave Kahn teamed up with two new partners to incorporate the Edgar Cayce Petroleum Company.

Major Wilson handled the lease agreements and Martin Sanders paid for the partnership agreement, signed by all four on Sept. 20, 1920.

Readings led them to Luling and property owned by Minnie Phillips, a white women whose passion was protecting blacks.

They reached an agreement to drill on five thousand acres for fourteen months, giving a percentage of the profits to Phillips and the black community. Unfortunately, they couldn't raise enough money to drill and had to give up their leases.

Edgar B. Davis bought the lease and had fabulous strikes on the property. Because Kahn had given Edgar's readings on the land to Davis, Kahn asked for a share of the profits, but David wrote back claiming other financial commitments.

Gratifyingly, he did share a large portion of his fortune with both black and white Luling people.

September 21

As the powers that were thine, are thine, are purified in the love of the Christ so may ye give out to those that seek, ever - ever in His name. "For if ye ask in my name, believing, it shall be done unto him for whom ye ask," if ye abide in His love.   281-23

Edgar may have given a reading for President Woodrow Wilson during a fundraising trip he and Dave Kahn took after their failure with Edgar Cayce Petroleum's first attempt to drill for oil.

Because the company had money to lease, but not enough to drill, they traveled to sell shares in their company. They first went to Birmingham, then Nashville, at which point Edgar was called to Washington, D.C.

President Wilson had suffered a stroke, and Kahn recalled that Edgar's reading in late 1920 for the President described his physical condition and said he would not get well. Having served as president from 1913 to 1921, he died on February 3, 1924.

If this presidential reading truly happened, Edgar never talked about it, just as he wouldn't talk about a Washington dignitary who consulted him in the 1940s.

After the stop at the capital city, they went on to New York and raised the necessary funds to continue their oil business. A reading led to a property for which the mineral rights were held by William Barrow, who became a major stockholder and officer of Cayce Petroleum. On May 18, 1921, a contract gave them rights to their first oil well, Rocky Pasture #1.

September 22

> (Q) What part did Jesus play in any of His reincarnations in the development of the basic teachings of the following religions and philosophies? First, Buddhism: (A) This is just one.
>
> (Q) Mohammedanism, Confucianism, Shintoism, Brahmanism, Platoism, Judaism. (A) As has been indicated, the entity - as an entity - influenced either directly or indirectly all those forms of philosophy or religious thought that taught God was One.   364-9

The revelation of the Law of One often came into the readings—a truth professed by the soul of Jesus in incarnations that influenced religious leaders of different eras.

"As the Spirit of the Master, the Spirit of the Son, was manifest - as was given - to each in their respective sphere. As it is today. As it was of yore. God calls on man everywhere to seek His face, through that channel that may be blessed by the Spirit of the Son - in whatever sphere this may take its form." (364-9)

The Forces scoffed at "present denominationalism, and each one crying, 'Lo, here is Christ - Lo, this is the manner of approach - Lo, unless ye do this or that ye have no part in Him.' 'He that loves me will keep my commandments.' What are the commandments? 'Thou shalt have no other GOD before me,' and 'Love thy neighbor as thyself.'

"In this is builded the whole LAW and gospel of every age that has said, 'There is ONE God!'" (364-9)

September 23

For what is bad? Good gone wrong, or something else? It is good MISAPPLIED, misconstrued, or used in a SELFISH manner - for the satisfying of a desire within self. And so is sin, so is illness; a lack of at-onement with a COORDINANT, COOPERATIVE force of a LIVING influence that may...become such a marvellous force for good, for a channel of manifestation of GOOD among its fellow man. The LORD is willing. Art thou, then, willing to accept and be guided, and be directed, by that in thy experience? 1089-5

Edgar's Forces consistently challenges us to be channels of good.

Doing so is easy if we are consciously in "contact with the universal-cosmic-God-Creative forces...by feeding upon the food, the fruits, the results of spirit, of God, of Life, of Reality: Love, hope, kindness, gentleness, brotherly love, patience. THESE make for the awareness in the soul of its relationship to the Creative force that is manifest in self, in the ego, in the I AM of each soul, and of I AM THAT I AM." (378-14)

"But keep the self unspotted from the world; that is, do nothing physically or in thought - that you'll be ashamed to present to thy Maker or to the woman you love. Don't be ashamed, and don't ask others to do something that you would not do yourself nor to be something that you are not yourself. Then keep the self unspotted from the World. This should not be as your system or policy but it should be your religion." (3689-1)

September 24

Magnify the virtues of all, as ye would have thy God, thy Maker, magnify thy trying, thy attempts to be holy - not righteous; so few can ever attain that - none in the material world - [but] they can try. All can be holy; that is, dedicating body, mind and purpose. That is being holy! Then, the try may be counted to thee as righteousness. For righteousness is of God. 3621-1

If we have setbacks in our attempts to lead a virtuous life, we should not be dismayed. On the cosmic scale, we gain whenever we try.

"Do not become discouraged in well-doing. Remember, no matter what others say, God looketh on the intent and purpose. Know that an honest try is counted to the individual entity as righteousness. For as He has given, to love and keep His commandments is the whole law." (3416-1)

"Just as breaking self from any other habit - if ye break over, try again! In the try, help will come. In the application there may be established the knowledge of the truth and the way, and help may come physically, mentally, spiritually. For, if ye know the truth - and apply it not, it is sin. And if sin lies at thy door, can ye have peace with self or with others?" (3078-1)

When you try but don't live up to your own moral standards, don't fret "if there is kept the purpose, the ideal... the entity may manifest the fruits of the spirit; patience, longsuffering, kindness, brotherly love, graciousness." (3416-1) Just keep trying!

September 25

For as the earth is ONLY a portion of a mighty array of forces and influences in our OWN little solar system, so man - though but a speck upon the earth and only as a grain in the universe - is a portion of that divinity that urges ON and ON and ON and ON! that makes for that eternal hope, that spark of light, that thread of soul in infinity itself! 1298-1

Edgar's wanted to make the availability of a helpful higher power known to the masses. Both in a waking state or a trance state, he often quoted the "Ask and ye shall receive" message that Jesus brought.

Our souls' interconnectedness with the infinite makes this divine assistance possible. "Each entity, as a spark of infinity, magnifies or uses its relationship NOT for self-indulgence or gratification but for the GLORY of that which is the source of light, of all that pertains to light.

"For every spark of light, whether in the spiritual, the mental or the material sense, must have its inception in infinity." (877-26)

The Creative Forces want us to succeed and will help us if our goal is good. "There is the ability within self to contact as high a soul as is sought, by will, by desire, by the use of that attained for THIS soul, for THIS entity to reach into the cosmic or the universal sources for its supply, for its needs, for its desires." (443-31)

If our goals are in keeping with the higher good, "there may be expected that wholehearted cooperation from the divine." (254-42) What a great promise!

September 26

Use thy abilities in the self-expression of that which has been...built in thy experiences in the earth, as to cause the fruits of thy efforts and abilities to become the helpmeets, the helpfulnesses to, and the incentives and motives of others in THEIR activities in their relationships of life. This will bring harmonious experiences, this will bring those material necessities in the material world that to so many become a burden and a stumblingstone. But these, if thy experience is founded in the spiritual import, will make this latter sojourn in the earth one of happiness.   811-2

Edgar helped Dave Kahn throughout his entire career, guiding him to the best jobs, the best acquisitions, the best partners. Dave reciprocated by lending financial support the many times Edgar faced monetary distress.

The Kahn family treated Edgar like a son, so much so that Edgar addressed Dave's mother as Mother Kahn. She consulted Edgar regularly for guidance for friends and family members. In his memoir Dave gave Edgar credit for adding at least ten years to his mother's life.

One time when a reading's prediction didn't happen, Dave's wife Lucille insisted that he stop listening to Edgar. Then the Forces insisted the prediction would absolutely happen, and it did. Lucille never wavered in her support after that. Strange then that when Edgar told Dave that a stock market crash was coming, he didn't sell stock. He lost a lot, but he certainly followed the Forces' advice after that.

September 27

In visions where spiritual awakenings, these most often are seen in symbols or signs, to the entity; for, as the training of self's consciousness in a manner of interpreting the visions would be in expressions of eye, hand, mouth, posture or the like, these are INTERPRETED in thine own language. When these are, then, in symbols of such, know the awakening is at hand.
262-9

Even after his physical death, Edgar continued to help Dave Kahn. He had told Dave many times that whatever happened, communication between them would continue. That communication usually happened at 3 a.m. when Dave had a particular dilemma tormenting his mind.

One instance occurred when a friend, Ed Nicholas, who was to buy half interest into a furniture factory, asked to meet Dave the next morning. When Dave probed, he said, "I don't want to talk about it on the phone." Oh! Was he going to back out of the deal?

That night Dave, a non-swimmer, dreamed he was on a bridge going into the Atlantic Ocean in total darkness, and he was frightened. He saw Edgar laughing on a beach with sunshine all around him, and he told him, "Don't worry. Everything is all right."

Nicholas was only upset at the factory's former owner who had protested Dave's 50/50 arrangement, but Ed himself was okay with it. Hearing the good news, Dave felt he was walking in sunshine, just as he did when he joined Edgar on the beach in his dream.

September 28

Then there should not be sorrow and sadness in those periods when the physical turmoils and strifes of the body are laid aside, for the moment, for the closer walk with Him. For indeed to be absent from the material body is to be present with the Lord. 1824-1

The physical body dies, but the soul transitions to another dimension with the Creator. That transition can be easy or hard, depending upon the kind of life led.

Ordinarily the prayers after a passing are for the family of the deceased, but Edgar said we should also pray for the one who left the planet. "Those who have passed on need the prayers of those who live aright. For the prayers of those who would be righteous in spirit may save many who have erred, even in the flesh." (3416-1)

Edgar told a woman who heard her brother calling her that he came to her not at the moment of death, but "when the entity could - and found the attunement such as to speak with thee….Much that he needs of thee. Forget not to pray for and with him; not seeking to hold him but that he, too, may walk the way to the light, in and through the experience. For this is well." (3416-1)

We should determine that we "will walk the closer with Him day by day. And then when the shadows…begin to close about, and there is the meeting at the river, there will be indeed no sorrow when this barque puts out to sea." (1824-1). The reading says that this truth is both an admonition and a promise.

September 29

Changing of the mental status is ever the builder, mental and physical.   257-53

    Helpful tips pop up throughout the readings, and at least one will be welcomed by those of us concerned about how we look while growing old.

    A woman asked, "How can people avoid aging in appearance?" The answer was, "The MIND!" (1947-4). How many times do we have to be told that mind is the builder before we start using it for every single thing we want? The lesson here is to tell ourselves we look young, feel young, and act young—then wait for our affirmation to manifest itself. A little help on our part might assist.

    The same woman asked how sagging facial muscles could be avoided, and the answer was to massage with cream over the chin and throat and around the eyes, and occasionally use Boncilla or a mud pack. Thank goodness the Forces mentioned a brand name product, leaving us free to find one in our present-day market.

    The woman's next question was about her occasional facial skin eruptions, and it is interesting to know that "These are the effects of poor eliminations or coordinations between the sympathetic and the cerebrospinal system." The advice was to take a teaspoon of Eno Salts before breakfast for ten days. Stop taking for five to six days, then take again for two or three more cycles. We must hope the effort would be worth it.

    See February 15 for a recommended facial cream.

September 30

> Do that which is good, for there has been given in the consciousness of all the fruits of the spirit: Fellowship, kindness, gentleness, patience, long-suffering, love; these be the fruits of the spirit. Against such there is no law. Doubt, fear, avarice, greed, selfishness, self-will; these are the fruits of the evil forces. Against such there IS a law.
>
> 5752-3

Patience is the most important of the fruits of the spirit, for without it, practicing all the others would be difficult. We should look upon opportunities for practicing patience as blessings, not just unpleasant burdens.

"FROM THINE OWN DISAPPOINTMENTS YE MAY LEARN PATIENCE, THE MOST BEAUTIFUL OF ALL VIRTUES AND THE LEAST UNDERSTOOD! Remember, it is one of the phases or dimensions through which thy soul may catch the greatest and the more beautiful glimpse of the Creator. For, as He came unto His own and His own received Him not, in patience He brought that awareness of what they had lost in their lack of appreciation of the opportunities given." (2448-2)

We must try to look upon any incident that makes us angry as a chance to master the art of patience. "Anger may upset the body and cause a great deal of disturbance, to others as well as to self. Be angry but sin not. You will learn it only in patience and in self-possession." (3621-1)

Let us pray that "in patience...I indeed may manifest the spirit of the Christ Consciousness." (262-11)

October 1

As it has so oft been given from the first, KNOW that the Lord, thy God, is ONE! KNOW that thy ability, thy service, begins first with COOPERATION in BEING that channel through which the Glory of the Lord may be manifested in the earth!   262-92

On this day in 1928 Edgar had a reading on himself to interpret a dream he had the night before.

He dreamed he heard a "noise drop on the floor and felt the presence of a cosmic entity whirling about him." That entity identified himself as the Old Testament prophet Habakkuk. This event occurred at Morton Blumenthal's New York home during the time he was financing the hospital being built in Virginia Beach, but Morton was not present.

Habakkuk told Edgar to tell Morton his Bible book's lesson was applicable to what was going on in Virginia Beach. That short book wondered why God is silent when the wicked succeed over the righteous, but prophecies that God's sovereignty rules and in the end will deal with the wicked and award the righteous.

The prophet chided Edgar for "laxness in following the lessons given through vision and dream, and not mindful of those lessons given as to the betterment.... with the more perfect application of self, more and more, may be the direct communication or understanding of the oneness and continuity of force, or life, or existence of individuals through their various experiences."

Was this a convoluted way of saying watch Morton?

October 2

What IS Meditation? It is not musing, not daydreaming; but as ye find your bodies made up of the physical, mental and spiritual, it is the attuning of the mental body and the physical body to its spiritual source. Many say that ye have no consciousness of having a soul - yet the very fact that ye hope, that ye have a desire for better things...that ye are able to be sorry or glad, indicates an activity of the mind that takes hold upon something that is not temporal in its nature -...not thy body, no - not thy mind, but thy SOUL was in the image of thy Creator. Then, it is the attuning of thy physical and mental attributes seeking to know the relationships to the Maker. THAT is true meditation.   281-41

Purification should precede meditation. "First, CLEANSE the room; cleanse the body; cleanse the surroundings, in thought, in act! Approach not the inner man, or the inner self, with a grudge or an unkind thought held against ANY man! or do so to thine own undoing sooner or later!" (281-13)

"Sit or lie in an easy position, without binding garments.... Breathe in through the right nostril three times, and exhale through the mouth. Breathe in three times through the left and exhale through the right."

Then, with either music or an incantation, let the body's centers (chakras) respond to the creative forces.

"Meditation, then, is prayer...from WITHIN the INNER self, and partakes not only of the physical inner man but the soul...aroused by the spirit...from within." (281-13)

October 3

(Q) How may I bring into activity my pineal and pituitary glands, as well as the Kundalini and other chakras, that I may attain to higher mental and spiritual powers?.... (A) ...first so FILL the mind with the ideal that it may vibrate throughout the whole of the MENTAL being! Then, close the desires of the fleshly self to conditions about same. MEDITATE upon "THY WILL WITH ME." Feel same. Fill ALL the centers of the body, from the lowest to the highest, with that ideal; opening the centers by surrounding self first with that consciousness, "NOT MY WILL BUT THINE, O LORD, BE DONE IN AND THROUGH ME."   1861-4

The kundalini is the life force coiled at the spine waiting to be risen to the head to trigger enlightenment. Practicing meditation or yoga activates its three centers: the third cervical in the neck (the throat fifth chakra), the ninth dorsal in the middle of the back (the leyden center third chakra), and the fourth lumbar (the lower back second chakra) where the kundalini coils and waits.

A wonderful meditation is to visualize the chakras awakening. See light starting at the root chakra at the spine's bottom. Visualize the light rising from the lower back, going through the leyden, through the solar plexus at the back midriff, to the heart chakra, to the throat chakra, to the crown chakra (the pineal) at the top of the head, then exiting through the pituitary center (the third eye chakra) in the middle of the forehead.

October 4

> (Q) When there is the beginning of Kundalini to rise or there is the circulation of Kundalini through the body, what should be the next step? (A) Surround self with that consciousness of the Christ-Spirit; this by the affirmation of "Let self be surrounded with the Christ-Consciousness, and the DIRECTIONS be through those activities in the body-force itself." Do not seek the lower influences, but the Christ-Consciousness. 2072-11

Energy channeled upward through the chakras in the pursuit of spiritual perfection can be very enlightening. However, be careful in using the new energy.

Edgar told one woman, "Easily may the entity, by entering deep meditation raise the kundaline [kundalini] forces in body to the third eye as to become a seeress; so that it may see the future and the past. But the law of such is that, unless these are used for constructive and never for selfish motives or purposes, they will bring more harm than good." (5028-1)

Edgar's method of visualizing chakras with the Lord's Prayer is popular among A.R.E. members. Our Father who art in heaven (third eye), hallowed be thy name (crown). Thy Kingdom come, thy will be done (throat) on earth as it is in heaven (root). Give us this day our daily bread (root) and forgive us out debts as we forgive our debtors (solar plexus). And lead us not into temptation (leyden) but deliver us from evil (heart). For thine is the kingdom (throat) and the power (crown) and the glory forever (third eye). (281-29) Amen! And so it is!

October 5

For, as has been indicated so oft in each body, no medicine, no mechanical appliance DOES the healing. It only attunes the body to a perfect coordination and the Divine gives the healing. 1173-7

Dr. Wesley Ketchum often contacted Edgar with his problem patients, asking him to sleep on it.

He diagnosed pellagra—severe malnutrition—for a brick works laborer who fainted on the job. That diagnosis helped Ketchum treat other cases he'd been stymied with, and the treatment was simple: a well-balanced diet with lots of green vegetables.

Edgar's Forces seldom recommended operations, but highly favored osteopathy—a rather new medical discipline at the time. Prescribed spinal adjustments or manipulations caused improvements that eliminated the need for surgery.

Recommended drugs were sometimes hard to find. In one complicated case doctors finally found balsam of sulfur in a 50-year-old catalog.

Edgar amazed Ketchum, who observed one reading when Edgar stopped at 3:20 p.m. in the middle of the reading and said, "He's gone." Ketchum found out later that the patient had died at that exact moment.

Edgar received nothing for diagnosing Ketchum's patients—not a penny and not a word of thanks from the patients. They couldn't thank him because they didn't know. Ketchum took all the credit for their cures.

October 6

All phases of thy bodily and mental and spiritual experiences, then, are to be considered in thy study and in thy application of thy abilities; meeting thyself, thy faults and thy virtues in such a manner as to make the experience a growth of thy soul.   1745-1

Edgar's subliminal advice sometimes informed Ketchum of patients' problems best solved by counseling. One was a millionaire's wife who was suffering from paralysis agitates, shaking palsy. Ketchum traveled many miles to the couple's home and was impressed that Edgar, from hundreds of miles away, had described the woman and situation perfectly: "in a wheelchair, rigid as a piece of marble, two trained nurses in white caps."

Ketchum, reading Edgar's transcript, said, "As a young woman, the patient had a secret sin." The pitiful patient showed the first sign of alertness, and Ketchum continued. "This secret sin was masturbation."

Because of this sin, she had delayed marriage until she was thirty-nine, but had married then, had two children, and then fallen ill, Ketchum recounted.

At this point the woman asked her husband to leave her alone with Ketchum, who counseled her to forgive herself and abandon feelings of guilt. Edgar's voice repeatedly told him the mind must want what the body needs. The woman took a few recommended drugs and lived a normal life for several years, proving again that spirit is the life, mind is the builder, physical is the result.

October 7

It is not all of LIFE to live, nor all of death to die - for the beginning of life is as of the spiritual DEATH, unless such life is lived in the spiritual understanding - and the death in the physical is the birth in the spiritual, see?
900-331

On this date in 1941 Edgar and Gertrude became grandparents. Hugh Lynn and wife Sally lost little time asking for a reading, which suggested the 8-pound 10-ounce boy be named Charles Thomas Taylor Cayce.

The reading gave many reasons for this choice, perhaps the most important being that the child was a reincarnation of Edgar's grandfather, the newborn's great, great grandfather, Thomas Jefferson Cayce. Thomas was also a desirable name because of Tom Sugrue, Hugh Lynn's best friend, who had written Edgar's biography which was about to be published.

Taylor was Sally's maiden name, and the baby had been named Charles in a previous, favorable incarnation.

***

On this date in 1935 a reading foresaw Austrians, Germans, and Japanese "joining in their influence—unseen—and gradually growing to those affairs where there must become, as it were, almost a direct opposition to that which has been the theme of the Nazis." Unless supernatural forces intervene, "the whole WORLD will be set on fire by the militaristic groups" seeking expansion. (416-7) Edgar urged nations to live as they prayed.

October 8

If the body-mental, the body-physical and the body-spiritual COORDINATE, ye have a body that increases in wisdom, in stature, in the growth of material things - and well-balanced! These are the results of keeping each portion throughout some experience cooperating and coordinating.   254-92

Doctors who thought Edgar was a fraud were always foiled in their efforts to expose him. Many joked about Dr. Wesley Ketchum's involvement with the mystic—even Ketchum's own father who worried that using Edgar would ruin his son's reputation.

Once anyone observed him in a trance and heard the medical terms that popped out of his mouth, they realized that this eighth-grade-educated country boy's mind was in touch with an extremely high intelligence.

Ketchum himself couldn't restrain himself from testing Edgar when he was hypnotized. Once he asked him to name the shortest muscle in the body. Without hesitation Edgar said, "Levator Labii superioris alaeque nasi—the upper lip."

Ketchum forged ahead, asking him to name the longest muscle and Edgar quickly replied, "Sartorius—the muscle flexing the hip and knee joints."

Edgar's Force could not be tricked or fooled with medical matters, but the Source itself said it could be wrong about foreseeing future events. Human's free will always had the option of changing anything. The Forces could only see what would happen if nothing changed.

October 9

When individuals apply themselves for the greater activity for self, in keeping with those things that bring only the activities of being true to self, it makes for the greater activities to the associations or family ties. For when one is true to self, one cannot be false to other - if the self is the SPIRITUAL self. 797-1

On a Sunday this day in 1910, the *New York Times'* front-page banner read: "Illiterate Man Becomes a Doctor When Hypnotized." With the sensational story were pictures of Edgar, his father Leslie, and Dr. Wesley Ketchum, whose association with Edgar brought about this unsolicited publicity.

Of the many Ketchum's patients diagnosed by the Forces, the most stunning was George Dalton, who broke his right leg, both above and below the knee. Edgar's inner voice said Ketchum was to bore a hole into his kneecap, nail the cap to the bone, and then put the patient in traction. Now with such unorthodox cures as this getting such widespread publicity, Edgar was no longer Ketchum's secret.

Unbeknownst to Edgar, Ketchum presented a paper about him at a meeting of the National Society of Homeopathic Physicians. That presentation prompted the front-page story which made both Edgar and Ketchum overnight celebrities. Hopkinsville was soon buzzing both with reporters and people seeking cures.

At last, Edgar would have the opportunity to do what he was meant to do: use his ability to help others.

October 10

In thy meditation, in thy seeking, know that the answer must come within.   **262-118**

Before national publicity made their cures well known, Edgar and Ketchum worked together in the doctor's suite, where Edgar lay on a black leather couch.

Ketchum promised him that any questioning in the readings would be only to help the patient, and Edgar was comforted that Ketchum had earned an actual degree in medicine at an accredited college. He was also gratified to see recommendations from the readings help people that other doctors had failed to help.

One of these early cases has become a Cayce legend. In a reading for a boy with a sore leg others doctors had been unable to cure, Cayce recommended using oil of smoke. Local drugstores didn't have it, nor could they find it in any catalog.

A second reading named a Louisville drugstore, but the druggist there did not have it, nor had he ever heard of it.

In a third reading Edgar told the druggist to go to the drugstore's back room, look on the top shelf to the left, remove a particular item which Edgar named, and find oil of smoke behind it.

The communications with the druggist had been by telegraph, and he wired back, "Found it!" The company that made it was out of business, so who knows how long it'd been hidden in that storage room?

The important thing was—it worked. The boy's leg healed.

October 11

(Q) Do the planets have an effect on the life of every individual born? (A) They have. Just as this earth's forces were set in motion, and about it, those forces that govern the elements, elementary so, of the earth's sphere or plane, and as each comes under the influence of those conditions, the influence is to the individual without regards to the will, which is the developing factor of man, in which such is expressed through the breath of the Creator, and as one's plane of existence is lived out from one sphere to another they come under the influence of those to which it passes from time to time. 3744-4

On this day in 1923 Edgar gave Arthur Lammers the horoscope reading he had requested. The reading expounded on the stars and planets at Lammers' birth, saying he was "ruled by Jupiter," with "Venus in the eleventh House."

The reading said Lammers was "one given to view matters with a great perspective view of conditions." It concluded with this shocker: "Third appearance on this plane. He was once a monk."

Edgar and Gertrude remembered a reading some four years earlier revealing that planets' location at the time of birth affected a newborn's nature through life, but this was the first time the idea of reincarnation had come up. The time had come to reserve their original notions that such beliefs conflicted with their religious faith. Because Edgar's readings had always told the truth, they were willing to pursue both subjects further.

October 12

Know thy ideal, spiritual, mental and material. Then study to show self approved unto same, a workman not ashamed; giving stress where stress is due, keeping self unspotted from the world.   2938-1

On this day in 1910 Edgar's partnership requirements were accepted, and a 5-year contract was signed. First, no one seeking his psychic help would be turned away, whether able to pay or not. Second, all readings would be conducted by his father Leslie. Third, half of all income generated would go to Edgar and his father.

Ketchum and Noe would receive the other half, pay all overhead expenses, and set up a photography studio for the Cayces to run independently. Albert Noe was the manager and later owner of Latham Hotel, which was expected to do a booming business from people coming to Hopkinsville to seek readings from Edgar.

After the four had signed the contract at the Latham Hotel, an East Indian man came in and gave each a warning, but each had the same underlying message: They must avoid greed and self-serving interest or the good that could happen in this partnership would be destroyed. Their diagnosing of disease should not be for profit, but for their patients' health and their own spiritual lives.

No one knew this man, who left quickly after delivering his message. One of the men present for the signing went after him, but couldn't find him.

October 13

For ALL have fallen short of the grace of God. And all need to learn, "As ye do it today to the least of thy brethren, ye are doing to thy Maker." For in what manner ye measure, it must be measured to thee again. 3003-1

The new partners paid $12 a month for upstairs rooms on Hopkinsville's Main Street in a red brick building adjacent to Hopper Bookstore.

Outside a sign pointing up read "Cayce Photo Studio." Upstairs a sign reading "Psychic Diagnostician" marked the area where Edgar would do readings.

The suite was one block from Ketchum's office where he would carry out the recommendations given in the readings.

A guideline fee of $25 was set for the readings. Noe was to give Edgar and Leslie ten percent of hotel income derived from Edgar's patients.

This arrangement proceeded smoothly from late 1910 to 1911 when Leslie broke his kneecap, and Ketchum started conducting the readings. Gertrude became suspicious when Ketchum bought a farm and racehorses and was the first in town to buy an automobile.

Edgar wrote to a patient asking if her reading had been beneficial, and she replied she had never received one. Ketchum had put Edgar in a trance for horse racing tips.

That breach of trust dissolved their partnership. Ketchum left town and Edgar never saw him again.

October 14

The attitudes have much to do with the general physical conditions. Let the attitudes be more of a constructive nature; more of patience, more of brotherly love, more of "give and take." 1819-1

Edgar and Ketchum were in different social circles in Hopkinsville. Ketchum was a social climber, while Edgar had no interest in belonging to the Elks, the Masons, or the Odd Fellows. He used the train tickets Ketchum bought to get him home from Alabama to diagnose his patients, and once he had done so, he was interested only in being with his family.

Happy to be able to help Ketchum himself, he gave him a reading about his frequent lower abdomen pain. Two fellow doctors agreed with Ketchum that the symptoms were like appendicitis, but he still wanted Edgar's psychic opinion.

Edgar said someday he would have to undergo a very difficult appendectomy, but his present pain was also related to having wrenched his spine some years ago. The readings prescribed manipulations to relieve it, and after nine osteopathic treatments, he was pain free.

FAST FORWARD: Years later Ketchum admitted that information from the readings about Elk's Club members helped him get admitted to the prestigious organization. Years later he also had to have an appendectomy, which was as complicated as Edgar had predicted.

October 15

But, as God's purpose is to GLORIFY the individual man (or soul) in the earth, so the highest purpose of an individual soul or entity is to glorify the Creative Energy or God in the earth...for He hath given His angels charge concerning thee, and THY god, thy face, is ever before the Throne of the Infinite. 338-3

On this day in 1900 Edgar took a picture of Theodore Roosevelt—a campaigning Republican vice presidential candidate—who was in Hopkinsville to speak at the Union Tabernacle.

Wearing his well-known Rough Rider hat and flashing a big smile, Roosevelt arrived by train and was transported by carriage to the Hotel Latham. Edgar captured him as he stepped out of a carriage at the hotel. This picture's negative may have been among many later destroyed by a fire in Edgar's studio.

***

On this day in 1933 the Archangel Halaliel made his first reading appearance at a study group meeting. They were on their fourteenth lesson, "Day and Night," the title spiritually symbolizing good and evil.

At the close of the reading Archangel Halaliel introduced himself and said they had no doubt gained from the words spoken "through this channel; Halaliel, that was with those in the beginning who warred with those that separated themselves and became as naught." (262-56) Halaliel spoke out in several future readings. Edgar's voice always changed when an angel spoke through him.

October 16

> Then, KARMIC forces - if the life application in the experience of an individual is made towards constructiveness, it grows and grows. For the individual entity GROWS to a haven of peace and harmony and understanding; or ye GROW to heaven, rather than going to heaven. Ye grow in grace, in knowledge, in understanding. 1436-1

Two days before on the last day of Edgar's New York visit, David Kahn conducted the first of four life readings for Morton Blumenthal, predicting worldly wealth in 1930 when he would be thirty-five. The reading advised him to use his worldly possessions correctly.

His incarnation as Achilles in Egypt was during the same era that Edgar, Gertrude, Hugh Lynn, and Gladys had dwelled there. He had killed Hector the Trojan prince, who the Cayces knew was now reincarnated in the body of Arthur Lammers.

He and his brother Edwin had been co-workers in the building of Jerusalem.

The reading said he had great power to help the lives of multitudes of people and to make the "realm beyond" better understood throughout the world.

In his incarnations he had developed so well that if he lived the present life well, he might not have to incarnate again.

FAST FORWARD: A later reading revealed he and his brother Edwin were Edgar's imaginary friends, visiting him as a child to prepare him for his future work.

October 17

Ye must be born in flesh, in spirit again, that ye may make manifest that ye have experienced in thine own soul.   262-60

By autumn of 1923 the universal consciousness that spoke through Edgar apparently decided he was ready to hear about reincarnation.

After the subject was first introduced in Arthur Lammers' October 11 reading, Edgar was surprised that it came up in a physical reading for himself. Insight of all questions manifested through other minds or souls could come through Edgar apparently because he had developed these psychic skills in previous lives. "For this soul has seen its seventh manifestation upon this physical earth plane."

References to prior lives kept popping into readings, even connecting Edgar and his four partners as previously working together for "destructive purposes."

An even bigger breakthrough came when Edgar discovered that the Forces were willing to answer questions. Soon he was receiving detailed information about earlier lives—the era, the nationality, the sex, the name, the occupation, the social status. Whether or not the entity had gained or declined during each incarnation was also revealed, and sometimes what karmic debt needed to be worked out in this life.

Edgar now knew his knowledge could do more than cure people's illnesses. Sharing that knowledge would become an important part of "the work."

October 18

> *...the Destiny of the Soul - as of all creation - is to be one with Him; continually growing, growing, for that association. What seeth man in nature? What seeth man in those influences that he becomes aware of? Change, ever; change, ever. Man hath termed this evolution, growth, life itself; but it continues to enter. That force, that power which manifests itself in separating - or as separate forces and influences in the earth, continues to enter; and then change; continuing to pour in and out. From whence came it? Whither does it go when it returns? So the Soul's activity in the earth, as it is seen in this or that phase of experience, is that it may be one with the Creative Forces, the Creative Energies.* 262-88

Edgar's reluctance to believe in reincarnation disappeared as readings repeatedly stressed a soul's purpose on earth was to become worthy of returning to companionship with God.

Readings kept confirming that the soul evolves through many lifetimes on earth until it reaches perfection. They either repeated what was said before or added new details. One reading never contradicted another, and they also agreed with recorded history.

Souls have free will, and they choose when and where to re-enter the earth according to the karmic debt they need to pay. They keep coming back until they owe no debt; then they've reached their goal of acceptance into eternal bliss in the company of God.

October 19

For HOME represents that of permanency, to the mind, to the body; in peace, in harmony, yet in doing good for goodness' sake...becomes as the overflowing blessings in many, many ways.   416-11

On this day in 1925 the Cayces completed their move into their Virginia Beach cottage. Though they considered the $35 a month rent exorbitant, they were happy to have their first house.

They didn't realize until cold November winds blew in that the living room fireplace was not adequate to heat the house. At Edgar's request, Morton financed a portable oil stove to help until they could afford a furnace.

Their first Sunday on the beach introduced them to unwelcoming Christians. After the Baptist service, Edgar asked about joining. The minister said he'd have to consult the congregation. They would never go back.

They had tried the Baptist Church because Virginia Beach didn't have a Christian Disciples of Christ church. The next Sunday they tried the Presbyterian Church and were warmly welcomed by the 40-some members.

As one would expect, Edgar taught a Bible class. Gladys sang in the choir, Hugh Lynn taught a Sunday school class, and Edgar Evans met at the church with a Boy Scout troop.

Just as their Sunday activity was always the same, so was Saturday's. On that day they took the trolley to Norfolk, went shopping, had dinner, and saw a movie.

Life at Virginia Beach was going to be just fine.

October 20

> (Q) What specific work did I come to this planet to do, and how much longer do I have to stay? (A) You have to stay so long as there are the needs for the unfoldment of those that have come to rely upon the entity! Where failure has come - not failure, but rather the neglect to hold to the opportunity presented at times. How long remain in this sphere? This alone may the inner consciousness dedicate, or indicate. 69-6

Edgar was pleased when a reading discounted the superstitious notion that humans could reincarnate as animals. He had read that the Hindus refused to kill cows because they may be their reincarnated grandfather or some other relative. They wouldn't kill beetles for the same reason.

This idea of transmigration was exposed as a false belief of ignorant people, but some sects in India still believe it. Hinduism does not support it, but does believe that all living beings have souls, even animals and plants.

Buddhists' belief stated in the *Bhagavad Gita* is that worn-out garments are shed by the body, and worn-out bodies are shed by the dweller within the body. New bodies are donned by the dweller (the soul) like new garments being donned by the body. They believe that a soul desires to be born to enjoy worldly pleasures, but Edgar's information says otherwise.

The cycle of rebirth ends when desire vanishes, when the soul has learned its lessons, paid its karmic dues, and earned the right to return to its original home.

October 21

> Be it true that there IS the fact of reincarnation, and that souls that once occupied such an environ are entering the earth's sphere and inhabiting individuals in the present, is it any wonder that - if they made such alterations in the affairs of the earth in their day, as to bring destruction upon themselves - if they are entering now, they might make many changes in the affairs of peoples and individuals in the present? Are they...BEING born into the world? If so, what WERE their environs - and what will those environs mean in a material world today?
>
> 364-1

The above quote was to a man who had lived in Atlantis, a highly evolved civilization that was wiped off the face of the earth because of their own misuse of advanced technologies.

As Atlanteans were reincarnating then in 1933, one can assume many former Atlanteans continued to come back to earth up to and including the present time.

They are here to pay their karmic debt, but the admonishment above poses the unspoken question: will they learn their lesson and gain in this reincarnation, or will they again follow a destructive path, hurt the earth, and need to come back again?

Readings pointed out if a client had gained or lost in specific lives on earth. Edgar's inner voice told one housewife who had persecuted the church and was a friend of Nero, who fiddled while Rome burned, that she "had advanced from a low degree to that which may not even necessitate a reincarnation in the earth." (5366-1)

October 22

(Q) Is the Celestial Sphere a definite place in the Universe or is it a state of mind? (A) When an entity, a soul, passes into any sphere, with that it has builded in its celestial body, it must occupy - to a finite mind - space, place, time. Hence, to a finite mind, a body can only be in a place, a position. An attitude, sure - for that of a onement with, or attunement with, the Whole. For, God is love; hence occupies a space, place, condition, and IS the Force that permeates all activity. 5794-4

On this day in 1935 the ghost of Edgar's close friend visited him at his Arctic Crescent home.

Edgar was in the living room listening to the radio when he became aware that Byron Wyrick had joined him. Byron, who had died on April 28, just six months earlier, had met death too early because of an accident.

He came to Edgar to deliver a message, and he called him by his last name. "Cayce," he said, "there is the survival of the personality. . . but [the life of prayer] is the only life to live."

The incident might have frightened most people, but Edgar probably accepted it as just one of his many clairvoyant experiences.

If Gertrude was surprised at this ghostly visitor, she would soon accept the strange lifestyle of living with a man who carried on one-sided conversations with visitors she couldn't see. Byron visited every Sunday night for many weeks, listening to the gospel hour with Edgar.

October 23

> *(Q) What is the soul of a body? (A) That which the Maker gave to every entity or individual in the beginning, and which is seeking the home or place of the Maker.* 3744-1

Before Edgar could fully accept reincarnation, he needed to be sure it was not contradictory to Biblical teachings.

A reading about Gnosticism revealed it was commonly accepted until outlawed by early church leaders who didn't want individuals to have a choice of blaming a past life for this life's inadequacies.

They perpetuated the belief that good actions and attitudes in *this* life would be the only thing needed to have a blissful afterlife. That belief may have encouraged many to walk the straight and narrow, but a reading said there are no shortcuts.

In the Bible Peter writes about one's earthly sojourn —by definition a temporary stay—and mentions "being born again."

Jesus told Nicodemus, "Except a man be born again, he cannot enter the kingdom of heaven." (John 3:3)

Three disciples saw Jesus transfigured as Elijah and Moses appeared. (Matthew 17:1-13) Jesus told them to tell no one about the vision and implied that Elijah had already come back as John the Baptist.

Disciples asked about a blind man, "Master, who did sin, this man or his parents, that he was born blind?" (John 9:1,2) They not only believed in reincarnation, they understood karmic law.

October 24

Little by little does ONE come to the understanding of the PURPOSE for which they came into the earth. Purpose is of the MAKINGS of the individual, PLUS that GIVEN in the beginning, and as souls seek the Father, in that companionship that one may have through communion with Him....　　　　　　　　　　　　　99-8

An edict in 553 by the Emperor Justinian may have been the reason the Bible contained so few references to reincarnation.

He called the Second Council of Constantinople for the express purpose of condemning the writings of one of the era's most renowned theologians, Origen of Alexandria.

Origen believed the canons adopted in the Council of Nicea in 397 and—probably some that were not chosen to be included—supported the pre-existence of souls, multiple ages of souls, and the eventual restoration of all souls to a state of dynamic perfection with the godhead. In a simpler word: reincarnation.

Emperor Justinian's wife Theodora had been sexually promiscuous and wanted the canons to assure her of heaven, without the need for coming back to earth again. She elicited a deathbed promise for Justinian to grant her this wish. He fulfilled her wish.

Origen's writing and those of his followers were denounced and declared evil, and references to reincarnation were purged from the canons. Fortunately, they missed a few, probably many more than those cited on the October 23 page.

October 25

Each soul that enters, then, must have had an impetus from some beginning that is of the Creative Energy, or of a first cause... The first cause was, that the created would be the companion for the Creator; that it, the creature, would - through its manifestations in the activity of that given unto the creature - show itself to be not only worthy of, but companionable to, the Creator.
5753-1

Readings found that souls choose the mothers they expect will be best for them to learn necessary lessons in this incarnation. Souls retain memories of all their lives and know how they gained or lost in those incarnations.

They enter a mother either shortly before birth, at the moment of birth, or shortly after birth—as much as 24 hours. The fetus is like an auto that can be built and started, but not driven until the driver enters the car.

A pregnant woman asked Edgar, "What mental attitude should I keep during the coming months?" The Forces replied, "It depends upon the type of entity you desire. If you wish a musical, artistic entity, then think about music, beauty, and art. Do you wish it to be purely mechanical? In that case, think about mechanics—work with such things. And don't think this won't have its effect! Here's something every mother should know. The attitude held during pregnancy has much to do with the character of the soul that would choose to enter through this channel." (2803-6)

Edgar was so right to want to share the information!

October 26

Then seek associations first with those whose principles, whose motto is first and foremost: "I serve that I may be the more able to serve better" and in those lines, those channels that have to do with the building up of materials, their structure, their construction, their application in the part such plays in the lives of individuals.
4341-1

On this day in 1929 Morton came to Virginia Beach for a reading to clarify actions in the stock market.

During the summer and autumn, both Morton and his brother Edwin had received several readings warning them of a coming stock market catastrophe. Morton's trip this day was to pinpoint details.

In a previous reading a spiritual guide speaking through Edgar had told Morton that one of his largest well-margined accounts could be wiped out. A reading this day confirmed it could happen the next day.

Morton bemoaned that the client's portfolio in question held the same stocks as the Blumenthals' account which was "well margined" and could be "wiped out."

The spiritual guide said it was best to sell and then buy back later at a lower price.

Morton, who had asked for readings frequently during the past five years, didn't contact Edgar again until November 15. He continued with readings for many months after the crash.

In February of 1931 he began proceedings to undo all the good he had helped Edgar accomplish.

October 27

(Q) What relation has karma to my present development, and how can I overcome karma? (A) This possibly to the entity, to the body-consciousness of [257]would require a whole dissertation in itself. The body little understands the MEANING of karma - but to answer same in a few words: That depends upon whether the ACTUAL of the innate forces are kept in accord with that not as HEARSAY, but as to that KNOWN by the body to be GOD'S way! Karma is, then, that that has been in the past builded as INDIFFERENCE to that KNOWN to be right! Taking chances, as it were - "will do better tomorrow - this suits my purpose today - I'll do better tomorrow." Karma is that; making that correction.
257-78

In his altered state of consciousness, Edgar was able to tell people how karmic debts accumulated in past lives were causing problems in this life. He gave much advice on how to correct the problems and much counsel on the proper attitude to take.

"The approach," he said, "should always be in the attitude of 'Not my will, but thine, O God, be done in and through me.'"

Karma is a debt, or a deficit, or a deficiency caused by the lack of awareness of one's spiritual identity, leading to the absence of spiritual qualities. Because most humans forget from whence all came, most also forget their purpose on earth is to qualify to return.

What goes around comes around. Readings define karma as action-reaction. It is universal law.

October 28

As self enters into that consciousness where the influences from without are being tempered by that desired and willed within the soul of self, there may come that which will be both helpful and beneficial, and constructive in the experience of self for others. 443-3

On this day in 1933 a turbaned East Indian appeared in a vision to Edgar for the second time. Several years had passed since he came to him years before to deliver a message about his health. This time Edgar was in New York, alone in the library of the Zentgraf family whom the Cayces and Gladys were visiting. He had been fighting a cold for three weeks.

When he joined the others and asked Gladys to cancel all his New York appointments, they knew by looking at him that something momentous had occurred.

Soon he ran a fever that forced him to bed. A doctor came, diagnosed him with pneumonia, ordered him taken to a hospital, and called an ambulance.

He told Hugh Lynn to lock him in the bedroom and not let anyone in until he awoke. He went into a trance and perspired so much that sweat dripped off the sheets to the floor. The doctor pounded on the door for admittance, and the Zentgrafs demanded to be let in, but Hugh Lynn obeyed his father.

When Edgar awoke, the confused doctor couldn't understand how, but he confirmed that he was well.

Edgar never revealed what message the East Indian brought that day, but it seems to have saved his life.

October 29

For, remember, it is not all of life just to live nor yet all of death to die. For it is self that one has to meet. And what ye sow - mentally, spiritually, physically - that ye WILL eventually reap. And the laborer is worthy of his hire; or that effort, that purpose for which ye as an entity plan, consider, has already brought in eternity its own shadow of things to be.   257-249

Edgar's readings are sprinkled with phrases pinpointing where and when present karmic debts originated. What happened "on that plane" influenced "this experience." Attitudes in "that sphere" caused turmoil in "the present sphere."

Karma is a psychological law, and physical circumstances are merely the means of fulfilling a psychological purpose. A reading with Edgar could be compared to having a psychiatrist help work out one's unwelcome predicaments.

Readings never suggested that any present-life affliction had been instigated by a former victim of the individual. Karmic dues seem to be accurately apportioned—an accident kills one not another, disfigures one, leaves another unscratched.

The test for determining if one's present dilemmas are because of past-life errors is to ask: "Have I done something in this life to deserve this?" If not, what past-life action might have precipitated the problem?

Logic might lead us to find one's karma and overcome it.

October 30

> Man should learn - should learn - it is God that giveth the increase. Man as he labors, as has been given of old, is worthy of his hire. To take advantage, then, of an employee because of circumstance, because of surroundings - or for the employee to take advantage of the employer because of any condition that arises - must be met in the experience of them all. For it is the law; and the law shall not pass away until it is fulfilled to every whit and every tittle in the experiences of each individual! 257-182

Readings said individuals may correct karma by gaining spiritual qualities they lack and embracing their own spiritual identity. They must approach this redemption in a spirit of willingness, not rebellion.

Of course, individuals create their own karma in this present life and have opportunities to correct mistakes and not carry them into a reincarnation.

The treatment for afflictions caused by karma is to make an honest acknowledgment of a past obligation, have an honest willingness to meet that obligation, and finally affirm having the needed strength which—being absent before—led to the karma to begin with.

The readings' point of view is: This is your karma. Here is what you can do about it.

The continuation of the above quote said, "For the Lord thy God is a living God. Man's soul, man's activity, is a living experience. Begin to build constructively in the beginning, if you would have the success in all phases of the endeavor."

October 31

Evil only creates fear and hate and sorrow and the lack of tolerance, the lack of faith and the lack of patience, the lack of hope, the lack of love and longsuffering and brotherly kindness. These only have their shadows in the activity of individuals toward their fellow man. DIVINITY blossoms as in the morning sun of light and hope of immortality....   1298-1

In 1892 at the age of fifteen Edgar attended a rally in Hopkinsville for presidential nominee Grover Cleveland, who was trying to regain the office he had lost to Benjamin Harrison.

The event was festive, with banners and flags creating a carnival atmosphere. Saloons were doing a booming business, and outside one Edgar observed two drunk men in a fight that led to a bloody shooting.

That incident took the fun out of the event for Edgar. Always soft-hearted, he had no desire to witness more violence. He immediately went home.

In future years he learned that the Forces felt the same way about violence, saying that "Anger causes poisons to be secreted from the glands. Joy has the opposite effect." (281-54)

"The spirit of hate, the anti-Christ, is contention, strife, fault-finding, lovers of self, lovers of praise. Those are the anti-Christ, and take possession of groups, masses, and show themselves even in the lives of men." (281-208)

November 1

As the Law of the Lord is perfect, so be ye perfect in desire, in purpose, in aim; that the glory of the Father may be made manifest more and more in the lives of others. Well hast thou chosen in Him, for as He blesses thee so may YE bless others.   281-23

In this month in 1911 Ketchum made a huge bet to prove Edgar's credibility. The gesture was not to advance Edgar's interests, but to save his own medical license. The Christian County Medical Society had charged that the treatments Ketchum gave patients based on Edgar's diagnoses were all fake.

Before sending the resolution to revoke Ketchum's license to the governor and attorney general, the CCMS scheduled a local meeting to discuss suspending his license. With fifty-some doctors in attendance, the meeting started with an announcement of the names of doctors who would take the resolution to the capitol at Frankfort. Ketchum was given a chance to defend himself.

He arranged two stacks of $500 each and, after a brief discourse about Edgar's unusual capabilities, he made a bet. He asked that six doctors choose their most complex case and have Edgar go into a trance to diagnose each one. If any diagnosis was wrong, he would donate the $1,000 to a Christian County charity of their choice.

A motion was made for further investigation before taking the resolution to Frankfort. His license was saved.

November 2

For, the soul seeks growth; as Truth, as Life, as Light, IS in itself. God IS, and so is life, light, truth, hope, love. And those that abide in same, grow. Those that abide in the shadow of the night, or the conditions that become or make for the fruits of these, do not grow....Study to show self approved.   257-123

On this day in 1924 Morton Blumenthal visited the Cayces in Dayton and was appalled to find them living in what he called "sheer poverty."

Edgar and Morton were immediate friends, and he invited the Cayces and Gladys to New York, where they were his guests at the Hotel Cambridge in early 1925.

He treated them to a Broadway play and a jaunt to the Silver Slipper nightclub. Edwin Blumenthal's wife took Gladys and Gertrude on a shopping expedition, buying them new dresses and picking up the tab for lunch at a fancy restaurant.

Morton was attracted to Adeline Levy but worried because she scoffed at Edgar's psychic powers. A reading said she was ideal for Morton.

Morton became Edgar's benefactor, paying a weekly $50 retainer and Gladys $25 weekly for transcribing and sending the readings to New York. He wanted readings on the stock market and on the life of Jesus.

FAST FORWARD: Morton and Adeline married in June 1925. A reading identified her as Helen of Troy, and Morton as Achilles had waged war on Troy to rescue her.

November 3

MANY have the entity contacted, both those of state and church; those of art, those of the music, those of...experiences that may be taken of that as necessary to make for an exceptional individual.   403-1

On this day in 1925 Edgar Evans started school at Professor Francis H. Green's School for Boys in Virginia Beach. Edgar's psychic skills had not gained notoriety among the locals, so Edgar Evans didn't have to contend with tormenting taunts from his fellow students, as Hugh Lynn had been forced to endure.

He was an excellent, detail-oriented student who kept careful records of everything he did, down to the last dime he spent.

By age ten he was building mechanical devices without any help. He was a good writer and would graduate as valedictorian with the highest grades ever accomplished at that school.

Although while making gunpowder, he accidentally caused an explosion, it wasn't fooling around with his inventions that injured him: it was a cinder from the fireplace.

The family had been at the beach around a year, when a cinder caught his flannel pajamas on fire. Gertrude came to his screams and put out the fire, but his left side was scarred for life. A reading said not to cut a tendon, as doctors recommended, knowing it would leave him with a limp. Scarred or not, he didn't limp and became very athletic, excelling in both football and golf.

November 4

Remembering, even though He were the Son, yet learned He obedience by...things... He suffered. Not, then, in vain-glorying; not then in the amount of moneys, lands, holdings, houses, cattles, nor gold - but in that ability to serve thine brother lies strength, security, and the perfect knowledge of God.   900-370

After many early Virginia Beach readings for Morton Blumenthal and his brother Edwin, dreams started becoming the focus in Edgar's time in a trance.

The brothers had almost exclusive use of Edgar's skills, just as Morton wanted. He financed the family's relocation to the beach to have Edgar closer for private meetings and for quicker mailing of their transcripts.

Because both brothers were stockbrokers, their questions to the Forces usually involved the stock market, but they were also highly interested in Jesus—perhaps unusual for two Jewish New Yorkers.

A reading way before Virginia Beach told both to "pay more attention to dreams, for truths are given."

Readings named close to two hundred symbols they contained: A baby (new venture), blood (person's health), fire (fear), hair (reasoning process). However, symbols could mean different things—according to their relevance—to different people.

Dream interpretation helped the Blumenthal brothers become millionaires. Once Morton started a fundraising campaign to build the hospital: next he had enough money to finance it himself. He truly believed in "the work" and supported it—mentally and physically.

November 5

Let them: power, might, position, whether that of in money, in prestige, in social or authority not be first and foremost. "Money," I use same to better expression, to better manifest my conception of my Creator or myself, for truly, does not one build that which it (self) occupies? Then in the change there is good to come, for bound about the narrowness of others, self finds little opportunity for expression.   **4341-1**

In 1926 the Blumenthals were very generous with the Cayces, buying them a 35th Street house and their very first automobile, a new Ford. Plus, the brothers seemed serious about wanting to build a hospital.

By mail they solicited paid memberships for the Association of National Invesigators, but ended up with only $5,500, plus lots of resentment for new clients for having been asked.

They came up with the idea of opening in Edgar's name a stock market account dedicated to financing the hospital. People who knew Edgar well invested almost $20,000 for the fund which was left entirely in Morton's hands.

Most stock market tips didn't come through Edgar's usual sources, but from their dreams about the brothers' deceased relatives and financially astute friends.

Whatever the source, the advice worked, for in a short time both brothers were millionaires. They paid for the hospital. With or without Edgar's dedicated fund is not certain.

November 6

This is the greatest trouble of most, my friend, in saying that conditions are imposed by God when they are the demands of errors committed in self! The command has always been to show ourselves worthy not only to the natural laws of the Creator of God, but "If ye will be my people I will be thy God." 257-128

Parents were concerned that their boy started bed-wetting when his baby sister was born. They made sure the sister got no more attention than he did, but he kept bedwetting.

When he was three years old, they took him to a psychiatrist. Five years passed with a wet bed nightly.

The parents took him to many specialists, then psychiatrists again, and then to Edgar at age eleven.

The boy had been a Puritan minister at the time of the witchcraft trials. He was a stool-dipper, performing the accepted custom of strapping supposed witches on stools and dipping them into a pool of cold water. He was now receiving what he had given: unwanted wetness.

Edgar's Forces told parents to use suggestions of a spiritual nature before he went to sleep at night.

His mother told him, "You are going to make many people happy. You are going to help everyone with whom you come in contact." She continued with the same idea for five to ten minutes. For the first time in nine years, he didn't wet the bed. She gave such suggestions for several months, then only once a week, and then not at all. His karma was overcome.

November 7

For as is seen and as has been given, one (each entity) must give an account of every idle word spoken, see? To whom? To self and self's service to others, and to the Creator of All Things. For we are co-operators with the divine forces as are seen, as are manifested in the physical world, that this entity loves the phenomena of so well. 257-10

A Catholic's parents wanted him to be a priest, but he did not feel the call. He was concerned that he had an urge toward homosexuality.

He had been a satirist and a gossip-monger in the French court, and he especially loved exposing gay scandals in the court with his cartoonist skill.

His reading said something applicable not just to him but to all of us: "Condemn not, then that you be not condemned. What measure you mete it shall be measured to you again. And what you condemn in another, that you become in yourself."

Edgar's inner voice repeated the same message time and time again to person after person, admonishing that actions should be "founded in the truth as of the spirit, and ever in the ways 'as I would have my fellow man do to me,' then that's the way and manner in which thou will be acted towards by thy fellow man! That is all the command of God. Do that." (257-128)

A very similar Bible command is "Judge not, that ye be not judged. For with what judgment ye judge, ye shall be judged."

November 8

To do wrong never will make good come of it... Good is like a leaven that eventually leaveneth the whole lump. How is evil? Usually smeared on as some kinds of paints that cover and yet - How did He put it? - are as a whitened sepulchre, beautiful to look at but inwardly full of dead men's bones! So are the relationships with individuals. You cannot whitewash that which is in import and intent evil and have good come from same. 257-182

A woman caught a venereal disease because of her husband's infidelity. Several times he had even brought other women into their home.

Edgar's Forces found that she had been shamelessly unfaithful during a French court experience when her present husband had been her principal lover.

In another incarnation she was the illegitimate daughter of one of Commodore Perry's sailors and a Japanese girl. Feeling an outcast, she abandoned herself to sensual pleasure, infecting many men.

Infidelity sometimes occurs through karmic necessity. Immoral behavior will have its payback.

It's best to be good! Edgar said, "This has always been...the laws given thy peoples; that if the manifestations given to thee in trust as to the world's forces are used in the manner that thou givest out peace and harmony, then the fruits of the spirit are the result; not imposed by God but the actual results of the endeavors in self, as to what thou doest in...thy relationships to thy God and thy fellow man." (257-182)

November 9

Then, let thy steps be in the way of light, that these may bring - not only to self but to those that are dependent upon self - those things that make for the worth while. For, as given, a good name is to be chosen rather than great riches.   257-123

On this date in 1928 whether or not Edgar should give a psychic demonstration at the upcoming dedication of the hospital was settled by a reading which said, "It would not be in keeping the [the hospital's] best interest...Let that as may be accomplished be well spoken of, and do not parade that that is holy."

Edgar always felt his psychic ability was God-given, and this reading indicated the Forces that spoke to him held the same opinion. He knew that his psychic abilities should be used only for a higher, moral purpose. When he'd been tricked into using them for a bad reason, he had suffered headaches.

When he sought higher intelligence for locating oil, a reading told him that the oil ventures would not succeed unless all involved sought a worthy purpose.

A reading had given him the go-ahead to give stock tips to Morton Blumenthal, whose wealth was now financing the hospital. Now doctors would be close by to administer the readings' cures on ailing patients whose own doctors had given up on them.

The information Edgar received while in a trance was always right.

November 10

Be not discouraged because the way seems hard at times. Know that He heareth thee. For as He hath given, "If ye will keep my law - " And what is His law? It is to love the Lord, to eschew evil - which is the whole duty of man - love they neighbor as thyself.   1747-5

On this day in 1931 Edgar, Gertrude, and Gladys were arrested for pretending to tell fortunes in a New York hotel.

They were there to give readings for A.R.E. members because after the hospital closed, they were once again struggling financially.

Edgar's health went downhill, and in three months he lost twenty pounds. Readings told him to stay in Virginia Beach, but warned to make changes or his health could become a serious condition. One change needed was more monetary security.

Gladys appealed by mail to A.R.E. members and some money came in October for train fare to New York, to give readings arranged by David Kahn and other members.

A hotel guest Bertha Gorman begged throughout the day for an appointment, so when the 3 p.m. appointment cancelled, Gladys gave her that time slot.

After her reading, she and her companion announced they were undercover policewomen, and an officer arrived and arrested Edgar, Gertrude, and Gladys for pretending to tell fortunes. The press had been alerted and gave their arrest spectacular coverage.

All three went to jail.

November 11

Thy prayers, thy supplications have been heard, and...as these are manifested in thy...associations with thy fellow man, so does that assurance grow in the knowledge and the wisdom of the Most High. 1301-1

On this day in 1928 Morton Blumenthal, who had financed construction of the newly built hospital, formally turned it over to the Association of National Investigators.

Crowds who filled the lecture hall for the dedication ceremony were touched when Edgar said with great emotion, "When your prayers are answered, you find out that prayers are about the only things that words are good for, so there's nothing to say, except to give thanks."

The keynote speaker was Dr. William Mosely Brown, Hugh Lynn's psychology professor from Washington and Lee University, who noted the years of effort, work, perseverance, and devotion to "a new and little-recognized cause...for the benefit of mankind" that preceded this special day.

***

On this day in 1931 Edgar, Gertrude, and Gladys went on trial, charged in New York for pretending to tell fortunes.

Judge Francis J. Erwin took only a few minutes to hand down his verdict of not guilty. "I find as a fact that Mr. Cayce and his co-defendants were not pretending to tell fortunes...." The verdict didn't get the same publicity as the arrest.

November 12

Purpose is of the MAKINGS of the individual ….communion with Him means DOING; not shutting self away from thine brother, from thine neighbor, even from thine self - rather APPLYING self to the duties material, mental AND spiritual, as IS known. 99-81

A New York City telegraph operator became curious about the strange telegrams she was asked to send to Virginia Beach. She decided to come to Virginia Beach for a life reading for herself.

Edgar told her she was wasting her time as a telegraph operator. She should study commercial art because she had been a noted artist in several past lifetimes. She took this advice seriously and put herself through art school. She became a successful commercial artist and transformed her personality in the process.

Readings often gave vocational advice "in developing a plan, or a manner of seeking ways in which individuals might give expression of the latent faculties and powers from their material sojourns." (5753-3)

A retired Navy inspector finally understood his obsession with gems. He had traded trinkets and firewater with Indians, had been a Persian merchant who dealt with pearls, opals, and lapis lazuli, and had sewn precious stones into priests' garments in the Holy Land. He devoted the rest of his life to lines of research suggested in his life reading. We all might have latent talents or attractions just waiting to be explored.

November 13

Study to show thyself approved unto God, a workman not ashamed, rightly dividing the words of truth, and keeping SELF unspotted from the world - of condemnation. For, with what judgement ye mete it is measured to thee again…. Keep the faith.   2800-2

On this day in 1888 at age eleven, Edgar officially became a Christian and was baptized by immersion in the Little River close to Beverly.

He had been a member of Liberty Church since January 1887 and surprised members by attending the adult Bible study and even the church elders' meetings.

They were surely impressed by the lengthy scriptures he could recite from memory and the interpretations that came so easy to him.

Reading the Bible had become a natural habit for him, and he was determined to keep his vow to read it all the way through every year of his life.

He was appointed as the church sexton, a position no child before him had ever held.

Being sexton was hard work. He was responsible for cleaning the outhouses and stocking the coal bin. On winter Sundays he built the fire in the stove and on all Sundays he prepared communion.

Before long he would also become one of the church's youngest Sunday school teachers. The Cayces had not been churchgoers, and whether their son's interest in religion lured them to attend church is not known.

November 14

For the home is the nearest pattern in earth (where there is unity of purpose in the companionship) to man's relationship to his Maker. For it is ever creative in purpose from personalities and individualities coordinated for a cause, an ideal. Keep it. 3577-1

On this day in 1925 Gertrude, Gladys, and 5-year-old Edgar Evans joined Edgar in Dayton. Hugh Lynn stayed in Selma to finish his junior year in school.

When Edgar hired Gladys, he had told her they might be leaving Alabama, and he surely must have been pleased for her to move with the family.

Edgar met them at the Cincinnati train station and took them to Dayton's Phillips Hotel where they would stay until their furniture arrived for a small efficiency, which would be their crowded home for many months.

Arthur Lammers was responsible for Edgar's decision to give up his photography and psychic diagnostician business in Selma. But now Lammers had not given the expected financial support, and he had not referred friends and family to get Edgar's skills known in this new location.

The family was almost broke and clients were in very short supply. Though they lacked money, they had an abundance of time. What better way to spend it than to have readings about their past lives?

They discovered they were all connected in previous lives. They began to realize that souls traveled to earth in groups. Edgar wanted to provide better for his.

November 15

Repeat three times every day, and then listen: "LORD, WHAT WOULD THOU HAVE ME DO TODAY?" Have this not as rote. Mean it! For as He has spoken, as He has promised, "If ye call I will hear, and answer speedily." He meant it! Believe it! 3003-1

On this day in 1929 Jesus came through Edgar's mouth in a reading for Morton Blumenthal, a Jewish stockbroker who asked for two kinds of readings: some to get tips on the stock market, and others to ask questions about Jesus.

Today's reading said, "Take this and keep it with thee in thy heart, and in thine mind always. With power of money, with position, and wealth, comes great responsibility."

Morton asked if the voice came from Jesus. The answer was: "He speaks with thee often in thy meditations and prayers."

Morton had asked Edgar in a previous November 2 reading if he should get out of the market and was told to stay out for a few days. "Let not the minds be troubled," the Froces said. "Let not the bodies become overwearied. Let not the mental come unbalanced by the clamor or the unsettledness as is arising at this time."

In Morton's November 16 dream, a diver was trying to save people from downing in the sea. The reading said the dream was about the plunging stock market.

Morton continued readings with Edgar until March 30, 1930—five months after the stock market crash.

November 16

> *(Q) Did I come here to do a specific work? (A) As ALL have a specific work, so are the activities of self to be in cleansing self's own understanding and enabling others to find the way to know themselves and Him.*   69-3

    Individuals in earlier societies still had enough soul memory to know that they had a purpose in this existence. This certainty became obvious in many readings of people who had been ancient Egyptians.

    Priests and priestesses in the Temple Beautiful advised students of vocations appropriate to their karmic problems and karmic gifts. Then they made a life seal representing the entity's past pattern of development to serve as a reminder of their objective in this life.

    A young woman who came to Edgar had provided music in the Temple Beautiful to raise vibrations for meditating and healing. She had also devised body-beautiful diets and designed elaborate life seals.

    Edgar advised her to be either a nutritionist or a musician and to use meditation to reach super-consciousness and see other souls' histories. Music became her profession, and she made life seals non-commercially.

    Readings explained that each soul passes from one sphere to another, becomes conscious about itself in that sphere, and becomes conscious of what the soul attained "in a materially manifested way or manner."

    Individuals either gain or lose, grow or remain stagnant in their ongoing journey back to their maker.

November 17

Do not allow the worry of business to overshadow spiritual development. Do not think that these may be separated, or that these may be run as one - no! for each in its own sphere, each in its own pace, apart - yet ever one; for in applying self comes understanding of business, and also spiritual knowledge comes through application of spiritual truths.   39-4

The Forces within Edgar sometimes told people things they didn't want to hear.

A dissatisfied real estate agent came to Edgar for advice about what new field he should pursue. He did not like his job, and his customers did not seem to like him—a bad situation for someone whose paycheck depended upon commissions.

His personality difficulties were the problem. He had been a harsh, dictatorial teacher in a past life, and those traits had carried over to the present, making it difficult for him to be social and outgoing.

"Don't change jobs," the reading told him. Instead he should make every effort to become more congenial.

Edgar said, "For, while it is not always easy, you are learning a needed lesson."

If he didn't learn the lesson in this life, he would have to learn the lesson in a later life.

Many similar cases are in the readings, making it very clear that individuals cannot run away from their karma. The more one tries to avoid rather than overcome karma, the longer it takes for the journey home.

November 18

Remember thou art the God within thine own self that may make or break thine own spirit to accomplish that as is set before thee, for ever is it true, "I am with thee, and will not forsake thee, even though you are compassed about by shadows, doubts, and many rabbles," yet keep thine heart in attunement, and EVERY condition will open in the right time, place, and manner. Keep thine self aright - all will come well! 39-4

Some people ignore the profession they chose before incarnation. A 31-year-old man consulted Edgar wanting to know if he were too old to pursue a medical career.

His father was a doctor, and he had every opportunity to study medicine, but he had not. Now he badly wanted to be a doctor, but feared it was too late.

The reading told him his determination to be a doctor arose during the American Revolution when he was an orderly and messenger.

He was filled with pity at the suffering he witnessed and longed to know how to relieve it. For that reason his soul chose a doctor as a father, but he got off track.

"Yes!" The voice coming from Edgar was emphatic. The man was not too old. He should definitely enroll in medical school.

Many readings expressed that individuals should follow what their hearts tell them to do. The reason for a particular yearning may be good karma pointing the way to something that will bring great achievement and satisfaction.

November 19

Let that mind be in thee as was in Him, "Thy will, O God, be done in and through me; yet I claim, I desire, I EXPECT His strength to sustain me." 1614-2

On this day in 1882 Edgar's baby brother Thomas was born, but he lived for only ten days, plunging his mother Carrie into a deep depression which lasted all winter, and asthma bothered her all her life.

FAST FORWARD: In the 1920s Edgar's reading on his best friend's baby, Cayce Jones, said the baby could provide proof of reincarnation. "Let your mother see the child; she will recognize him as he will her."

Edgar's mother died before Edgar had a chance to get her together with the Jones baby. Would she have recognized him as Thomas, the baby she had lost?

When Edgar visited his friend in 1927, little Cayce begged to go home with him, saying he wanted to be with his family. The boy was so insistent that Edgar could not leave that night until the boy was asleep.

He didn't see the child until eight years later. Little Cayce wouldn't go into his room without one of his parents. Even without a reading Edgar realized little Cayce was manifesting psychic abilities and was fearful of a ghost. Edgar told the boy that any living thing accompanying him to his room would stop the ghost's vibrations—a caged bird, a potted plant, a pet—because "life is God." The boy could enter his room alone now, but he didn't want to. He packed his suitcase to go home with Edgar.

November 20

GC: You will give at this time information which may stimulate in the hearts and minds of those gathered here a greater appreciation of the true spirit of Thanksgiving...and which may be to all those to whom it is sent an inspiration and an explanation for Thanksgiving even in the face of personal problems and spreading worldwide fears and hatreds that seem to dominate so many minds today.

EC: Yes, we have the subject here; and many there be that appear with the desire to give their own interpretation upon such a subject. But rather would we choose - from the more universal need of those here, as well as mankind everywhere - that thought, that purpose, that attribute of man's choice to show, to give thanksgiving for not only the blessings as may be the experience of many but the fuller meaning of the appreciation of Life itself and the opportunity which is offered to all through same to become more and more aware of their relationship to the Creative Force or God.

On this day in 1938 Gertrude's request and Edgar's answer in this reading (3976-21) for the A.R.E. study group are just as applicable today as is his message: "Let this day of Thanksgiving be not only that wherein to enjoy that which may satiate the body, that which may make for the gratifying of appetites of the body, but that day when each of you may give thanks to God for BEING alive - with the opportunities to raise thy voice in prayer, in praise, in thanksgiving for the love He hath shown, that He showers upon thee day by day!"

November 21

While storms and trials are necessary in every soul, as we see manifested in nature, only in contentment does GROWTH make manifest. Not contentment to that point of satisfaction, for a satisfied mind or soul ceases to seek. But only in contentment may it receive and give out. In GIVING does a soul grow, even as a tree, even as a rock, even as a sunset, even as a world GROWS in its influence upon that about it. So has that force grown that we find manifested in the earth that we worship as constructive influence of God.   699-1

On this day in 1944 Edgar's wish to return to Virginia Beach for his final days was granted.

Edgar Evans, a captain home on leave from a long overseas military duty, arranged for Virginia Beach's new rescue squad to bring an ambulance for the trip. Norfolk's Dr. C.W. Irvin came along to care for Edgar en route.

The Forces had told him in his last reading: "Let not your hearts be troubled, neither let it be afraid, for, 'Lo, it is I, and I have promised to be with thee, even unto the end of the world.' Ye have much work to do. Ye have many helpers. Be not dismayed or troubled." (294-212)

Throughout his lifetime Edgar had known that things would work out for him, and here was one final proof.

He may have looked pitiful being carried from the ambulance to his house on a stretcher, but his heart must have leapt with thanks. He wept, but he was very happy.

November 22

It will be found that there has been no experience that may not be used as a steppingstone for greater successes, whether for the advancement for the material side or for the mental and spiritual aptitudes and forces of the entity's experience. 2136-1

Whatever is happening at any moment is completely appropriate for one's inner development. No matter how terrible a bad experience feels, you can choose to grow from it, rather than sink into its misery.

No effort is ever wasted. Karma penalizes us for evil conduct, but it also rewards us for constructive effort. At every moment we are creating our own future and dictating the terms of how it will happen.

If we had to choose just one bit of wisdom from Edgar's reading, it should be: "Spirit is the life, mind is the builder, physical is the result."

Think good thoughts. That's the advice. Chase away bad ones. Remember Edgar's favorite mantra, "Not my will, but thine, O God."

A well-to-do woman asked how she could best serve humanity. Edgar told her, "In those ways that open to you day by day. It isn't always the individual that plans to accomplish some great deed that does the most. It is the one who meets the opportunities and privileges which are accorded it day by day."

Another was told, "Be what you should be where you are, and when you have proven yourself, He will give you better ways!" That promise is for all of us.

November 23

Hence the entity develops THROUGH the varied spheres of the earth and its solar system, and the com-panions of varied experiences in that solar system, or spheres of development or activity; as in some ways accredited correctly to the planetary influences in an experience. The entity develops THROUGH those varied spheres.   5753-1

Between sojourns on earth, souls learn lessons on other planets.

On Mercury we become gifted in writing, com-munication, and understanding. Venus is the planet of love, especially brotherly love for our fellow humans.

Entities go to Mars to learn how to manage anger and wrath. Jupiter is the planet of strength.

Saturn is purgatory, where souls go to cleanse themselves of negative traits.

Uranus is the planet of extremes, and souls who sojourn there tend to be either very good or very bad people. Neptune is the planet of mystics, the closest souls come to clairvoyance.

This reading also said, "the sun, the moon, the stars, the position in the heavens or in all of the host of the solar systems that the earth occupies—all have their influence in the same manner (this is a very crude illustration, but very demonstrative) that the effect of a large amount of any element would attract a compass. Drawn to? Why? Because of the influence of which the mind element of a soul, an entity, has become conscious."

November 24

...one may apply ... these conditions in the earth's experience and develop toward that mark of higher calling as is set in Him - for it is not all of life to live, nor all of death to die; for one is the beginning of the other, and in the midst of life one is in the midst of death - in death one begins in that birth into which the earthly application of the inmost intents and desires as applied in respect to will's forces, that given by the Creative Energy, that one might make self equal with that Energy.
2842-2

The sun and the moon are also common sojourns for souls, but the readings do not spell out what lessons can be learned there. The Forces said t souls sojourning on the moon may be at the mercy of their emotions. They may have abrupt changes of mood, and—as children—are often accused of being fickle. Their moon sojourn may be to discover what they want from life.

Arcturus was a "usual but unusual step for an entity." Those going there were given permission to leave the solar system. They may come back either to learn certain lessons or to share their knowledge on earth.

To overcome negative karma, souls sometimes choose what we humans would call a bad life. To souls, though, a lifetime on earth is as quick as fireworks in the sky. Put in perspective, consider how short an earthly life of seventy-five years actually is in comparison to eternity.

Each soul that enters earth has an impetus to finish its schooling and return to its original home with God.

November 25

Desire! DESIRE! Hence Desire is the opposite of Will. Will and Desire, one with the Creative Forces of Good, brings all its influence in the realm of activity that makes for that which is constructive in the experience of the soul, the mind, the body, one with the spirit of truth.   5752-3

In 1964 many years after Edgar's earthly death, his readings saved a doomed composer-conductor who, in his mid-fifites, gave up all hopes of continuing with his renowned career.

Alan Hovhaness suffered with bursitis and arthritis, both taking over his arms so badly that he could no longer lift them above his waist. His conducting career that was enjoyed by audiences around the world was finished. He wanted badly to be a maestro again.

His wife persuaded him to see Harold J. Reilly, a physiotherapist who began treating Edgar's referrals in 1931. Patients arrived at his door with a transcript of their readings, with very explicit instructions about what Reilly was to do. He and the patients had consistently been very pleased with the results, and Reilly continued to use Edgar's treatments with similar diagnoses.

For Hovhaness he adjusted his vertebrae and limbs, massaged him to stimulate blood, lymph, and glands; prescribed pine oil fume baths and colonics to eliminate toxins, and put him on an exercise routine.

The composer recovered with the ability to compose ten to twelve hours a day and travel the world conducting symphonic orchestras.

November 26

But ideals are not your mind - ideals are principles acted upon BY the mind. But remember, just as that expectancy - because your great, great, great, great grandfather died you will die too - is there, and is part of the expectancy of every cell of your body! It can be eradicated, yes. How? By that constant activity within self of expectancy that this condition does not HAVE to happen to you!   2533-6

Longevity could be ours if we truly expected it and lived a life worthy of getting it. When one client asked how long he should live in this incarnation, the Forces said, "To a hundred and fifty! If there is the turning. Here we find much may be said aside from these:

"There is the fault in the flesh of not housing the soul, by the abuse of the body. If there is the feeding of the body that the soul may find the greater expression by the activities of the mental mind, the soul and spiritual mind may have the greater opportunities to express itself.

"For, as has been given in that command with the promise, 'Honor thy father, thy mother, that thy days may be long in the land which the Lord, thy God giveth thee.' Who is thy father? Who is thy mother? They that do the will of thy Father in heaven; they that do that which makes for the glorifying, the purifying, of the lives, the associations of one with another." (866-1)

As we honor these with our fellow man, we lengthen our own earthly days and "make THEM aware also of THEIR relationship to their God." (866-1)

November 27

Just as the impressions to the whole of the organism, for each cell of the blood stream, each corpuscle, is a whole UNIVERSE in itself. Do not eat like a canary and expect to do MANUAL labor. Do not eat like a rail splitter and expect to do the work of a mind reader or a university professor, but be CONSISTENT with those things that make for - even as the UNIVERSE is builded.   341-32

    Dr. Reilly summed up Edgar's holistic approach to healing in one sentence: "You get everything working right, body and mind, and illness hasn't got a chance."

    So true! And the readings gave the recipes for making everything work right.

    Dr. Reilly learned that massages needed to vary. For epilepsy, peanut oil and olive oil from brain's base to spine's end. For diabetic, peanut oil alone across small of back, sacral, hips, and sciatic area. For anemia, a more vigorous massage with peanut oil each morning on abdomen and stomach, spine, and sacral.

    Edgar often recommended purifying baths. One should soak tired feet in coffee made from old coffee grounds to stimulate better circulation and aid elimination, and also to eliminate heaviness in the throat and head. Acupuncturists have always known the connection between feet and the brain.

    He diagnosed the cause of stomach ulcers long before doctors had a clue, professing it was better not to eat at all than to eat when upset. As he said, the mind builds.

November 28

There is the physical body, there is the mental body, there is the soul body. They are One, as the Trinity; yet these may find a manner of expression that is individual unto themselves. The body itself finds its own level in its OWN development.   416-11

The importance of the readings' holistic health advice was proven with the case of Marjorie Barney's daughter, Emily. She and her daughter were in an automobile accident in 1948, three years after Edgar's death. Emily's face and body were badly scratched and her foot wobbled on a stick-like leg as she walked.

Watching some children at play at A.R.E. headquarters, Dr. Reilly asked about the poor little limping one and found she was Marjorie's daughter.

"If something isn't done about that leg pretty soon," he told her, "the muscles will atrophy completely, and she'll be crippled for life."

Marjorie bemoaned that doctors had been unable to help her. Dr. Reilly suggested she ask Gladys Davis, Edgar's secretary, if she remembered any reading about wasted muscles. Gladys found some that recommended massage with peanut oil and camphorated oil, applied on alternate days, rubbing muscles from the toe toward calf, thigh, and groin. Marjorie on her own decided to use the oil also on her scarred face. Success wasn't immediate, but two years later Emily had no scars and she walked without a limp.

The readings clinched Edgar's title as the Father of Holistic Medicine.

November 29

Remember above all, as He hath given, "As ye do it unto the least of thy brethren, of thy associates, of thy companions, day by day, ye do it unto thy God; yea, the God within THYSELF! 1436-1

On this date in 1931 the Norfolk Study Group came up with a plan for preserving the lessons they learned to help others, following their spiritual challenge to give "light to the waiting world."

Esther Wynne, the group's secretary who had recorded Edgar's psychic messages from all meetings, presented a summary of their first lesson, Cooperation.

The group decided upon a format for future lessons. Each would begin by reading Esther's written account of Edgar's last trance message after which they would memorize the prayer in that reading.

They would then meditate to prepare themselves to carry out the message in their daily lives.

Edgar's Forces that day were pleased with the group's decision and started them on their second lesson, "Know Thyself."

These original study group members were a remarkably dedicated bunch who, though in their own homes, meditated collectively at the same time every day seven days a week.

Many years passed before the lessons were compiled, published, and made available to others. They are now studied by Search for God study groups throughout the world.

November 30
Smile always - and LIVE the smile.   1819-1

On this day in 1935 Edgar, Hugh Lynn, Gertrude, and Gladys were arrested in Detroit for practicing medicine without a license. They were fingerprinted, relieved of all their clothes and possessions, and jailed—leaving them only three dollars for candy and cigarettes.

A father and his doctor who couldn't understand a reading's treatment advised for his asthmatic child had filed charges for fraud, claiming the reading was worthless.

In the jail Gertrude and Gladys were confined in the women's section and Edgar and Hugh Lynn in the men's section with some twenty-five other inmates.

Their leader demanded and took their three dollars and asked if Edgar was guilty of the charges against him.

Edgar said he had—like them, besides what he was e accused of—a real reason for being in jail.

He told the leader he was accused of hitting a child with an automobile, but his real reason for being in jail was an argument he'd had with his wife. He'd been so angry he didn't look when he pulled out his car.

As many gasped, knowing what Edgar said was true, the leader ordered them to put the two best mattresses in Edgar's and Hugh Lynn's cubicle. Before they needed to use them, they, Gertrude, and Gladys were released on $800 bail put up by two previous patients. A plea-bargain agreement freed everyone but Edgar, who pleaded guilty and was released on probation.

December 1

First seek an answer consciously for any question within thine own environ, thine own surroundings, and let thine own development, thine own ideas, answer yes or no. Then take the answer - yes or no - to the inner consciousness and let thy ruling influence in the Spirit answer. And ye may know, and the truth in same sets you free. For, when one is used by the environs that make for a questioning within self as to its ideal, know the ideal is questioned - even by the better self. Let the answer be in the highest - mental, and then in the spirit itself from within. 443-3

In December 1893 Carrie and Leslie Cayce moved with their daughters to Hopkinsville, where they rented a log home on Seventh Street, with a stable for their cow, a barn, an outhouse, and a well for their water.

Edgar went back to the country to live with his Uncle Clint and to continue working for him.

On Sundays he visited his family and attended Sunday school at the Ninth Street Christian Church, sitting quietly and keeping to himself.

He and his unusual skills were not known in Hopkinsville, and he probably preferred to maintain the status quo.

Later the voice of an angel told him his mother needed him in Hopkinsville, and he moved there. The move was fortuitous because it necessitated him getting a new job, and it was because of his bookstore job that he met Gertrude, the love of his life.

December 2

Study well, then, the influence ye have upon those ye meet day by day. For, again, with what measure ye mete, with what judgment ye act, so comes it back to thee. For, to have love one must manifest and show love in one's life and one's dealings with others. To have friends one must show self friendly.   2560-1

In this month in 1913 Edgar did a reading conducted by Dave Kahn, who would later become an influential friend and supporter of his work.

Edgar had traveled from Selma to Lexington to help Amanda Fay DeLaney, the crippled victim of an automobile accident. She was swollen, couldn't feed herself, couldn't move without pain, and carried more than 200 pounds on her 5'5" body.

She lived with her husband, Kentucky Lumber Company owner, in a large home next door to the Kahns, a Jewish family.

Edgar gave Dave a list of questions and gave him instructions on conducting the reading, which traced Amanda's problem back to a horse-and-buggy accident many years before the auto accident.

Six months later Edgar visited and found she could feed herself and her swelling had decreased. In another eight or nine months, she was walking and driving her own car.

Amanda became Edgar's staunch advocate, and Dave Kahn became his lifelong friend.

December 3

Then, act ever in the way ye would LIKE to be acted toward. No matter WHAT others say, or even DO, do as ye would be done by; and then the peace that has been promised is INDEED thine own.   1183-3

Faint not at waiting, for in patience ye become aware of thy soul.   2144-1

As ye are shown to do from within, considering all, weigh thy judgments well - and let thine conscience be thy guide.   699-1

Keep and be able to see - keep that ability to see the ridiculous even in the most sacred thing. Not that it may be used, of course, as to hinder others, but in thine OWN life. These keep.   2560-1

    In a trance Edgar helped many clients with their inventions, but on at least one occasion, he obtained invention knowledge while wide awake.

    First Christian Church in Selma had too many members to fit into a group photo. To solve the problem, Edgar designed and made a tripod to swivel his camera and click the shutter so that all could appear.

    The delayed action allowed Edgar to get himself in the picture before the camera stopped.

    Young members of Edgar's Bible study class couldn't resist the urge to do the same. From their position on the left, they'd run behind the congregation, take a position on the right, and appear in the picture two times.

    That photo shoot may have been the most boisterous of Edgar's photography career.

December 4

The abilities lie before thee to make a mental, material and - above all spiritual success in the present experience. Choose thou. Use that thou knowest today in the way and manner that will build for that which answers the motivating force within self; not unto self-glorification, but for that thou settest before thyself as thine ideal. 361-4

The Forces within Edgar stressed repeatedly that each one of us is a soul, a portion of the Divine Energy that brought us into being. The heritage of each soul is to know itself to be itself, yet one with the Creative Forces. In the beginning, we had companionship with God, lost that companionship by choice to satisfy material desires. Thus we must enter again and again.

John 14:2 in the Bible says, "In my Father's house are many mansions." Edgar said, "Dwell on that, not for an hour or a minute but for a day—as you go about your work. Who is your father?...What does he mean by mansions? And that there are many mansions in his house? What house? It is indeed thy body—that is the temple. Many mansions are in that body, many temples. For the body has been again and again in the experience of the earth, and they are sometimes mansions, sometimes huts, sometimes homes...." (3578-1)

Know that in whatever state you find yourself—of mind, of body, of physical condition—that is what you have built, and is necessary for your unfoldment.

December 5

The study from the human standpoint, of subconscious, subliminal, psychic, soul forces, is and should be the great study for the human family, for through self man will understand its Maker when it understands its relation to its Maker, and it will only understand that through itself, and that understanding is the knowledge as is given here in this state. 3744-5

On this day in 1923 Edgar gave a life reading for Gertrude. The family had moved to Dayton at the urging of Arthur Lammers, who convinced Edgar to move beyond readings for curing people's physical problems and delve into the metaphysical realm.

Gertrude's reading told her she'd have great blessings for three, maybe four years.

It devoted much time to her astrological signs. She had been affected by many planets because her physical birth happened in the morning and her soul didn't enter until the afternoon.

She had incarnated in France as Lurline during the exile of Charles II. Other incarnations placed her in ancient Greece and in the Egyptian hill country when she was a beautiful Bedouin dancer.

Life readings always seemed to key in on previous incarnations that had the most bearing on the present one. Gertrude now knew why as a child she had named her favorite doll Lurline. She smiled, remembering that her favorite pastime back then had been dancing in the woods, imagining an audience enjoying her on stage.

December 6

Know that all strength, all healing of every nature is the changing of the vibrations from within - the attuning of the divine within the living tissue of a body to Creative Energies. This alone is healing....it is the attuning of the atomic structure of the living cellular force to its spiritual heritage. 1967-1

The first doctor to recognize that Edgar could help him with difficult patients was Dr. Wesley Ketchum. In the early 1900s, young Ketchum opened his first practice in Hopkinsville, eager to fulfill his Hippocratic oath and become a physician of note.

From Ohio, he met another Ohioan, C.H. Dietrich, who told him how Cayce had miraculously helped his daughter whom doctors had determined lacked any capability of developing intellectually. The man called "freak" had diagnosed her problem, prescribed treatments, and the daughter was now a normal, mentally capable child. Ketchum thought maybe he should give this oddball Cayce a try.

His problem patient was a college student who suddenly dropped unconscious during a football scrimmage and had been incoherent ever since. He alternated between violent seizures and staring speechlessly. Ketchum hadn't helped, but with only the student's name and address, Edgar went into a trance, described his brain, and prescribed a little-known drug.

No improvement happened for more than three weeks, but in the fourth week Ketchum received a call from his mother, who said, "Good morning, miracle man."

December 7

...there is that existent influence; that He, the Father, has not willed that any soul should perish. He does not have joy in suffering, in death, in disappointment, in hate, in those things that make individual souls or entities afraid, but has with ALL the willfulness of an entity, a soul, prepared a way of escape.   263-13

On this day in 1925 Edgar started readings that resulted in a design for which he never received credit.

Edgar laid out the basic color-filtration system for a fog light to help pilots and ship navigators. A reading four months later refined the high-intensity system.

By 1929 such lights were commonplace at airports and on waterways.

The same lack of credit occurred with his design in 1926—"elastic glass," which was marketed as Plexiglas when it came out in the 1940s.

Tim Brown, who always yearned to make a profit for both himself and Edgar, was incapable of interesting any industry in producing these innovative products.

One wonders how many technological advances resulted from inventors receiving information from the same infinite intelligence that communicated with Edgar.

One also might wonder why Edgar didn't hire a more competent marketing man, but he was in no position to do so. He still hadn't built his practice in Dayton and was still struggling financially.

Brown achieved one wonderful thing for the Cayces. He arranged a full scholarship for Hugh Lynn at the very exceptional Moraine Park School.

December 8

(Q) What is meant by learning the Law of Love? How may I do this? (A) It is that ye make applicable in thy daily experiences. "Love me" is ever the command. "A new commandment I give, that ye love one another even as I have loved you." It is the willingness to sacrifice all of self, even the abilities of self, that others may know the Lord better. 3945-1

We are called to remember that God is in everyone, and that we must love everyone no matter how loathesome they might be.

We gain when we "Do good, as He gave, to those that despitefully use thee, and ye overcome then - in thyself - that ye HAVE done to thy fellowman!" (1650-1)

Love toward others should be consistently demonstrated. "In thy daily walks let His light so shine in thine own self that those ye contact may know that the love of the Father is being shown in thy daily conversation, thy daily activities." (262-47)

We practice the Law of Love every time we treat others in accordance to our ideal. "Study to show thyself approved in all good conscience to that thou dost set as thy ideal, and know - as has been indicated - that thy ideal is only in Him who is the keeper, who is thy Brother, who is thy Friend, thy Lord - even the Christ!

"Then as ye pattern thy life by His, ye will mete the fruits of the Spirit to thy fellowmen day by day, in whatever field of service is chosen." (1650-1)

As Edgar has said, what one metes out, one gets.

December 9

So live that thy friend, thy foe, thy neighbor, may also - through patterning his expressions after thee - find the way to that mercy which is manifested in Him, who gave "I stand at the door and knock-by thy biddings I will enter - by thy rejection I will leave- I hold no grudge." 1747-5

The day after this day in 1910, Edgar and Ketchum's relationship would be tested when Frank Mohr came into their lives. Mohr had a successful coal mine in Nortonville Kentucky because Edgar pinpointed coal underground. He came to Edgar for help with his toddler niece, whose doctors held out no hope for her surviving polio.

Edgar's advice for her was so successful Mohr wanted to buy out his contract, and, if not that, expand the existing agreement he had with Ketchum and Noe to include a hospital. The idea of having a hospital for treating out-of-towners—was very appealing to Edgar, but Ketchum and Noe seemed more concerned with their monetary cut than the patients' help.

By the middle of 1912, the hospital's foundation had been poured, but Ketchum and Noe still hadn't signed the contract. Mohr had a serious accident which Edgar said, if corrective measures were not taken, would result in blindness..

Ketchum belittled that notion, two lawsuits were filed, but Mohr left town and the cases were never heard. The hospital's foundation still stands, overtaken by weeds and thick brush.

December 10

There comes that necessary force for the quieting within, that the abilities for reasoning powers may be enabled to see the opposites, or the different phases or angles from which there may be an approach to the questions - whether these be as to relationships, things, conditions, emotions, and general influences.   538-59

On this day in 1923 Edgar gave a life reading for Hugh Lynn, who was not present to react one way or another.

It was predicted he could be successful as a "writer, composer, historian, or compiler of data." He was strong willed and would attain much financial success, and his "life love will enter after years of maturity."

The reading listed six incarnations. He had been a monk named Olaf Ericson in England during the reign of Alfred the Great and was a knight in the Crusades.

His most impressive incarnation was as Andrew, one of Jesus's disciples "in the days when the Prince of Peace walked by the seashore."

His remains from an Egyptian incarnation were still at a pyramid's north corner. The reading placed his soul at the beginning of life on earth "when the morning stars sang" at humanity's first indwelling on earth.

FAST FORWARD: Back from school for Christmas, Hugh Lynn was infuriated with his reading. He had never heard of reincarnation, and he was appalled at the very idea. He ordered Edgar to stop giving life readings.

December 11

The influences from astrological aspects come as innate urges in the mental or the dream state, while the influences from the appearances in the earth come as the emotions of the entity.... Thus we find that the emotions - the senses, or the sensing of influences - may become a stumbling-stone; as they... tend to satisfy the physical without due...consideration of spiritual aspects....
2021-1

Dreams aren't simply idle fiction to keep us entertained while we sleep. If we will only think about our dreams, we will find they're telling us something to help our spiritual, material, or mental enrichment.

Edgar pointed out the difference between dreams and visions. "When only dreams, these TOO are significant - but rather of that of the physical health, or physical conditions. In visions there is oft the INTER-BETWEEN giving expressions that make for an awakening between the mental consciousness, or that that has been turned over and over in the physical consciousness and mind being weighed with that the self holds as its ideal." (262-9)

For recurring dreams, "First the body should analyze in self that which is - as given the body oft - the basis from which the activities of the mental self are given...as may be correlated with the body. The BODY may analyze same, interpret same, BETTER; for it can do it better for its own activity than were it done by the most wonderful of all interpreters." (257-138) Again, our minds build!

December 12

In the normal force of dreams are enacted those forces that may be the fore-shadow of condition, with the comparison by soul and spirit forces of the condition in VARIOUS SPHERES through which this soul and spirit of the given entity has passed in its evolution to the present sphere. In this age, at present, 1923, there is not sufficient credence given dreams; for the best develop-ment of the human family is to give the greater increase in knowledge of the subconscious, soul or spirit world. This is a DREAM. 3744-5

Dreams can both guide us toward goals we want to achieve and deter us from pursuing the wrong path.

Edgar's Forces suggest that to interpret a dream "Correlate those Truths that are enacted in each and every dream that becomes a part of...the entity of the individual, and use such to the better developing, ever remembering develop means going toward the higher forces, or the Creator." (3744-5)

Dreams arise from three sources: poor assimilations, reaction from foods or drink, and "Then there are those visions of the character to be sought, rather than rejected; as the experiences of the unconscious self or subconscious self that may come as warnings or as helpful experiences, or of that through which those influences acting about self become a part of self." (1472-10)

Stop bad dreams by coordinating "the assimilating and eliminating systems of the body." Then happy dreams!

December 13

He that leads, or WOULD direct, is continually beset by the forces that WOULD undermine. He that endureth to the end shall wear the Crown. He that aideth in up-building shall be entitled to that that he BUILDS in his experience. He that faltereth, or would hinder, shall be received in the manner as he hinders. No difficulty exists in the man's soul. There exists difficulty in the minds of individuals who, with monetary MEASURES, see all forces hindered as to their concept of success.   2897-4

On this day in 1916 Edgar found out that Edwin Williamson had queried the head of Universal Pictures with a proposal to have Edgar psychically plot a screenplay for a Hollywood movie.

Williamson, who wanted a Hollywood writing career, often brought his two children to the Cayce apartment. Their favorite game was movie-making, with Hugh Lynn as the director and cameraman and his children Ethyl and Malcolm as the stars.

The game became more fun when Edgar finally agreed to plot movies for them while in a trance. Little did he dream that Williamson would try to advance his career the same way.

Edwin's proposal to Universal was to arrange an experiment with a well-known actress at Churchill's, a New York nightclub. Edgar would not have to be there—he had done many readings at a distance.

Weirdly enough, Universal Pictures liked the idea, and the experiment took place on February 8, 1917.

December 14

Hence we may find that an individual may from sorrow SLEEP and wake with a feeling of elation. What has taken place? ...There has been, and ever when the physical consciousness is at rest, the other self communes with the SOUL of the body, see? or it goes OUT into that realm ...of all experiences of that entity that may have been throughout the EONS of time, or in correlating WITH that as it, that entity, HAS accepted as its criterion... or justice, within its sphere of activity. Hence through such an association in sleep there may have come that peace, that understanding...by that which has been correlated through that passage of the selves of a body in sleep. Hence we find the more spiritual-minded individuals are the more easily pacified, at peace, harmony, in normal active state as well as in sleep.
5754-2

On this day in 1944 Edgar awoke from a coma which had lasted from early last evening through the night. He looked and felt better than he had since coming back to Virginia Beach on August 10 to spend his final days.

However, for the rest of his life, he never slept more than thirty minutes at a time. His doctor said because Edgar didn't want to go to a hospital, the hospital should be brought to him. A hospital bed came from Willis Furniture in Norfolk, and oxygen and nursing services were arranged.

Gladys was told to discontinue daily massages and simply allow him to rest. Gertrude was told not to give him anything apt to strangle him. He was at peace.

December 15

For as He hath given, "If ye call, I will hear - if ye seek, ye shall find. I stand at the door and knock. Open and I will enter in." But ye yourself - yes, ye thyself - must open. He opens it not for thee, until thou hast determined in thine heart, "Others may do as they may, but for me I will serve the living God"   2795-1

In mid-December 1911 a prestigious Harvard University dean of psychology came to Hopkinsville to expose Edgar as a fraud. Dr. Hugo Munsterberg showed up at Edgar's front door and asked to see his crystal ball or any other psychic items of trickery he used.

Edgar explained how his psychic insights came only by his going into a trance and records were kept in typed transcripts of his readings. They arranged to meet at Edgar's studio the next day. Munsterberg observed Edgar give a typical physical reading to August Boehme, who had a stomach disorder because of chronic malnutrition. After the reading the professor interviewed Boehme, who was very pleased with the diagnosis and recommended treatments.

During this time period Edgar's clients went to Dr. Wesley Ketchum, who implemented treatments, and stayed in a hotel managed by Albert Noe.

Munsterberg spent two more days talking to Ketchum's patients and before leaving admitted to Edgar's unusual power and legitimacy. He told Edgar in private that he was "running with the wrong bunch."

Gertrude thought so, too. She never trusted Ketchum.

December 16

(Q) Is the Darwinian theory of evolution of man right or wrong? Give such an answer as will enlighten the people on this subject of evolution. (A) Man was made in the beginning, as the ruler over those elements as was prepared in the earth plane for his needs. When the plane became that such as man was capable of being sustained by the forces, and conditions, as were upon the face of the earth plane, man appeared not from that already created, but as the Lord over all that was created, and in man there is found that in the living man, all of that, that may be found without in the whole, whole world or earth plane, and OTHER than that, the SOUL OF MAN is that making him above all animal, vegetable, mineral kingdom of the earth plane. Man DID NOT descend from the monkey, but man has evolved, resuscitation, you see, from time to time, time to time, here a little, there a little....   3744-5

In the same reading as above, Edgar explained that to the human family, evolution means rather resuscitation of "understanding the law of self from within" and man's evolving "has only been that of the gradual growth upward to the mind of the Maker."

Evolution, then, brought enlightenment that delivered "the better force in man to bring about the gradual change that has come to man, known through all the ages...and brings forth to meet the needs of the man...many thousands and millions of years... for the needs of man in the hundreds and thousands of years to come."

December 17

(Q) In the physical plane, do the thoughts of another person affect a person either mentally or physically? (A) Depending upon the development of the individual to whom the thought may be directed. The possibilities of the developing of thought transference is first being shown, evolution, you see. The individuals of this plane will and are developing this as the senses were and are developed. 3744-3

Telepathy is a skill we once had, but lost. Still, most of us have experienced instances when the very person in our minds calls only a moment later. Many siblings and close friends share this phenomenon frequently.

Edgar emphasized that thoughts are deeds, and they have the power to manifest. The following quote from the same reading as above seems to explain how angry thoughts instigate a mob mentality while holy thoughts spur others to sacred solace.

"The THOUGHT held against an individual directs the mind either of masses or classes, whether toward good or bad. Thought is reached through the physical forces, and by becoming a part of the physical or conscious mind either lends the strength of subconscious forces or allows the subconscious to direct."

We can use our minds to benefit humanity "by developing the mental or physical mind toward the uplift of mankind toward the Maker...By the training of...the faculty of doing in the right or direct way, and lending assistance to the uplift of all." Thus, good evolution!

December 18

In the flux, then, of life - keep thine paths in the way of sound judgment, as is reasoned with the love's influence in the experience of self.   1735-2

The Forces were wonderful at quick soundbites:

"Analyze thyself. Judge not harshly. As ye would find love, give it. As ye would make peace, live it. As ye would have friends, be one." (2581-2)

"Keep the whole mentality in that way as to build the best development." (33-1) "Keep the body occupied MENTALLY-- for others, and not self." (1000-1)

"Faint not at waiting, for in patience ye become aware of thy soul." (2144-1) "Do learn music." (3659-1)

"Be not impatient, but love ye the Lord!" (262-63) "Doubt not, but seek. Seek in His name." (440-4)

"Judge not that ye be not judged." (281-8) "THINK—THINK—on these things!" (254-68) "Hate not." (262-121) "Be not dictatorial, nor lording in thine own activity." (900-428) "As ye sow, so shall ye reap." (440-4)

"Soul development should take precedence over all things." (3357-2) "Think twice before you act once." (341-32) "In thy meditation, in thy seeking, know that the answer must come within." (262-118)

"Study to show thyself approved unto thy conscience." (1669-1) "Let thy light so shine that others may take hope also." (3393-2) "Rise and pray—facing east!" (3509-1) "Keep thine body fit. Keep thine mind attuned to beauty." (257-53)

What a taskmaster! But unquestionably good advice!

December 19

> *For, "as ye do it unto the least, ye do it unto thy Maker." That should be the attitude, ever. But LIVE, each soul, in SUCH a manner as to implant not the bigness of the individual but the love of God made manifest among men!*   3976-24

On this day in 1906 Blackburn—wanting doctors to see how Edgar could help them diagnose illnesses—had Edgar give a demonstration for the E.Q.B. Literary Club.

Gertrude made Blackburn promise no pins or monkey business, but Blackburn couldn't control what happened.

After Edgar made a diagnosis of one doctor's patient at a nearby college, and three doctors rushed to Potter College to see if the diagnosis was correct. It was!

Immediately, other doctors, suspecting an elaborate hoax, came onstage where Edgar was still in a trance.

One stuck a needle in Edgar's arms, hands, and feet, but got no response. Another thrust a hatpin through his cheek, and another pushed a penknife under a fingernail. Edgar didn't budge. He awoke with a groan and blood pouring from his cheek.

Edgar had wanted to prove how his skill could help doctors, and this was the response he received.

"I'm through," he said. "I'll never give another reading unless it's for someone who needs help and believes I can give it to him."

His finger was forever disfigured.

December 20

Minimize the faults. As ye would be forgiven, forgive others. Magnify the virtues, for the Lord thy God is a jealous God. So in thy own experience a soft word turneth away wrath, grievous words stirreth up anger. The sowing of the seed of the spirit bringeth peace. The sowing of the seed of strife bringeth contention. 1541-11

Adaptations of Bible verses like in the above quotation often appear as advice in the readings, and sometimes Edgar recited them verbatim.

When asked what present printed version of the Bible was nearest to its true meaning, the answer was: "The nearest true version for the entity is that ye apply of whatever version ye read, in your life. It isn't that ye learn from anyone. Ye only may have the direction. The learning, the teaching is within self.

"For, His promises have been, 'If ye love me ye will keep my commandments. If ye seek, ye shall find. For, behold I stand at the door of thy heart, of thy mind, of thy consciousness, and knock. If ye will open, I will enter - and abide with thee.'" (3051-2)

Regardless of what version one reads, remember that the whole gospel of Jesus Christ is: "Thou shalt love the Lord thy God with all thy mind, thy heart and thy body; and thy neighbor as thyself."

Do this and have eternal life. The rest of the book is trying to describe that—the same in any version.

December 21

The THOUGHT held against an individual directs the mind either of masses or classes, whether toward good or bad. In this state the conscious mind becomes subjugated to the subconscious, superconscious or soul mind; and may and does communicate with like minds, and the subconscious or soul force becomes universal. From any subconscious mind information may be obtained, either from this plane or from the impressions as left by the individuals that have gone on before.
3744-4

One day Edgar was about to pass a very distinguished looking gentleman walking in the opposite direction and probably surprised even himself when he said, "Hello, Richard."

The man tipped his hat and started past him, but then he stopped and said to Edgar, "How do you know my name?"

Edgar told him the truth: that he had the ability to read minds and had access to knowledge of the universal consciousness.

Richard scoffed in disbelief. "I am a bank manager and the only person who knows the combination to the bank's safe. I will believe your wild story only if you can tell me that combination."

Edgar pulled a small notebook from his pocket, wrote some numbers on a page, tore is out, and gave it to Richard. Of course, it was the combination, and the two men became friends for life.

December 22

The fruits of the spirit of the Christ are love, joy, obedience, long-suffering, brotherly love, kindness. Against such there is no law. The spirit of hate, the anti-Christ, is contention, strife, fault-finding, lovers of self, lovers of praise. Those are the anti-Christ, and take possession of groups, masses, and show themselves even in the lives of men.   3976-24

On this day in 1906, an arsonist burned down Edgar's Bowling Green studio. Although the perpetrator was never definitely identified, authorities suspected the blaze was probably set by one of Dr. David Amoss's Night Riders. That hooded vigilante group of tobacco farmers burned many homes and businesses in the county during this era.

Because insurance did not cover the many prints Edgar and his partners had on consignment from a New York art gallery, they were left in debt for $8,000. Thankfully, insurance did pay for his photographic equipment, but even so, one of Edgar's partners declared bankruptcy.

Gertrude was pregnant, and Edgar was still recovering from the trauma inflicted on him three days earlier by Blackburn's committee of doctors, so the timing of this new catastrophe was bad.

Gertrude's mother came from Hopkinsville to help them move into a less expensive rental, and it was there their firstborn Hugh Lynn was born.

December 23

(Q) What, then, is the purpose of the entering of a soul into material manifestations? (A) In the beginnings, or in the activities in which the soul manifested individually, it was for the purpose of becoming as a companion of Creative Force or God; or becoming the whole body of God itself, with the ability - even as thy Pattern, as thy Savior, as thy Guide and Guard - to know thyself to BE thyself, yet one with Him! 1650-1

As described above, souls knew in the beginning of their oneness with God, but that knowledge degenerated during each successive generation.

Many do not realize that our journey on earth iasts but a few seconds in the timelessness of eternity. That truth is perhaps one reason souls choose dire circumstances for an earthly lesson. When choosing it, the time needed for that lesson seems insignificant. Once on earth and learning it, a lifetime is measured in mortal, not immortal, hours.

"For, in the comprehension of no time, no space, no beginning, no end, there may be the glimpse of what simple transition or birth into the material is; as passing through the other door into another consciousness.

"Death in the material plane is passing through the outer door into a consciousness in the material activities that partakes of what the...soul has done with its spiritual truth in its manifestations in the other sphere." (5749-3)

While here on earth we need to practice the fruits of the spirit to work our way back to the holy sphere.

December 24

(Q) May we have a Christmas message from the Master at this time? (A) Let not your hearts be troubled, neither let them be afraid. For the Lord is in the Holy Temple - let the earth and those that love the Lord rejoice, that the Father-God in the Christ is mindful of men, and He will not let thy loved ones - nor those with and for whom ye pray - be tempted beyond that they are able to bear. But live daily as ye pray, and pray as ye would have thy brother, the Christ, to praise thy life before the throne of mercy. Show ye mercy and love one to another, then, if ye would have love and mercy shown to thee. For this is the beginning and the end of wisdom. 5758-1

The above Christmas message of loving assurance to all humankind came directly from the Master.

A message to be sent to the Glad Helpers' prayer list was: "Dearly Beloved: As the Season of Joy comes, that came to the world through the gift of the Child, the Christ, to the world, may we - as those that have such as our purpose - give to thee that blessing which comes to all that seek to be a channel of blessings to others!" (281-22)

The true meaning of Christmas? "Let patience, love and mercy be thy watchwords. PRACTICE them in thy daily life. For in so doing ye bring into thy experience all the joy, all the expectancy, all the anticipation of a closer walk with Him - which is indeed the Christ-mass spirit." (262-116) "His joy be thine this day...for He is nigh unto thee, He is in thy midst." (262-103)

December 25

In the Piscean age, in the center of same, we had the entrance of Emmanuel or God among men, see? What did that mean? The same will be meant by the full consciousness of the ability to communicate with or to be aware of the relationships to the Creative Forces and the uses of same in material environs.   1602-3

  On this day in 1923 the Cayce family faced a bleak Christmas. They had spent most of the little cash they had moving Gertrude, Gladys, and Edgar Evans to Dayton. Gladys had been working without a paycheck even before the move.
  They had come to Dayton expecting financial support from Arthur Lammers, who had not come through for them as he had promised.
  Edgar had a stack of unpaid Cayce Art Company bills his father Leslie had failed to pay. Edgar had not been paid for most of the 34 medical readings he'd given since arriving in Dayton—many for friends or family.
  The family was so destitute that Gertrude had to cash out the last gold coin from her dowry to bring Hugh Lynn to Dayton on Christmas Eve.
  None had winter coats to wear to meet Hugh Lynn at the train station. Edgar stuffed newspaper under his coat and sleeves to help keep him warm in the freezing weather.
  When father and son hugged, Hugh Lynn heard the crackle of paper and noted the tired lines in Edgar's face.

December 26

He that is angry and sinneth not controls self. He that is angry and allows such to become the expression in the belittling of self, or the self-indulgence of self in any direction, brings to self those things that partake of the spirit of ... the product or influence of anger itself.　　　　　　　　　　　　　　361-4

After that meager 1923 Christmas dinner during the family gift exchange, Hugh Lynn received a surprise gift—the life reading conducted for him on December 10.

The word "reincarnation" might as well have been a foreign language to him. Once he understood that to incarnate meant to take on body form, he at least began to grasp that his life reading (also a term he'd never heard) would tell him about the different times his soul had come to earth.

The very idea! Preposterous! Had the stress of being a misunderstood psychic caused his father to go bonkers? Still, dutiful son that he was, he began reading about his six lives. He was okay when he was a monk during the era of Alfred the Great and when he was a knight in the Crusades. But when he got to his third incarnation as one of Christ's disciples, he flipped his lid.

The very idea! Such a claim disgusted him! He could never have been worthy to pal around with Jesus!

Hugh Lynn confronted his father, demanding him to stop giving life readings. Edgar probably had read his mind and expected his juvenile explosion, but he also probably knew Hugh Lynn would change his mind, for he—like his dad—knew the readings were always right.

December 27

When thou hast chosen... that activity thou would take, know that thou art kept in a balance...of the material, mental and spiritual influences near to right. Then lay it not aside until it, the activity, has borne fruit in thine mental and material experience. 361-4

Even when on the verge of poverty, Edgar was always optimistic. "The money will come," he said of the family's financial problems in Dayton. Sure enough, an associate in Chicago sent a check for $50, and a friend from Oklahoma sent $100 advance against future oil profits. Edgar checked out of the Phillips Hotel and moved the group to a 3-bedroom duplex.

Gladys was surely the happiest of the bunch as she would no longer have to share a bedroom with Edgar Evans and Hugh Lynn.

In later years she would reminisce that "the divine hand of providence" seemed to watch over them.

Once when they were trying to decide who would get their only remaining bowl of soup, a stranger arrived and paid $25 in advance for his son's reading. Until then, they had only thirteen cents to spend for more food. Only a few hours later, Edgar found another $25 in the mail from a stranger in Chicago.

The next break they received was an opportunity for Edgar to ask the Forces to plot a screenplay, and he did so on January 3, 1924. A previous screenplay he'd done had led to individuals who believed in and supported "the work." He welcomed another shot at pleasing Hollywood.

December 28

Keep the whole mentality in that way as to build the best development. 33-1

A dispute over the publication of a proposed book about a series of readings led to Edgar's very last meeting with Arthur Lammers, who had lured him to Dayton and then virtually deserted him.

Lammers Printing and Engraving Company was approaching bankruptcy, and creditors had foreclosed on his mansion and repossessed his automobiles. Printing Edgar's book was out of the question, but Lammers was irate when he discovered that other associates were negotiating with another publisher.

The book was the last of Edgar's concerns. He owed money on a room he had kept at the Phillips Hotel to do his readings, which averaged only one a day for a $5 fee. He couldn't consider giving readings at their small, overcrowded flat. Besides, his only clients came from the hotel's personnel knowing about him.

The one check he'd received from Lammers since resettling in Dayton bounced. The family was broke, in a city of strangers who couldn't come and pay for readings because they didn't know he was there to give them.

One bright side was the idle time they had to spend in the Dayton Public Library. There they researched all the geographical and historical information given in the readings, finding them 100% accurate. Now more than ever, Edgar needed a way to share the infinite intelligence with more of humankind.

December 29

The physical body, as we find, is as a shadow, as a shell, made up of those growths of the ego in the egg of the force or power that has emanated from the union of those plasms that have brought into materiality a dwelling place for physical organisms - as in all the forces in a physical body, and dwelling with same is the soul-body.   531-2

On January 1, 1906, after taking photos at an unheated furniture factory warehouse, Edgar sat by his studio fire, passed out, and fell to the floor. Two men found him and had the nearby Dr. McCraken on the scene quickly. Attempts to pour whiskey down his throat didn't awaken him, but broke his lower front teeth.

Other doctors arrived, and injections of morphine, strychnine, and nitroglycerin didn't help, nor did heated bricks on his feet's soles. They declared him dead.

Dr. John Blackburn arrived and was furious at all they had done to him. He told Edgar in his ear that his blood was circulating normally and his pulse was increasing, continuing these suggestions for some twenty minutes. Finally, Blackburn could feel his pulse, and Edgar whispered, "Ask me in a trance what to do."

Blackburn hypnotized him as he had done so many times to help others. Edgar said to give him suggestions that his body not assimilate the poisons, that his burns be healed, and that his body return to normal. Blackburn did, and then withdrew drugs through a needle from his swollen, discolored arms.

Edgar woke up and Blackburn walked him home.

December 30

And these become then thy mission. Open the door for those that cry aloud for a knowledge that God is within the reach of those that will put their hand to DOING; just being kind - not a great deed as men count greatness, but just being gentle and patient and loving even with those that would despitefully use thee. For the beauties of the Lord are with those that seek to know and WITNESS for Him among men.   1436-1

On this day in 1927 Tom Sugrue, who first had visions of exposing Edgar as a fraud, decided that Edgar's communication with higher, all-knowing sources was genuine. He vowed to dedicate his life to "the work."

He had come to Virginia Beach with his college friend Hugh Lynn, who had become like a brother to him. He often spent weekends at the beach, perusing transcripts of the readings, becoming more and more convinced that such profound wisdom could not possibly have come from Edgar's own unassuming mentality.

When Edgar in trance mentioned his gonorrhea, he knew for a fact that no living person other than himself knew about his contracting that despicable venereal disease. Never again did he doubt Edgar's authenticity.

The reading warned that disease from his past could have disastrous consequences, but he could prevent problems with a special diet, medicinal injections into his uretha, and "clean and pure living."

Later in life he didn't follow that advice, and he died at age 45 during a surgery to help him walk again.

December 31

> In the mental self, there is as much reason to dwell upon the thought from whence the soul came, as it is upon whence the soul goeth. For, if the soul is eternal, it always has been - if it is always to be. And that is the basis, or the thought of Creative Force, or God. He ever was, He ever will be. And individuals, as His children, are a part of that consciousness. And it is for that purpose that He came into the earth; that we, as soul-entities, might know ourselves to be our-selves, and yet one with Him; as He, the Master, the Christ, knew Himself to be Himself and yet one with the Father.
> 3003-1

On this night in 1899 Edgar and Gertrude welcomed the new century watching dazzling fireworks glittering in the sky above Hopkinsville.

Only a few days before on Christmas day, Edgar had returned from Louisville, where he worked, and found his beloved fianc'ee emaciated, unhealthy, and unhappy.

He most assuredly knew that he had caused her decline for Gertrude's health had plummeted as his relationship with Margaret had ascended.

Their engagement had been threatened by the unlikely liaison of a poor country man with a rich city girl. But it was threatened no more.

Edgar and Gertrude were back in each other's arms and would stay devoted to each other on earth until death divided them.

Both were confident their souls would meet again. Edgar's readings had provided proof of that truth.

Lenore Vinyard Bechtel

s a frequent presenter at Edgar Cayce retreats and teaches classes about him, including one on creation, for the Academy of Lifelong Learning at Lone Star College in Conroe, Texas. She has been a public relations consultant, teacher, guidance counselor, journalist, and playwright with 13 plays produced by community theaters. She is author of *Heart in Her Pocket,* a historical suspense novel, and *Thank You, Elvis,* a romantic comedy, and has co-authored several others. She was born in Indiana and educated at Indiana University and University of Michigan.

Find information about Edgar Cayce events and retreats, including *Search for God* study group meetings, at www.edgarcayce.org

The Association for Research and Enlightenment offers opportunities for personal transformation of body, mind, and spirit based upon the wisdom found in Edgar Cayce's readings. Many remedies recommended in his health readings are offered at the onsite A.R.E. Health Center & Spa at the Virginia Beach headquarters.

Edgar Cayce's A.R.E.
215 67th Street
Virginia Beach, VA 23451-2061
1-800-333-4499

www.ingramcontent.com/pod-product-compliance
Lightning Source LLC
LaVergne TN
LVHW041606070426
835507LV00008B/156